A Different Medicine

O | R | S Oxford Ritual Studies

Series Editors
Ronald Grimes
Ute Hüsken, University of Oslo
Eric Venbrux, Radboud University Nijmegen

THE PROBLEM OF RITUAL EFFICACY
Edited by William S. Sax, Johannes Quack, and Jan Weinhold

PERFORMING THE REFORMATION
Public Ritual in the City of Luther
Barry Stephenson

RITUAL, MEDIA, AND CONFLICT
Edited by Ronald L. Grimes, Ute Hüsken, Udo Simon, and Eric Venbrux

KNOWING BODY, MOVING MIND
Ritualizing and Learning at Two Buddhist Centers
Patricia Q. Campbell

SUBVERSIVE SPIRITUALITIES
How Rituals Enact the World
Frédérique Apffel-Marglin

NEGOTIATING RITES
Edited by Ute Hüsken and Frank Neubert

THE DANCING DEAD
Ritual and Religion among the Kapsiki/Higi of North Cameroon
and Northeastern Nigeria
Walter E.A. van Beek

LOOKING FOR MARY MAGDALENE
Alternative Pilgrimage and Ritual Creativity at Catholic Shrines in France
Anna Fedele

THE DYSFUNCTION OF RITUAL IN EARLY CONFUCIANISM
Michael David Kaulana Ing

A DIFFERENT MEDICINE
Postcolonial Healing in the Native American Church
Joseph D. Calabrese

A DIFFERENT MEDICINE

Postcolonial Healing in the Native American Church

JOSEPH D. CALABRESE

OXFORD
UNIVERSITY PRESS

OXFORD
UNIVERSITY PRESS

Oxford University Press is a department of the University of Oxford.
It furthers the University's objective of excellence in research,
scholarship, and education by publishing worldwide.

Oxford   New York
Auckland   Cape Town   Dar es Salaam   Hong Kong   Karachi
Kuala Lumpur   Madrid   Melbourne   Mexico City   Nairobi
New Delhi   Shanghai   Taipei   Toronto

With offices in
Argentina   Austria   Brazil   Chile   Czech Republic   France   Greece
Guatemala   Hungary   Italy   Japan   Poland   Portugal   Singapore
South Korea   Switzerland   Thailand   Turkey   Ukraine   Vietnam

Oxford is a registered trademark of Oxford University Press
in the UK and certain other countries.

Published in the United States of America by
Oxford University Press
198 Madison Avenue, New York, NY 10016

© Joseph D. Calabrese 2013

Library of Congress Cataloging-in-Publication Data
Calabrese, Joseph D.
 A different medicine: postcolonial healing in the Native American
Church / Joseph D. Calabrese.
   p. cm.
Includes bibliographical references and index.
ISBN 978–0–19–992784–5 (pbk. : alk. paper) – ISBN 978–0–19–992772–2
(hardcover : alk. paper)   1. Native American Church.   2. Peyotism.
3. Indians of North America—Religion.   4. Indians of North America—
Medicine.   5. Navajo Indians—Religion.   6. Navajo Indians—Medical care.
7. Navajo Indians—Rites and ceremonies.   I. Title.
E98.R3C35 2013
299.7—dc23
2012035237

Contents

Preface: Hard to Swallow: The Challenge of Radical Cultural Differences   vii

Acknowledgments   xiii

PART ONE: *Anthropological and Clinical Orientations*

1. Introduction: Peyote, Cultural Paradigm Clash, and the Multiplicity of the Normal   3

2. Expanding Our Conceptualization of the Therapeutic: Toward a Suitable Theoretical Framework for the Study of Cultural Psychiatries   24

3. Clinical Ethnography: Clinically Informed Self-Reflective Immersion in Local Worlds of Suffering, Healing, and Well-Being   51

PART TWO: *Cultural and Personal Healing in the Native American Church*

4. The Unfolding Cultural Paradigm Clash: Ritual Peyote Use and the Struggle for Postcolonial Healing in North America   77

5. Medicine and Spirit: The Dual Nature of Peyote   101

6. The Peyote Ceremony: Psychopharmacology, Ritual Process, and Experiences of Healing   116

7. Kinship, Socialization, and Ritual in Navajo Peyotist
Families   150

8. Postcolonial Hybridity and Ritual Bureaucracy in New Mexico:
Participant Observation in a Navajo Peyotist Healer's
Clinical Program   175

9. Decolonizing Our Understandings of the Normal and the
Therapeutic   190

Notes   199
References   203
Name Index   221
Subject Index   225

Preface

HARD TO SWALLOW: THE CHALLENGE OF
RADICAL CULTURAL DIFFERENCES

IT IS SEPTEMBER 1998. I have returned to the Navajo reservation, taking a break from a clinical training year at the University of Chicago Hospitals to visit Navajo friends and attend a conference on Traditional and Western Medicine in the Northern Navajo town of Shiprock. The conference is in the gym of a local high school. I have just finished my own presentation, describing my studies of clinical care among the Navajos, and I am attending the traditional Navajo food sampling event. As I make my way down the serving line, I am suddenly shocked and stop to contemplate what is in front of me: a tray full of blackened, whole-roasted prairie dogs (a traditional Navajo delicacy as I had just discovered).[1] I notice that my response is simultaneously mental and physical, combining astonishment with revulsion in a way that I find fascinating.

"Study that!" the Navajo food server suddenly interjects with glee, displaying characteristic Navajo wit as he gestures at the charred rodent bodies with his tongs. After a moment of deliberation, I shrug and extend my plate. As I munch on prairie dog meat back at my chair with my Navajo friends and former clinical coworkers, I reflect on the experience. This is what the ethnographer ideally does: approaches radically different and often seemingly unhealthy or distasteful cultural experiences with an open and self-reflective mind in an attempt to extend intercultural understanding. Ethnographers answer the challenge "study that!" as so memorably stated by this Navajo man. Rather than sidestep the cultural difference, ethnographers immerse themselves in it. Rather than sticking to initial gut reactions, which are often saturated with cultural assumptions, ethnographers tend to question them. This questioning process leads ethnographers to many interesting and informative predicaments, such as mine at the Navajo food tasting event. Prairie dog did not become my favorite treat. However, I learned that eating rodent meat is not as bad as I thought it would be. And I learned something about the hunter-gatherer past of the Navajos in a uniquely experiential way.

I begin with this short ethnographic vignette from my field notes because, for me, this story is emblematic not only of the brute fact of cultural differences but also of the powerful experiences of shock and revulsion that they can elicit and how these reactions can be interpreted as reflecting mere common sense (in areas of health or morality, for example). These experiences often reveal deep cultural paradigm clashes rather than deviations from some universal "common sense" reality. Given their potential to foster intercultural discord, social injustice, and even ethnocentric violence, these clashes cry out for detailed study wherever they arise. As my ethnographic vignette illustrates, experiences of cultural difference can also be opportunities to stop and reflect. Unsettling experiences often throw us into the sort of reflexive state that can allow us to take a step back from our own cultural assumptions and analyze their roots. In this process, what one had understood to be "common sense" may be called into question or even replaced by an enlarged field of possible alternatives. To illustrate this, I will narrate my own process of reflection on the "semantic network"[2] mediating my initial reaction to my prairie dog snack. This took the form of a self-questioning:

Why is the idea of eating prairie dog distasteful to me? Is it because human consumption of rodent meat is universally unhealthy? There are, admittedly, many historical reasons for Euro-Americans to assume this is so, from the filthy and rat-infested alleys of contemporary large cities to the bubonic plague, spread by rats in the Middle Ages. But a mental association that is accurate (or merely functional) in one cultural context may be completely irrelevant in another. An alley full of plague-carrying city rats is not the history of the desert-dwelling Navajos and their free-range prairie dogs. Here, rodents were wild game rather than pest. Maybe they weren't the preferred food of the Navajos but they no doubt helped the Navajos survive through some lean seasons, and thus are valorized. And after all, is it so different a meal than the more culturally familiar rabbit? I conclude that the revulsion arises primarily from the projection of distinctly Euro-American realities onto another cultural context to which these realities do not apply.

Here we see that cultural paradigm clashes are not merely elements of a sociocultural theory. They are brute facts of reality that press on us the need to make a decision: do I do that or do I not? Do I follow my Navajo friends in consuming prairie dog or do I follow my preconceptions, conclude that it is unhealthy, and refuse it? And how do I judge those who engage in practices that I reject?

I faced a similar situation of choice in relation to a cultural paradigm clash when I attended my first Sweat Lodge ritual, led by the elderly Road Man (a ritual leader of the Native American Church) whose rural family I lived with during the summer of 1990. Here the clash in question was between different cultural paradigms related to intense heat and physical discomfort. In a Sweat Lodge ritual, heated stones are placed into a pit in a small hut. Water is often poured on the rocks to produce steam. The small earthen Sweat Lodge that was built on the family's rural ranch was barely large enough for the Road Man, his two grandsons, and me. This was a traditional Navajo Sweat Lodge rather than the Sioux-style intertribal sweat. The searing heat was unlike anything I had experienced. The discomfort was intense and close proximity to the red-hot stones resulted in several leg burns. My decision in this case was not to stay and explore the paradigm clash but instead to bolt from the Sweat Lodge fearing for my life. However, even given this beginning, my ability to sit in a Sweat Lodge improved over the years of my Navajo fieldwork. My fear of the Sweat Lodge decreased as my appreciation for it increased. I could even look forward to the comments about my "White Man" status, such as the usual joke by my friend and teacher Hoskie: "One of you needs more browning."

Just as experiences of culture clash often force the individual to make a personal decision, societies faced with cultural diversity also choose which practices to tolerate and which to outlaw. Each nation fashions its own balance of multicultural tolerance and forced assimilation to the dominant culture based on its own criteria. This often occurs in the context of polarized discourses in which those in power ethnocentrically cling to their own cultural prejudices as providing the "correct" answers to life while those from contrasting cultural backgrounds may claim that virtually any traditional practice, even a harmful practice, is vital to cultural survival and dignity. However, researchers in the social and clinical sciences can and should draw important rational distinctions between different forms of cultural practice. For example, cultural practices through which one class of people within the society disempowers or seriously harms another class of people can be considered human rights violations and, as such, have no place in a liberal democracy no matter how culturally valued they are. Conversely, a special ethical issue is raised by traditional forms of therapeutic intervention that can be shown to support health, social harmony, or effective socialization for members of the group in question. Even when these practices offend the sensibilities of the dominant culture, if they can be shown to support health without causing significant harm, there is a strong ethical case that they should be tolerated. Given the divergent cultural paths of human development, including unique local approaches to understanding and maintaining health, the right to access culturally appropriate therapeutic modalities may be more of an imperative than freedom of religion or other rights. Instead of advocating clinical imperialism, the most ethical approach might be to understand cultural differences in treatment expectations and systems of intervention and, in addition to offering the best of modern biomedical health care, work to support diverse social groups in their own efforts at self-healing.

This book explores a traditional Native American spiritual and health care practice that is distasteful, even intolerable, to many Euro-Americans, based largely on their cultural assumptions and projections rather than on serious personal research, but that nevertheless throws light on a unique Native American context and cultural heritage: ceremonial consumption of the psychedelic cactus Peyote[3] (*Lophophora williamsii*). This case takes us into an area of cultural antithesis and conflict that has a long history in North America and to which very strong—and often diametrically opposed—moral interpretations and emotions are attached on both sides of the cultural divide. In fact, given my ethnographic findings and their challenge to current "War on Drugs" and "Drug-Free America" ideologies, sacramental consumption of the Peyote cactus by Native Americans is arguably the most misunderstood cultural practice in the history of North America. Since my first summer of ethnographic field research on this tradition in 1990, I have been amazed by the complexity and vitality of the tradition and its followers, as well as the variety of emotional reactions and cultural assumptions that are stirred when I describe the tradition in my classes and lectures. It is, in so many ways, a Rorschach for the many positions Euro-Americans take in relation to Native Americans, minority health practices, use of psychoactive plants, minority religious traditions, proper conduct within families, and cultural otherness generally (positions ranging from mystical romanticism to ethnocentric scorn).

Ethnographic research reveals that pharmacological or behavioral alteration of the neurochemical substrate of experience (consciousness modification), often paired with education (as in initiation ceremonies) or therapeutic emplotment[4] (as in healing ceremonies), is a mainstay of human life in its many manifestations (Bourguignon 1973; Grob and Dobkin de Rios 1994; Schultes and Hofmann 1992; Fernandez 1982). However, many non-Peyotists, both Euro-American and Native American, would respond with shock, revulsion, or disbelief when I describe my witnessing of family Peyote Ceremonies that are conducted to help children in their school-based education, in which Peyote is passed from grandparent to parent to child. Many would be offended by the story of the father who gave his young son a small amount of Peyote to help him learn to tie his shoes, or the fact that I myself, as a clinician working at a Navajo-run facility, have written Peyote Ceremonies into my treatment and aftercare plans for Peyotist adolescent clients, following standard local clinical practice, as tolerated by the US Indian Health Service. The extreme cultural divergence is obvious when, on the one hand, Native American Church members uniformly refer to Peyote using the English word "Medicine" (Schultes 1938) and say that it is necessary for their continuing health and stability while, on the other hand, the US government classifies Peyote as a Schedule I drug, defined as a dangerous drug of abuse with no therapeutic uses.

This particular situation of culture paradigm clash was thrust into the spotlight in 1990 as a result of the US Supreme Court case of Al Smith and Galen Black, two men who did not think attending a Peyote Ceremony conflicted with their role as substance abuse counselors (Calabrese 2001; H. Smith and Snake 1996). However, the clash is as old as the Spanish Inquisition in colonial Mexico (Leonard 1942). My finding in this book is that, when we bracket our ethnocentrism and strive to understand this cultural tradition on its own terms and from a broad anthropological perspective, and especially when we get to know Peyotists personally in the contexts of their family and professional lives, as I have done, the bulk of the evidence reveals the Native American Church to be a cultural system of therapeutic, developmental, and spiritual intervention. This form of intervention utilizes ancient and widespread ritual-based forms of healing and socialization, including ritual symbolism, consciousness modification, and relationship with divinity, to address particular problems of contemporary Native American communities living in the (post)colonial era.[5]

This argument will be, like the bitter Peyote cactus itself, "hard to swallow" for some readers. For certain readers, this may simply reflect an inability to recognize, or a refusal to question, the cultural assumptions and ideologies in which they have been trained. The reader, in other words, may experience the cultural paradigm clash and choose to mentally bolt from the Sweat Lodge rather than stay to explore the cultural difference. For other readers, the topic of psychoactive plant use will simply seem exotic and thus peripheral to serious scholarship.[6] However, saying that something is "exotic" is just another way of automatically marginalizing it, often with ethnocentric or colonial implications. "Exotic" should immediately imply the questions "For whom?" and "From which cultural perspective?" Practices are not inherently exotic. The practices of the Native American Church are certainly not exotic and peripheral from the perspective of the people who use them to sustain their health and their families. For readers who have the ability to question their own preconceptions and cultural training, they may discover in this book a fascinating example of the diversity of human ways of being, the continuing resilience of indigenous societies, and the continuing vitality and clinical utility of healing rituals in the modern world. This study is meant to challenge the reader with cultural difference in the hope that the reader will come to grasp its significance and in the hope that cultural understanding and support for personal and cultural healing (both within and between societies) are extended.

Acknowledgments

MY GREATEST APPRECIATION goes to the many Native American people who shared their stories, opinions, mutton stew, and homes with me. Foremost among these is Hoskie Benally, Jr., the retired president of the Four Corners Chapter of the Native American Church, who supported this project from the beginning. There are many other Native American people I would like to thank by name but whose identities I must protect. My sincere appreciation to all.

I am very grateful to the team at Oxford University Press for their thoughts on the book, including Sponsoring Editor Cynthia Read, Series Editors Ronald L. Grimes and Ute Hüsken, Assistant Editor Lisbeth Redfield, the other editorial staff involved, and the two anonymous reviewers of the manuscript.

Deepest thanks also to the many scholars who taught me and have influenced my work. These include the members of my dissertation committee at the University of Chicago: my anthropological mentor and dissertation chair Raymond D. Fogelson, my clinical mentor Bertram J. Cohler, and anthropologists George W. Stocking, Jr., Waud Kracke, and Anne Terry Straus. Other very important teachers at the University of Chicago included Gilbert Herdt, Richard Shweder, David Orlinsky, Martha McClintock, and James Fernandez.

My sincere thanks to Byron Good, Mary-Jo DelVecchio Good, and Arthur Kleinman at Harvard for their foundational work in medical anthropology, their crucial examples, and their encouragement and valuable training during my time as a National Institute of Mental Health Fellow in their department. I have also been greatly inspired by the work of other Harvard anthropologists, especially Robert A. LeVine and Paul Farmer.

I would also like to thank the many other anthropological scholars who have influenced my work through their writings, conversations, and lectures, including Susan Tax Freeman, Benjamin Colby, Mel Spiro, Anthony Wallace, Joseph Gone, Alex Cohen, Cheryl Mattingly, Thomas Csordas, Janis Jenkins, Robert Desjarlais, Marlene Dobkin de Rios, Michael Winkelman, Laurence Kirmayer, Allan Young, Tanya Luhrmann, Robert L. Hall, Lawrence Keeley, Paul Hockings, and many others. I owe special thanks to the late David Aberle for his laudatory comments in his peer review of my first paper in *Ethos*, which encouraged me to continue my study of the Native American Church.

Many thanks to my friends and colleagues at University College London, including David Napier, Roland Littlewood, Sahra Gibbon, Alexandra Pillen, Charles Stewart, Susanne Kuechler, Martin Holbraad, Sushrut Jadhav, Rodney Reynolds, Murray Last, and Allen Abramson, and all the faculty and staff of the University College London Department of Anthropology. At the University of Oxford, where I was the Cannon Fellow in Patient Experiences and Health Policy, I am grateful to Louise Locock, Sue Ziebland, Ann McPherson, and the Health Experiences Research Group; David Gellner, Elisabeth Hsu, Caroline Potter, and the rest of the Anthropology faculty; and Colin Bundy, Sir David Watson, and all the Fellows and staff at Green Templeton College.

I also owe a great debt to all my clinical teachers, including Saul Rosenthal, Marla Eby, Peter McEntee, Jean Fain, Emily Bailey, Vida Kazemi, Larry Rosenberg, Rebecca Rosenblum, Matthew Leeds, and Jim Lindsley at Harvard Medical School's Cambridge Hospital; Patrick Corrigan, E. Paul Holmes, Princess Williams, Stanley McCracken, and Mark Reinecke at University of Chicago Hospitals; Charles Stiava and Marge Melstrom at the Chicago-Read Mental Health Center; and Candice Sabin, my clinical supervisor on the Navajo reservation.

Last but not least, I would like to acknowledge the importance of the support and encouragement I received from my family, including my parents, Joseph and Ann Calabrese; my brother, Shawn; and my wife (and partner on visits to the Navajo Nation and other adventures), Tracey Denton-Calabrese.

This project was partially supported with funds from the University of Chicago Human Rights Program, the University of Chicago Committee on Human Development, the Society for Psychotherapy Research, the Association for Religion and the Intellectual Life, the Institute for Humane Studies, and the Acton Institute for the Study of Religion and

Liberty. I was able to devote effort to writing during my time as a National Institute of Mental Health Fellow in Medical Anthropology at Harvard Medical School and during my fellowship at Green Templeton College, University of Oxford.

The symbolic analysis of the Peyote Meeting presented here was previously published in *Ethos* (© 1994 American Anthropological Association) and is reprinted here (in a revised form) with permission from *Ethos* volume 22, number 4. In addition, certain sections of chapter IV are reprinted with permission from *Anthropology of Consciousness* volume 12, number 2, published by the American Anthropological Association (© 2001).

This book is dedicated to those who are open-minded. This group of people is an important source of hope for humanity at a time when the world seems threatened by narrow-minded capitalist economic domination and equally narrow-minded religious fundamentalisms. The book is also dedicated to critical thinkers who question received wisdom while preserving ideas and practices that, after a careful, critical evaluation, can be shown to have enduring value.

A Different Medicine

PART ONE

Anthropological and Clinical Orientations

1

Introduction

PEYOTE, CULTURAL PARADIGM CLASH, AND THE MULTIPLICITY OF THE NORMAL

Cultural anthropology has the healthiest of skepticisms about the validity of the concept of "normal behavior."...It is valuable because it is constantly rediscovering the normal....[P]ersonalities are not conditioned by a generalized process of adjustment to the "normal" but by the necessity of adjustment to the greatest possible variety of idea and action patterns according to the accidents of birth and biography

—EDWARD SAPIR *(1932)*

...an abnormality of our culture is the cornerstone of their social structure.

—RUTH BENEDICT *(1934, 65)*

THIS BOOK IS an attempt to create a bridge of understanding between very different experiential worlds: antithetical poles in a clash of cultural paradigms surrounding the ritual use of the Peyote cactus by Native Americans. The book uses a dialectical approach, striving to bring opposed perspectives (Euro-American/Native American, collective/personal, study of cultural meanings/embodied practices, anthropology/psychology/psychiatry) into the same analytical space and view them critically in relation to each other and in terms of the ethnographic data. The ethnographic data in this case are the personal experiences and practices of members of the Native American Church, a postcolonial revitalization movement and healing movement among Native North Americans.

The book takes an anthropological approach to central questions for the clinical sciences, especially as they increasingly interact with culturally diverse populations: What is normal? What is therapeutic? What is medicine? Do these things vary across different cultural contexts? My approach to these questions is informed by studies of the dialectical relationship between the collective and the personal, which problematize standard understandings of the mind and psychology (Stigler, Shweder, and Herdt 1990; LeVine 1982; J. Bruner 2008; Obeyesekere 1981; Cole 1996). Scholars working in this tradition increasingly draw attention to collective forms of suffering (Kleinman, Das, and Lock 1997), often in postcolonial contexts (M-J. Good et al. 2008). In this book, I approach the postcolonial world as a site of social suffering but also as a site of personal and collective healing. This leads to questions that are more anthropological: How do traumatized postcolonial populations heal themselves? What are the emotional and relational dynamics of cultural revitalization? What role can rituals play in this process?

To begin to understand the indigenous healing movement called the Native American Church and its medicine Peyote, we must first understand the circumstances of the Native American societies in which this tradition developed. Though the encounter of Europeans and Native Americans in the New World is often celebrated with optimistic terms like *discovery* and *exploration*, this encounter also resulted in what has been called "the greatest genocide in human history" (Todorov 1984, 5) and an American Holocaust (Brave Heart and DeBruyn 1998; Thornton 1987; Stannard 1992). As many as 100 million indigenous people died as a result of the European colonization of the Americas (Stannard 1992). Perhaps 90 percent of the indigenous population was wiped out by European diseases for which there was no immunity, including smallpox, measles, influenza, typhus, bubonic plague, yellow fever, and malaria. Europeans were not always innocent bystanders in this biological process. It appears that they sometimes supported the process by making gifts to the Indians of blankets infected with smallpox, an early example of the use of a biological weapon (Cook 1998, 206–213).

To this biological onslaught was added the indiscriminant murder of men, women, and children; subjugation; forced labor; and cultural destruction. Bartolomé de las Casas, a Spanish historian and Dominican friar writing in sixteenth-century colonial Mexico, gave many eyewitness accounts such as the following:

> The Spaniards found pleasure in inventing all kinds of odd cruelties, the more cruel the better, with which to spill human blood. They built a long gibbet, low enough for the toes to touch the ground and prevent strangling, and hanged thirteen [natives] at a time in honor of Christ Our Saviour and the twelve Apostles. When the Indians were thus still alive and hanging, the Spaniards tested

their strength and their blades against them, ripping chests open with one blow and exposing entrails, and there were those who did worse. Then, straw was wrapped around their torn bodies and they were burned alive. (Las Casas 1971)

This account has a special hypocrisy in the fact that thirteen victims were tortured to death to glorify the "Prince of Peace" Jesus Christ and his twelve disciples in a perverse mockery of his central message. Other disturbing accounts from this time describe infants being torn from their mothers' breasts and smashed against rocks, women and children being thrown to hungry dogs to be torn apart, dismemberments, killings for sport, large-scale massacres, and brutal enslavement.

The conflict between Europeans and Native Americans was also a conflict in radically different views of the world and approaches to life. These two human groups, separated for millennia by oceans and by divergent developmental histories, experienced shock at their mutual discovery. As the Canadian anthropologist Bruce Trigger (1991, 1200) writes, Native Americans had never previously had to deal "with anything like the bearded, white-skinned beings who began haunting their seacoasts. The latter's huge ships, abundant metal goods, brightly colored clothes, and thundering guns and cannons placed them in a different category from any known or imaginable native group." Europeans were also shocked by the cultural differences. They often saw Native Americans as inferior to Europeans and perhaps less than human. They sometimes reassured themselves with arguments that the domination of Native Americans was actually to their spiritual benefit because the Native Americans did not know about Jesus Christ, an ancient Jewish religious teacher and healer born on a continent they never knew existed. Europeans pursued the destruction of indigenous cultures while holding an ethnocentric view of the metaphysical and moral superiority of their own identity and beliefs. Even Bartolomé de las Casas, who worked to expose the atrocities of the Spanish against Native Americans, was in favor of their Christianization.

The extreme cultural differences must have led to very strange feelings for both Europeans and Native Americans. The Spanish obviously did not like the feeling of strangeness and set out to exterminate it, bringing the techniques of the Inquisition to Mexico (Perry and Cruz 1991; Chuchiak 2012). Torture, incarceration, public humiliation, and burning at the stake were used to enforce a Spanish Catholic vision of the normal and the sacred. As Carrasco (1988, 153) puts it, "A massive program to obliterate strangeness was initiated in sixteenth-century Mexico and carried out until the present." Many of the Inquisition cases against Native Americans were for idolatry, superstition, and sorcery as defined by the Spanish. Through these charges, indigenous spiritual and healing practices were punished, as was the use of various psychoactive plants that had a spiritual or medical significance for the indigenous populations.

It is in this context of conquest, colonial domination, and ethnocentric cultural antagonism that Europeans formed their first opinions of the Peyote cactus. Peyote was seen by the Spanish as a strange substance that was used in heathen rituals to contact evil spirits. Its use reinforced indigenous spiritual traditions and thus blocked the dominance of Christianity. Ethnocentric persecution of indigenous people who use Peyote began soon after Europeans arrived in the New World. The Inquisition likely created the first Euro-American antidrug law in 1620 by proclaiming Peyote the work of the Devil (Leonard 1942). Government-sanctioned witch hunts against Peyotists living within the area that would become the United States go back to 1632, when anti-Peyotist Inquisition hearings were held in Santa Fe (Stewart 1987, 22–24). This is a short distance from the Navajo Peyotists with whom I did my fieldwork.

North of Mexico, in the area that was to become the United States, the post-contact period was also marked by the decimation of indigenous populations through diseases and wars. In the nineteenth century, the Manifest Destiny doctrine arose, in which the citizens of the United States convinced themselves that they were ordained by Providence to rule North America from the Atlantic Coast to the Pacific Coast. This particularly grandiose and self-serving strand of American exceptionalist ideology, not completely dead today, used the idea of the unique virtue of the democratic form of government as practiced in the United States to justify a territorial expansion that was frequently violent and predatory (and not very democratic). In this context, Native Americans were often cast as barriers to Manifest Destiny that had to be eliminated and were, in fact, destined to fade away in any case:

By 1845 the Indian population of California was down to no more than a quarter of what it had been when the Franciscan missions were established in 1769. That is, it had declined by at least 75 percent during seventy-five years of Spanish rule. In the course of just the next twenty-five years, under American rule, it would fall by another 80 percent. The gold rush brought to California a flood

of American miners and ranchers who seemed to delight in kill-
ing Indians, miners and ranchers who rose to political power and
prominence—and from those platforms not only legalized the
enslavement of California Indians, but, as in Colorado and elsewhere, launched public campaigns of genocide with the explicitly
stated goal of all-out Indian extermination. (Stannard 1992, 142)

In addition to removal by outright murder, the United States also removed
tribes from their traditional lands through forced death marches of up to
a thousand miles. The most famous of these are the "Long Walk" of the
Navajos to Fort Sumner and the "Trail of Tears," in which many Cherokees,
Muscogees, Seminoles, and Choctaws died as they were marched from
the southeastern United States to Oklahoma. From the mid-nineteenth
century, Native American children were also removed from their families
and placed in government-run boarding schools designed to strip them
of their cultural identities. They were beaten for speaking their tribal languages and abused in a variety of other ways (Adams 1995).

The Native American peoples who survived these events were mas-
sively traumatized by the violent conquest, death of loved ones, loss of
their lands, and forced acculturation. Their societies were destabilized and
their understandings of the universe and hope for the future were likely
thrown into question. Today, Native Americans face health problems, pov-
erty, and social disorder that are, compared to many other groups within
the United States, uniquely severe. These problems include elevated rates
of death from alcoholism, suicide, homicide, unintentional injuries, tuberculosis, and diabetes (Surgeon General of the U.S. Public Health Service
2005; Indian Health Service 2004).

This situation of disrupted social harmony and health is found in many
societies that have experienced conquest and colonialism. In their book
Postcolonial Disorders, Harvard University medical sociologist Mary-Jo
DelVecchio Good and colleagues (2008, 3) argue that such situations
of societies traumatized by colonialism demonstrate "the political at the
heart of the psychological and the psychological at the heart of the political." For Native Americans specifically, Maria Yellow Horse Brave Heart
and Lemyra DeBruyn (1998), drawing from the literature on survivors of
the Jewish Holocaust, argue that "historical unresolved grief" contributes
to the high rates of disorder and illness found among Native American
peoples. They write that, like the children of Jewish Holocaust survivors,
"subsequent generations of American Indians also have a pervasive sense

of pain from what happened to their ancestors and incomplete mourning of those losses" (Brave Heart and DeBruyn 1998, 68).

Native American Efforts at Cultural Revitalization

In the wake of conquest and in the context of ongoing colonial domination, various attempts at cultural revitalization and self-healing developed among Native American communities. Many of these were intertribal in character, establishing connections even between tribal groups that had previously been enemies. The American anthropologist Anthony F. C. Wallace (1956, 265) introduced the term *revitalization movements* to describe "a deliberate, organized, conscious effort by members of a society to construct a more satisfying culture." This type of social movement is common in societies undergoing severe stress, such as in a situation of colonial conquest, and hundreds of such social movements have been identified throughout the world.

The pain of conquest often resonates in the ideologies and histories of these Native American revitalization movements. One of the most influential of the movements, the Ghost Dance, predicted that Native American people would be reunited with their dead loved ones, who would be resurrected, and predicted a transformation of the world involving the return of the previous ways of life, the return of the buffalo and other game animals, and the disappearance of the Europeans. This return to the life that existed before the Europeans came would be brought about through performance of a ceremonial dance and by living a righteous life. The most influential strand of the Ghost Dance originated with the Paiute spiritual leader Wovoka, who had a powerful vision during the solar eclipse on January 1, 1889. The movement spread to tribes throughout the western United States during a period in which Native Americans were confined to smaller and smaller patches of land with insufficient sources of food. Lakota participants in the Ghost Dance adopted the practice of wearing Ghost Shirts, painted with magic symbols, which they believed would protect them from harm, including the White Man's bullets. This practice was interpreted by most white people as a prelude to war. However, one White Man who was respected among the Lakota, Dr. Valentine McGillycuddy, urged restraint, wiring his superiors this message:

> The coming of the troops has frightened the Indians. If the Seventh-Day Adventists prepare the ascension robes for the Second Coming

of the Savior, the United States Army is not put in motion to prevent them. Why should not the Indians have the same privilege? If
the troops remain, trouble is sure to come. (Straub 2009, 46)

On December 29, 1890, the tensions surrounding the Lakota Ghost Dance
erupted in the tragic massacre at Wounded Knee on the Pine Ridge reservation. In this incident, well over a hundred Native American men, women,
and children were killed by the US Army, who used rapid-firing Hotchkiss
cannons on them. Those who attempted to flee were chased down and
killed by the soldiers. According to Brave Heart and DeBruyn (1998, 65),

This genocide was analogous to the Jewish Holocaust in that (a) it
was fueled by religious persecution of Lakota Ghost Dancers and
by federal policies of extermination (Brave Heart-Jordan, 1995;
Brown, 1970; Prucha, 1984; Tanner, 1982); (b) the victims of the
massacre were stripped and thrown into a mass grave "...like sar-
dines in a pit" (Mattes, 1960, p. 4) similar to the mass graves of
Jewish Holocaust victims; and (c) the suffering of the survivors and
descendants chronicled in the literature (The Lakota Times, 1990;
McDermott, 1990) and the challenges of mourning a massive group
trauma bear resemblance to the challenges facing Jewish Holocaust
victims and survivors.

After its Lakota practitioners were crushed at Wounded Knee, the main
Ghost Dance movement declined or at least went underground. However,
the friendly intertribal contacts that it helped to create remained. This set
the stage for the spread of another intertribal revitalization movement:
the Peyote Religion or Native American Church. This movement was
first described in the late nineteenth century as a new religious movement spreading among the Oklahoma tribes. Instead of focusing on a
transformation of the world through the disappearance of Europeans, it
focused on personal transformation that would allow one to survive in
the postconquest situation, build a stronger community, and avoid forms
of postcolonial disorder like addiction to the White Man's alcohol. This
personal transformation was achieved through ritual consumption of a
sacred Native American medicine: the psychoactive Peyote cactus.

Peyote use is among the most ancient Native American practices of
which we are aware. It was used in Mexico among the Aztecs and many other
tribes and is still a central aspect of life among the Huichol and Tarahumara

(Myerhoff 1976; Schaefer and Furst 1997). The word *Peyote* itself reveals the antiquity of the plant's use. The word derives from *peyotl*, the Aztecs' name for the plant in their language Nahuatl. Pre-Columbian use of the cactus extends back several millennia. The oldest evidence of Peyote use that we have, in fact, comes from sites within the area now occupied by the United States. Radiocarbon dating of Peyote buttons from the Shumla Cave excavation in Texas shows a mean age of 5,700 years (Bruhn et al. 2002). Another Peyote specimen from a prehistoric cave burial in Coahuila, Mexico, was dated at between 810 and 1070 AD (Bruhn, Lindgren, and Holmstedt 1978).

Purposeful human use of Peyote is indicated by the fact that the ancient specimens are identified as "buttons" (dried slices off the top of the Peyote cactus), were brought into caves, and, in the case of the Coahuila find, were strung together on a cord like a necklace. Two-thousand-year-old ceramic bowls from Colima, Mexico, depicting a human figure holding two Peyote plants, more clearly reveal the cultural significance of Peyote at this period and may even suggest prehistoric domestication of the plant (Schultes 1998, 3). Peyote use among tribes in the region now occupied by the United States and Canada diffused directly from the older Mexican forms and retains many Mexican traits, though it has developed its own unique ritual and community structure.

The Native American Church took hold, spreading to many tribes throughout the United States and Canada. As with the Ghost Dance and many other Native American spiritual practices, the Native American Church was misunderstood, charges against it were fabricated, and its followers were attacked or jailed. Nevertheless, the Native American Church survived and is now the most widespread Native American religion in the United States. For this reason, it is of interest to scholars in ritual studies, religious studies, and anthropology. The Native American Church should also have a special place in postcolonial studies as it is the largest indigenous revitalization movement operating within the internal colonies of the United States. In addition, the case of the Native American Church is a fascinating and important context in which to study cultural paradigm clashes.

A New Inquisition: The War on Drugs in Contemporary North America

As described previously, the culture clash over Native American use of Peyote, resulting in European punishment of the practice, began with the

Spanish Inquisition in Mexico. Today, Peyotists face another inquisition in the form a politically driven, anthropologically naive, and morally imperialist "War on Drugs." Dominant Euro-American norms limit psychoactive substance use to a few culturally familiar substances (tobacco, alcohol, caffeine, and the various approved psychiatric medications) all of which are manufactured, marketed, and sold as income-generating products within the approved ideological framework of those in power: capitalism. Another cultural norm is abstinence from consciousness-modifying substances altogether, which may be denounced in moral terms as "evil" or "sinful." Clinical psychopharmacology in the United States is limited to the exclusive use of lab-created psychological medicines that are profitable for drug companies and that are rationalized scientifically, though their efficacy is not straightforward or predictable and they often have significant negative side effects of their own (Breggin 1991). The psychoactive plant medicines of other societies have been labeled "drugs of abuse" or are assumed to be inferior to lab-created medicines in all cases, ensuring the hegemony of the Euro-American cultural norms. However, given the colonial history, many Native Americans and other cultural minorities continue to trust their sacred plant medicines, which are culturally familiar products of their natural environment rather than inventions of the Euro-American scientist.

This larger instance of cultural paradigm clash between dominant Euro-American pharmacological assumptions and the assumptions of other cultural groups (or even Euro-Americans who simply disagree with dominant assumptions) is of more than theoretical interest. Many argue that this situation has resulted in a human rights catastrophe within the United States and beyond (Calabrese 2001; Human Rights Watch 2003; Gray 2001; Nadelmann 1988). The War on Drugs has deprived hundreds of thousands of nonviolent Americans of their liberty and exposed them to the cruelties and commodifications of the US prison industrial complex (Schlosser 1998; Gilmore 2000; Leder 2004). In 1999, the Justice Policy Institute reported that, largely due to the War on Drugs, the number of nonviolent prisoners held by the United States had surpassed 1 million (Justice Policy Institute 1999). According to a report by Human Rights Watch (2003), nearly three-quarters of new admissions to state prisons were people convicted of nonviolent crimes. This report describes the War on Drugs as "perhaps the single greatest force behind the growth of the prison population....The number of incarcerated drug offenders has increased twelvefold since 1980."

The US prison population is now, in fact, the largest of any country in the world, both in absolute numbers and relative to the population. As data from the World Prison Brief of the International Centre for Prison Studies (2012) reveals, the United States imprisons the most people in the world, both in terms of the absolute number of prisoners held and the rate of imprisonment relative to population. In absolute numbers, the United States' imprisonment of 2,266,832 people dwarfs the number imprisoned by second-place-country China (with only 1,640,000 prisoners). This is in spite of the fact that China has a billion more people than the United States and the total population of the United States is only a quarter of China's. In terms of imprisonment rates per 100,000 people, the United States' rate of 730 easily beats the eighth-place Russian Federation (at 498). The United States is, in this sense, less free than Communist China or Russia. The disproportionate imprisonment of African Americans and other ethnic minorities is particularly troubling, especially when it involves slave labor by prisoners to benefit an expanding for-profit prison industry (Marion 2009; Wacquant 2001; Gilmore 2000).[1] Although African Americans account for only 12 percent of the population, they make up 44 percent of all prisoners in the United States (Human Rights Watch 2003). "The Land of the Free" has thus become a world leader in the imprisonment of its own citizens. This is an irony and an instance of hypocrisy, the injustice of which many Americans do not or will not recognize given their ethnocentric understanding of "drug use," persistent racism, and blind allegiance to "tough on crime" political campaign rhetoric.

It is clarifying to note that the annual number of deaths in the United States caused by either one of the *legal* substances alcohol or tobacco easily dwarfs the annual deaths related to all of the *illegal* substances combined (Mokdad et al. 2004; McGinnis, Michael, and Foege 1993). A study of the actual causes of death in the United States, sponsored by the Centers for Disease Control and Prevention and published in the *Journal of the American Medical Association*, found that, in the year 2000, tobacco use caused 435,000 deaths, alcohol use caused 85,000 deaths, and use of all illicit drugs combined caused a mere 17,000 deaths (Mokdad et al. 2004). The authors also point out that their illicit drug use category includes not only deaths caused directly by the substances in question but also those caused "indirectly," though why this is the case in a study of "actual causes of death" is not adequately explained and may itself reveal the ideological bias of medical knowledge. So what we have is not a rational policy related to the true dangers, or lack of danger, of particular substances but rather a moral reaction to the violation of particular Euro-American cultural taboos in which science is pressured to conform itself to fit with ethnocentric moral and political imperatives.[2]

Euro-American inability or unwillingness to understand Native American use of Peyote is symptomatic of a broader ignorance of world cultures. Almost absent from the Euro-American worldview is an awareness of the histories of ritualized sacred and medical uses in other societies of the substances that are outlawed in Euro-American society. Almost absent from popular understandings are positive accounts of the functional lives of people from such traditions who do not conform to the standard government-approved image of the "drug user" who must be severely punished. When viewed in the context of world cultures, far from being unnatural and pathological, consciousness modification, often involving more or less harmless use of psychoactive plants, has been found to be a near-universal human activity. Erika Bourguignon (1973) examined a diverse sample of 488 societies (57 percent of the human societies represented in Murdock's *Ethnographic Atlas*) and found that 437 societies (89 percent) were reported to have one or more institutionalized forms of consciousness alteration. She concluded that societies that do not utilize altered states of consciousness are the historical exceptions. The implication is that societies that forbid consciousness alteration practices are, in the context of the world's cultures, the "exotic" ones that require an explanation. Detailed studies of ritual psychopharmacological traditions have been done on use of the psychoactive *eboga* shrub among the Fang of Gabon (Fernandez 1982), therapeutic use of *ayahuasca* in the Peruvian Amazon (Dobkin de Rios 1972), ritual use of cannabis by Rastafarians in Jamaica (Barrett 1997), and the controlled use of coca in the Andes (Allen 1988), to name only a few. Given the greater prominence of psychedelic plants in the New World than in the Old World, their use is an aspect of the unique cultural heritage of the New World (Schultes 1998) that the War on Drugs mentality threatens to wipe out forever.

In the particular cultural paradigm clash that is the focus of this book, we have a situation in which the Euro-American response to a particular set of phenomena is nearly opposite to the indigenous response: a situation of cultural antithesis. Peyotists outlaw the use of alcohol and embrace the ceremonial use of a psychedelic plant. Euro-American society does the opposite, outlawing psychedelic plants and ritualizing wine (their culturally preferred intoxicant) in the Christian Mass. In the realm of psychopharmacological medicine, perhaps Euro-Americans, favoring an ideology of dominance *over* nature rather than interconnectedness *with* nature, merely trust the technologically manufactured substances while Peyotists trust a naturally occurring substance, which they take to be a medicine provided to them directly by the Creator through nature. Tobacco is a substance common to both systems, but in Native American societies it is a sacred means of communicating prayers to the spirit world, the use of which is ritualized and thus controlled. However, in Euro-American society, "freedom" means that tobacco is mass produced and commodified and is compulsively "chain smoked," with the unused portion thrown into the street. It is this pattern of compulsive rather than mindful use that makes tobacco a drug of abuse in the Euro-American context but not in the Native American ritual context. The problem is not in the plant itself but in the way it is used.

The Harvard University medical anthropologist Byron Good (1992, 1994) has drawn attention to the ideological component of all medical knowledge, emphasizing the networks of cultural associations that link illness to fundamental cultural values. He writes that medical narratives often represent as prototypical "not only a set of symptoms but a view of the person, social context, and life story that reproduces conventional knowledge about social relations" (B. Good 1992, 193). I argue that, in the domain of Euro-American clinical fields and policy related to psychopharmacology and "drug use," the view that medical knowledge reflects not simply "reality" but rather local ideological and moral commitments (as well as economic and political imperatives) is less a theoretical conjecture than an easily identified element of American society.

The Dialectical Study of Cultural Paradigm Clashes

The term *paradigm clashes*, inspired by the historian and philosopher of science Thomas Kuhn (1970) but defined more broadly here to include clashes of broad cultural paradigms, suggests not so much disagreements on a specific issue as major divergences in very basic approaches to conceptualization, action, and embodied experience. The paradigms in cultural paradigm clashes have long cultural histories, are assumed to be factually supported by either side, and remain largely unquestioned and impervious to conflicting evidence until a crisis arises. This term is usefully applied to cultural experience because socialization so often produces humans who accept the naive realist illusion that their cultural paradigms directly mirror reality rather than filter and construct it.

In taboo-laden cultural domains such as food choice, sexuality, parenting, spirituality, psychoactive substance use, and health care, cultural paradigms tend to be so ingrained by socialization, especially when paired with a totalizing moral ideology, that clashes in these areas can elicit complex psychophysiological, moral, and interpretive reactions. The extent of these cultural divergences can be striking. In some cases, to elaborate on Benedict (1934), the very practices and experiential states that are understood as pathological, immoral, or criminal in one society may be understood as beneficial and necessary, even as the foundation of responsible social behavior, in another society. In these cases, cultural paradigms are so dissimilar or mutually antagonistic that we may refer to them as "cultural antitheses."[3] These sorts of binary oppositions in cultural approaches to the understanding and practice of normal behavior, in which we find two radically different ways of being intelligent, healthy, or moral, frequently reveal domains of human life in which cultural constructions play a central role and in which a single universal level of "normal human functioning" is not apparent.

Given this book's focus on a situation of intercultural conflict and its tendencies toward holism and empathy in analysis, it is appropriate that this study was structured according to a dialectical philosophy. The dialectical approach taken in this study approaches conflicts and oppositions, bringing the opposed arguments into the same analytical space, where they are critically examined, along with the interrelationships, complementarities, and larger systems that link the opposed phenomena. The goal of a dialectical approach is a more encompassing understanding synthesized from the study of diverse and often contradictory perspectives and arguments (Basseches 1984; Nisbett et al. 2001). It involves a rejection of polarized thinking and simplistic extremist positions in favor of holism, complexity, contradictions, reciprocal relationships, and multiple points of view. For this reason, dialectical thinking is the "middle path" between the poles of universalistic and relativistic thinking (Linehan 1993, 120). To begin to resolve, or at least understand, a cultural paradigm clash, we must go beyond the level of the "insider's perspective" of either party in the clash to a more encompassing level that can comprehend both. The dialectical strategy adopted here is itself an attempt to get beyond a particular feature of Euro-American ethnocentrism: its tendencies toward polarization, founded in various Manichean traditions that dichotomize—Cartesian dualism, good-versus-evil Christianity, individual against society individualism, male as the opposite of female, and so forth. However, I also reject the assumption that there must be two equal sides on every issue or that the truth is always a synthesis of perspectives. Sometimes there is simply one correct answer to a question. Thus, the position of this book is not relativist but *meta-relativist*, holding that relativism itself must be relativized.

The overriding theoretical dialectic in this study is cultural psychiatry, a term that I use to refer to the dialectical interplay of culture and mental health. A related domain not specifically linked to clinical matters is "cultural psychology" (Stigler et al. 1990; Cole 1990), which focuses on the ways that culture and mind shape one another. My position is that good dialectical analysis in the human sciences does not reduce human life to either intrapsychic psychology or shared culture but instead encompasses the influence of human cultures on psychological functioning, as well as the influence of human psychology on the structuring of culture. We see this reciprocal relationship at work in revitalization movements: personal psychological needs contribute to the transformation of culture to better respond to those personal needs.

A dialectical approach to the study of human lives implies an interdisciplinary approach, given that perspectives bound to a single discipline are often very one-sided and incomplete. As such, in preparing to carry out my fieldwork on postcolonial healing in the Native American Church, I did not limit my training to a single academic discipline. Instead, I sought to bring together and balance anthropological and clinical disciplines. I felt that developing dual anthropological and clinical competencies was especially important for this study, given the fact that I was entering a sensitive domain of trauma, intercultural resentment, and personal and cultural efforts at healing. In my doctoral studies at the University of Chicago, I received training in fieldwork-based cultural anthropology (supervised by Raymond Fogelson and Gilbert Herdt) and studied the anthropological critiques of mainstream psychological and medical disciplines. I also engaged in clinical training and practice toward licensure as a clinical psychologist and, in turn, applied this clinical identity in the field, donating a year of my effort as a clinician as part of my fieldwork.

I have thus attempted to actualize Byron Good's (1994, 168) suggestion that anthropologists interested in the comparative study of illness and its treatment "do well to move dialectically between a critical analysis of biomedical categories and knowledge, on the one hand, and operationalizations of such categories for the purposes of comparative, cross-cultural analysis, on the other." I went beyond this, however, in moving dialectically between distinct disciplinary perspectives in the field, employing clinical psychological practice as a field technique while continually problematizing my practice using anthropological forms of critique. I also used reflexivity in many ways that were influenced by both my clinical training and my anthropological training.

In my clinical research and practice, I have specialized in the study and treatment of psychosis, severe substance abuse, and severe personality disorders. These areas relate to my ethnographic focus on major alterations of consciousness and how societies respond to people who inhabit these alternative states of consciousness, which relates to my other long-standing interest in stigmatized social groups. In the area of psychosis and in the use of psychedelic substances, aspects of social context and interpersonal response, such as emotions expressed by one's family, can have a crucial impact on self-experience and mental health outcomes (Calabrese and Corrigan 2005; Calabrese 1997, 2008). My goal has been to construct an interdisciplinary theoretical perspective that encompasses the best of both disciplinary traditions to achieve a dialectical balance between (1) a pluralist anthropological view of multiple cultural psychiatric *normalities* (we may call this view the "Sapir-Benedict hypothesis" of psychiatric relativity in light of their statements cited at the beginning of this chapter) and (2) perspectives that are less locally variable, such as the reality of the biological component of mental health and illness made apparent by my clinical experience, as well as an ethical perspective that emphasizes basic human rights beyond the conceptualizations of particular cultures.

The central methodological dialectic of this study is clinical ethnography, an approach to research that involves clinically informed and self-reflective immersion in local worlds of suffering, healing, and normality. Clinical ethnography seeks a dialectical understanding that encompasses thickly descriptive ethnography, as well as clinical evaluation and interpretation, allowing for some base of clinical competence from which to evaluate what is observed in the field. An *immersive* clinical ethnography, such as is attempted here, resists the reduction of complex human lives to an easily read statistical chart or a diagnostic category. Instead, what is sought in this study is a holistic, empathic understanding of actual persons in context and the structures of meaning and practice that form their ways of life. One conducts and analyzes interviews, but one also learns about practices through doing them (Wacquant 2004). One learns about cultural differences experientially, through establishing personal relationships, participating in social activities, and, in my case, observing and participating in clinical practices up close.

This research method produces data that are well suited to my overall goal: the creation of an empathy-facilitating document (a text that can serve as a guide for accurate empathic understanding across cultures, including more accurate clinical understanding and policy making). Empathic understanding develops out of concrete sensory experiences of interpersonal relationships over time and particular interactions and conversations, combined with critical analysis of one's own culturally shaped interpretations and emotional reactions (Cohler 1992; Cohler and Calabrese 1996; Devereux 1967; Kracke, 1994; Herdt and Stoller 1990).

Applying this dialectical framework in the structuring of my field research, I combined two years of immersive fieldwork among Navajo members of the Native American Church with a concurrent year of volunteer clinical work at a Navajo-run treatment program. I became involved in treating Native American adolescents with severe substance abuse and associated mental health problems. This clinical component immersed me in Native American clinical problems and experiences of suffering, as well as in the local treatment community. Because the CEO of the program was a Navajo Peyotist Road Man, the staff was almost completely Native American, and several of the staff members were also Native American healers, Peyotist and traditional, I had a unique opportunity to provide therapeutic intervention alongside Native American therapists addressing the forms of postcolonial disorder (substance abuse and antisocial behavior) that the Native American Church addresses through ritual. I was also able to observe Native American Church members in their professional occupations and see how various healing rituals were integrated into clinical programs. As such, though I approached a radically different tradition of psychopharmacology with an anthropologically informed open mind, I was also grounded in a clinical familiarity with the range of potential problems associated with substance abuse and in a familiarity with the standard Euro-American approaches to the treatment of mental illness. My anthropological relativism regarding traditions of consciousness alteration was thus balanced by continuous exposure to the clinical realities of substance abuse.

Discovering the Wider Context and a Contrasting Form of Normality and Psychiatric Intervention

The rationalizations that Euro-Americans use to justify their ban on the psychoactive substances of other societies and their imprisonment of those who use these substances include concerns about public health, safety, social control, effective child development, education, and, underlying it all, morality, with government authorities simply proclaiming "it's wrong" as if their job is to legislate morality based on their own ethnocentric convictions. However, my ethnographic research and clinical involvement revealed that what is an "illegal drug" for many Euro-Americans is, for thousands of Native Americans, an important source of support in all these areas: health, safety, social control, child development, education, and morality.

The US government designates the Peyote cactus as a Schedule I substance, defined as dangerous and without therapeutic uses. However (amazingly and ironically), I found that the same government that includes Peyote on its Schedule I also, in the context of the US Indian Health Service (IHS), codes the Peyote Ceremony as a valid therapeutic intervention for substance abuse! As Kunitz and Levy (1994, 202) document, therapeutic use of Peyote has its own IHS "client service code" on Code List 13, which is used for reporting provision of services to the Indian Health Service for reimbursement. The entry for Native American Church treatment reads as follows:

04: Native American Treatment: Participation in Native American Church Ceremonies (Peyote Church) led by a Road Man, who has been recommended by a local NAC chapter, and conducted primarily for the purpose of treating persons with alcohol and drug problems. This code should not be used for those Native American Church services conducted for general prayer service, birthdays, or other purposes. (IHS document reproduced in Kunitz and Levy 1994, 202)

This self-contradiction within US government policy itself calls for a questioning of the validity of Peyote's Schedule I status: Peyote obviously has accepted therapeutic uses within the United States, and if it was too dangerous to use, it is unlikely that a branch of the US government would be coding it as an intervention. In addition, the cultural and historical legitimacy of Peyote and its role in the stability of Native American communities has been supported by a host of reputable ethnographers, including Franz Boas, Alfred Kroeber, David Aberle, J. S. Slotkin, Weston LaBarre, Sol Tax, and Omer Stewart (Aberle 1991 [1966], 244; LaBarre et al. 1951), as well as psychiatrists like Karl Menninger (1971) and Robert Bergman (1971).

One recent study (Halpern et al. 2005), completed by researchers at McLean Hospital/Harvard Medical School, compared mental health and neuropsychological test results of three groups of Navajo people (one group of Native American Church members who regularly use Peyote, one group of Navajos with a past alcohol dependence but currently sober at least two months, and one group reporting minimal use of Peyote, alcohol, or other substances). Results of this study, which used the Rand Mental Health Inventory (RMHI) and a battery of standard neuropsychological tests, indicated that the group who regularly used Peyote showed no significant differences from the abstinent comparison group on most scales and scored significantly *better* on two scales of the RMHI. Furthermore, among the Native American Church members, greater lifetime Peyote use was associated with significantly better RMHI scores on five of the nine scales including the composite Mental Health Index. To put it simply, mental health *improved* with greater Peyote use.

In my own ethnographic research, I was able to live among, interview, and work alongside many socially functional and gainfully employed members of the Native American Church who use Peyote in a controlled, prosocial way. These included several clinicians, counselors, nurses, teachers, the CEO of a residential treatment program, and a district prosecutor. Witnessing the existence of multigenerational families of such people, including elders who have used Peyote regularly for fifty or sixty years with no apparent ill effects, was itself impressive evidence refuting Euro-American assumptions or moral convictions that Peyote use is inherently dangerous and socially disruptive.

The most convincing evidence to me of the role of the Peyote Ceremony in clinical intervention came from my year of clinical work at a Navajo treatment facility codirected by a licensed clinical psychologist and an influential Native American Church Road Man. Here I was expected to attend weekly Sweat Lodge rituals with my adolescent patients, which soon convinced me of the clinical utility of these sorts of rituals, especially in facilitating self-disclosure, emotion expression, and therapeutic goal setting. The Peyote Ceremony had also been reported to be clinically useful in these areas by other clinicians who worked with Native American patients. For example, Albaugh and Anderson (1974) noted for their Native American patients a "carry-over period" lasting seven to ten days after attending a Peyote Meeting that is marked by "increased openness and willingness to communicate." Given these realizations, and others that I will report, I had no ethical problem with writing Peyote Ceremonies into the treatment and aftercare plans of my clients, as was standard practice for patients from a Native American Church background who were willing to participate and whose parents had signed a Consent Form for Spiritual Participation. This was done with the approval of the patient, his or her family, and the clinical facility and is, once again, in line with what the Indian Health Service coding reveals: the Peyote Ceremony is a recognized treatment modality, as well as a prayer service.

These findings reveal that the ethnocentric understandings of psychoactive plants culturally unfamiliar to Euro-Americans, whose users they attack without mercy in their War on Drugs, may be shown to be seriously flawed when we observe the realities on the ground. Even the US government, which continues to imprison thousands of nonviolent users of these psychoactive plants, may be found to be aware of the safety and therapeutic value of this sort of medicine at the local level.

Toward an Understanding of Therapeutic Diversity and Postcolonial Healing

The increasingly multicultural composition of contemporary societies has foregrounded issues of human diversity as never before. In this new type of intercultural contact situation, marked by an unprecedented frequency of intercultural contacts and by an unprecedented number and diversity of cultures involved, health care providers, courts, law enforcement agencies, child welfare agencies, educational systems, and other institutions face a plethora of unfamiliar voices and claims that they are often ill equipped to comprehend. Nevertheless, these institutions carry on their task of separating "the normal" from all that is judged abnormal, pathological, criminal, and immoral. The problem is that, given the central role of local cultural-psychiatric adaptations in human history, "the normal," whether described as a moral, psychiatric, or even biological concept, is not one thing; it is many.

The multiplicity of the normal has been demonstrated in many domains of human life. Ethnographic research has documented significant diversity in cultural approaches to selfhood and person concepts (Fogelson 1979; Nisbett et al. 2001), childrearing (LeVine 1990; LeVine et al. 1996), gender and sexuality (Herdt 1987), management of emotions (Briggs 1970; Hollan 1988; Wikan 1990), illness expression (B. Good 1994; Kleinman 1977, 1988), dreaming (Kracke 1979, 1991), value orientations

(Kluckhohn 1956), moral functioning (Shweder, Mahapatra, and Miller 1990), and the relative emphasis placed on personal autonomy or communal interdependence (Shweder and Bourne 1984). Even biological reactions to psychiatric medications have been found to vary across ethnic groups (Lin, Smith, and Ortiz 2001). And the shifting, dynamic nature of Euro-American psychiatry's own definitions of the normal is revealed in the removal of homosexuality from our list of "mental disorders" and in the creation of new disease categories, such as premenstrual syndrome and chronic fatigue syndrome (Gaines 1992).

If this multiplicity is not recognized, unexamined cultural and moral biases of the dominant cultural group will continue to reign as the criteria by which representatives of the state unnecessarily separate families, discriminate against and imprison nonviolent offenders of victimless crimes for decades, provide culturally inappropriate clinical interventions, deny religious freedom and other cultural rights, and outlaw entire cultural traditions and ways of life. For this reason, accurate understanding of human cultural diversity and rational policies based on this understanding are ethical imperatives for any multicultural society, especially those that claim to be democracies. However, a very special ethical issue is raised in the case of the Native American Church, in which a conquering power has taken control of all the lands of an entire ethnic category of humanity, decimated these groups of people with diseases and murder, and facilitated their addiction to alcohol, and then attempts to deny them one of the few treatment approaches that has worked with their population.

This study argues that, in decisions about whether or not to attack those who practice a culturally different healing ritual or who use a culturally different plant medicine, there is a special ethical issue raised when the practice in question actually supports the health and social harmony of those who use it and when real harm associated with the practice cannot be demonstrated. A situation in which modern medical approaches and pharmacological ideologies are being forced on a population without clear data on their superiority for that population is simply one of cultural imperialism. In the case of conquered indigenous groups who are attempting to heal themselves after a genocidal onslaught, interference by the conquering power in this healing process can be seen as an element of continuing colonial domination and cultural destruction. In fact, it is like kicking the legs out from under someone whom you have already savaged and who is trying to lift himself to his feet.

This ethnography will go beyond the ethnocentrism to explore the Native American Church as a site of postcolonial healing. It will describe the meanings Native Americans attach to Peyote, the purposes for which it is used, the contexts and methods of its use, reports of therapeutic outcomes, and the challenges Native American Church members must deal with in the United States. Special attention will be given to several areas that my field experiences suggest warrant a much deeper coverage than they have received in the ethnographic literature thus far and that illustrate the multifaceted nature of the Native American Church. These include the use of Peyote in healing and health management (including its incorporation into mainstream clinical services on Indian reservations), the use of Peyote in the context of Peyotist families (including its use in the socialization of children with the goal of nurturing sober, responsible, socially valued lifestyles), the structure and symbolism of the Peyote Ceremony and its relationship with Peyotist spiritual and therapeutic experiences, the psychological significance of the widespread belief that Peyote is an omniscient spiritual entity, and the role of reflexivity or self-awareness in the Native American Church.

To understand postcolonial healing and the dynamics of revitalization, we must struggle to free our minds from ethnocentric dogmas and glimpse a truly different way of being. In following this path, I have come to see the Native American Church not as culturally valued "drug use," with all the cultural baggage of that Euro-American term, but as a complex system of medical knowledge and ritual-based psychopharmacological practice coexisting, somewhat miraculously, alongside hegemonic biomedical psychiatry within the War on Drugs–dominated United States. The extent of the divergence between European and indigenous cultural psychiatric paradigms creates a clash in which Peyotist cultural psychiatry is misunderstood as "drug use" or even "drug abuse." However, upon adopting a reflexive stance and questioning the universality of our own psychological and psychiatric paradigms, a whole new world of evidence and an entire psychiatric tradition become visible. The case of the Native American Church is thus a chance for us to, in Sapir's terms, "rediscover the normal," as well as an opportunity to broaden our understanding of therapeutic intervention, socialization, ritual, and human development across cultures.

2

Expanding Our
Conceptualization of
the Therapeutic

TOWARD A SUITABLE THEORETICAL FRAMEWORK
FOR THE STUDY OF CULTURAL PSYCHIATRIES

IN APPROACHING THE diversity of human cultural approaches to mental health and healing, we should simultaneously draw on understandings from the modern clinical disciplines and remain critical of them, seeing them as potentially reflecting particular cultural orientations and ideologies (e.g., individualism or biomedical materialism). We should realize that there is not one path to mental health, but many. This chapter uses clinical and anthropological concepts in an attempt to develop a conceptual framework broad enough to comprehend these diverse paths, encompassing both modern biomedical psychiatry and the interventions of ritual-based systems such as the Native American Church.

A central theoretical dialectic of this framework can be summarized in the term *cultural psychiatry*, a term I use to refer not to a particular disciplinary orientation but rather to the interplay of cultural and psychiatric realities as a focus of interdisciplinary investigation. This interplay involves two directionalities of influence. First, local cultural assumptions, ideologies, and forms of activity influence how illness is expressed, as well as which behaviors count as pathology, which behaviors indicate mental health, and which behaviors count as effective therapy (B. Good 1992; Kleinman 1988; Kleinman and Sung 1979; Gaines 1992). Second, the conceptual and activity structures of cultures themselves are shaped in response to human needs, including psychiatric and existential needs (Spiro 1965). Some of these needs arise in response to universals of the human condition, for example, the need for psychological adjustment to the awareness humans have of the finite span of our physical existence. This awareness, and the need to adjust to it, constitutes a very plausible explanation of the continuing power of religious conceptual systems in human societies, even in this age of scientific advances and secular ideologies (see Becker 1973). Other personal needs that help structure cultures relate more to specific social contexts with their own political and relational systems, values, and taboos.

In this chapter, I will briefly examine each aspect of the dialectic of cultural psychiatry: (1) the influence of cultural realities on clinical realities and (2) the influence of clinical realities on cultural realities. Together, these directionalities of influence help constitute distinct contexts of illness, suffering, healing, and "the normal" that we may refer to as particular "cultural psychiatries." I will also introduce two basic cultural psychiatric concepts that are central to this study: therapeutic emplotment and consciousness modification, the latter including diverse systems of psychopharmacology. In approaching the topic of psychopharmacological intervention, I will argue that any culturally informed approach should acknowledge other paradigms of psychopharmacology beyond biomedicine's agonist/antagonist paradigm, including what I call the semiotic/ reflexive paradigm of psychopharmacology (in which meanings and processes of self-reflection are central).

Therapeutic emplotment (B. Good 1994, 144; Mattingly 1994) is here defined as interpretive activity or social application of a preformed cultural narrative placing events into a meaningful story or otherwise supporting health, for example, by enhancing expectations of recovery or by discouraging unhealthy behaviors. This concept summarizes an array of anthropological theories related to the impact of meanings on health status, much of it deriving from the study of healing rituals and traditional medical systems (e.g., Lévi-Strauss 1963; Kleinman 1974; Moerman 1979; Dow 1986). Consciousness modification includes pharmacological and behavioral alterations of the substrate of experience. Cross-cultural research has shown institutionalized consciousness modification practices to be near universal in human societies (Bourguignon 1973). The interaction of these two human realities, the first implying structures of meaning and the second implying modifications of neurochemistry, exemplifies cultural psychiatry as I have defined it: the dialectical interplay of cultural and psychiatric realities.

A dialectic between emplotment and consciousness modification is at the heart of many cultural psychiatries, including Euro-American

psychiatry and Navajo Peyotist psychiatry. However, given a Cartesian dualist philosophical base, the psychotherapeutic and psychopharmacological interventions in the Euro-American system tend to be institutionally
separated (into clinical psychology and psychiatry) rather than integrated.
This tends to mask their interaction at the level of the lived experience of
patients. The dialectical relationship between emplotment and consciousness modification is more apparent in Navajo Peyotist cultural psychiatry,
in which emplotment and consciousness modification occur simultaneously and seem to work together as parts of the same ritual intervention.
Psychopharmacology is employed to achieve insight and emplotment in
a socially desired and health-facilitating narrative of transformation and
relationship with the spiritual presence of Peyote.

In this book, I argue that the use of Peyote in the Native American
Church, and the use of similar plants in many other cultural traditions,
represents a different paradigm of psychopharmacological intervention,
what I call a semiotic/reflexive paradigm. This is an experiential paradigm
of psychopharmacology in which the use of a psychoactive medicine is
aimed at higher-order mental processes (such as self-awareness, problem
solving, imagination, emotion, and suggestibility) and at transformative experiences rather than micromanagement of a person's mood state
and level of arousal (see Calabrese 2008). This paradigm contrasts both
with Euro-American psychiatry, which follows an exclusively materialist
agonist/antagonist paradigm, focused on fixing discrete neurochemical
imbalances at the molecular level, and with Euro-American psychothera-
pies, which, aside from hypnosis (itself dyadic and talk based), tend to
eschew consciousness modification and rely on rational discussions. The
Euro-American materialist paradigm results in psychiatric medicines
being administered with little effort devoted to emplotting their use in a
meaningful way, whereas, in a semiotic/reflexive paradigm, meaning is
a central aspect of the use of the medicine and perhaps the entire reason
why the medicine is used.

The Study of Cultural Psychiatries

A cursory glance at the ethnographic literature reveals that the calm,
rational discussions characteristic of Euro-American talk therapy are
not the approaches to healing used by the majority of human societies. Anthropological research reveals the centrality of ritual approaches
to healing in many societies outside the industrialized West. In these

traditions, a technique of emplotting the patient within sacred narratives, ritual symbols, songs, and myths is typically used, often in connection with a technique of consciousness modification. Ecstatic emotions and liminal symbolism predominate. From one perspective, Euro-American talk therapy may be seen as relatively decentered from a particular cultural tradition as compared to these ritual forms, being more secular and cosmopolitan and less explicitly based in cultural myths. But talk therapy is actually a very modernist/Euro-American cultural practice in that it tends to limit itself to calm, rational argumentation within individual-to-individual relationships and discussions.

Societies also differ widely in how the therapeutic modification of consciousness states takes place. Many societies have a system of psychopharmacology, though one society's psychiatric medicine is another's "drug of abuse" (Agar 1977; Dobkin de Rios 1977; Grinspoon and Bakalar 1986). Other societies prescribe such ritual behaviors as prayer, fasting, self-mortification, meditation, singing, or dancing, which also modify consciousness by altering psychophysiology and neurochemistry. Though psychoactive substances used safely and therapeutically in traditional contexts are being systematically attacked under modernist Euro-American society's War on Drugs (Calabrese 2001; Cohen 2003), there seem to be deep human needs for periodic or situational consciousness modification. The most popular explanations of the need for periodic consciousness modification, according to standard Euro-American viewpoints, tend to be intrapsychic and hedonistic, viewing use of consciousness-modifying drugs or practices as motivated by a desire to decrease stress or pain and increase subjective sense of well-being. These uses often have their own value in the individual's management of his or her own mental state. However, this study posits several very important purposes for which human *societies* (beyond isolated individuals) have developed technologies and traditions of consciousness modification. These purposes include psychiatric intervention, socialization, and social control. For this reason, reducing such traditions to hedonism is as misleading as reducing Euro-American psychiatric pharmacology to hedonism.

An orientation to cultural psychiatry provides a unique approach to general social theory, as well as to clinical theory. In addition to analyzing society through a Marxist focus on class conflict or a feminist perspective on gender, we can also study society as a therapeutic/antitherapeutic milieu. We can ask how society emplots the population and for what purposes. We can identify what sorts of differences (ethnic, political, sexual, and religious) are medicalized and pathologized. We can study how a society modifies and coordinates consciousness states or how it criminalizes and stigmatizes forms of consciousness modification that are not approved. We can ask questions like those of Kohut (1985, 224): "How does the social milieu provide stimuli or the lack of stimuli? How does it nourish the self or how does it undernourish the self, how does it warp the self, etc.?" We can also ask what memories are defensively driven out of a society's collective consciousness, such as the memory of American slavery or the violent conquest of Native American lands, and what the consequences of this repression are (such as a defensive inability to acknowledge past crimes or continuing victimization).

Not only do we need to understand the range of therapeutic and adaptive aspects of cultural psychiatries, but also we must develop an understanding of the pathological and conflictual aspects within and between them. Within a particular social context, one subgroup's psychological security may come at the expense of another subgroup's, such as in situations of ethnic or gender inequality. There are also fascinating clashes between culturally different systems of therapeutic emplotment, as manifest, for example, in clashes over conflicting religious convictions that are naively assumed to be accurate by either side or in clashes between religious explanations and those of science. The influence of the cultural on the clinical thus results in cultural psychiatric diversity, whereas the influence of the clinical on the cultural often results in people holding tight to their local ethnocentric "certainties" out of a deep need for psychological security. This sets the stage for powerful clashes of divergent cultural psychiatries.

The need to understand cultural psychiatries and their interactions is as strong as it has ever been. Beyond broad clashes of differing prescriptions for the good life, such as the clash between political Islam and capitalist democracy, the growing multiculturalism of contemporary societies means that Western-trained clinicians see a more and more culturally diverse client population. This typically takes place under the influence of biological reductionism and the psychic unity doctrine (Shore 1996, 15–41) and in the absence of a detailed knowledge of human cultural diversity. The result is that health care can be culturally inappropriate and ineffective. For example, Matchett (1972) reported that, for Hopi Indians, hearing the voice of a recently departed relative is normative. Clinicians working with Native American communities should know this or they may misdiagnose Hopis in mourning as suffering from a psychotic illness.

Clinicians also need some level of cultural knowledge to be able to distinguish personal delusions from shared belief systems into which the person has been enculturated by his or her society. What we need are clinically informed "thick descriptions" (Geertz 1973) of cultural psychiatries in all their diversity combined with a reflexive focus on the clinical investigator's own ideological and cultural psychiatric baggage.

Therapeutic Emplotment as a Synthesizing Concept in the Study of Cultural Psychiatries

Emplotment, a term that generally refers to the placing of events into a plot structure or story, has the potential to be a very useful synthesizing concept in the study of cultural psychiatries. The term *emplotment* has been used by historians like Hayden White (1981) to describe the ways in which historical events are incorporated into a coherent story by the historian. Narrative and reader response theorists (Iser 1978) tend to use the term *emplotment* to describe the imaginative activity of a reader or listener, who constructs an understanding of the story and its imagined outcome. Applied to the person in the social world, emplotment describes the person's ongoing narrative engagement with lived reality, such as a patient's struggling after a hopeful, or at least coherent, story of his or her illness or the clinician's struggling after a narrative that facilitates treatment (Mattingly 1994). As Byron Good (1994, 145) writes,

> From the perspective of readers or hearers of stories that are in process, plot is less a finished form or structure than an engagement with what has been told or read so far in relation to imagined outcomes...outcomes that are feared, longed for, or seem ironically or tragically inevitable....The activity of "emplotting" thus has a special affinity to the experience of persons with debilitating chronic illness.

As Mary-Jo DelVecchio Good and colleagues (1994, 855) argue, the activity of "emplotting" is not limited to the reader or hearer of stories but is a central feature of the way we make sense of life, as well as "a crucial imaginative response of those who face the sudden threat of an illness." In addition, emplotment is not merely an intrapsychic process; the term also captures the fashioning and deployment of narratives as a purposeful *social* activity. Anthropological data from a variety of societies around the world and throughout history have shown that the telling of stories is a powerful means of embedding culturally valued ideas in human minds. Experimental studies of narrative persuasion (Green and Brock 2000, 2002) find that absorption into a story (labeled "transportation") increases experimental subjects' subsequent story-consistent beliefs and favorable evaluations of the story's protagonists. This effect did not change depending on whether the story was identified as fact or as fiction.

Therapeutic intervention frequently aims at changing the ill person's emplotment of his or her situation, even in certain Western biomedical contexts. Mattingly (1994) and Mary-Jo DelVecchio Good and colleagues (1994) observe the ways in which clinicians place events into a story that not only is coherent but also reflects the goals of the clinical intervention, preserving hope and moving the patient toward a more therapeutic outcome. Mattingly's research illustrates the ways in which contemporary occupational therapists help to guide the experiences of patients, putting them into a plot structure or story that supports the treatment process. According to Mattingly, patients and healers not only tell stories about their work together retrospectively but also form the story of their interaction as they work together. So lived experience already has a narrative structure that forms the bases of retrospective accounts.

In her paper "The Concept of Therapeutic Emplotment," Mattingly focuses on a very short therapeutic encounter that many people would find uninteresting: an occupational therapist taking a patient with a spinal cord injury on a tour of the hospital. But she identifies several subtle interventions by the occupational therapist that begin to shape the patient's story in a way that, the therapist hopes, will get him motivated for treatment and recovery. The occupational therapist encourages the patient to comb his hair, initially describing the activity as good practice for balance and then placing the activity into a story about him preparing himself to see his girlfriend (foreshadowing his reincorporation into social relationships). A casual glance at the exercise mat begins a story of their future work together that will lead to his improvement. A pain in his shoulder allows the therapist to imply that their work will require some pain at first, thus preparing him for the pain of hard therapeutic work, but will result in more strength and flexibility. Mattingly (1994, 811) argues that

> clinical encounters involve clinician and patient in the creation and negotiation of a plot structure within clinical time. This clinical plot gives meaning to particular therapeutic actions by placing them

within a larger therapeutic story. No therapeutic plot is completely pre-ordained, however. Improvisation and revision are necessary to its creation.

In the following paragraphs, I will argue a bit with the last two sentences of the previous Mattingly passage, seeking a more encompassing model of therapeutic emplotment suitable for the study of diverse cultures of healing. Mattingly's model of therapeutic emplotment is one of a co-constructed improvised narrative between the patient and clinician. This model is very compatible with the dyadic therapeutic encounters between a patient and a clinician that we find to be typical of modern Euro-American medical contexts. However, the approach to emplotment I take in this book aims to include traditions in which therapeutic emplotments are much less negotiated or improvised and more "preordained" or prestructured by cultural narratives, for example, closely following the narrative structure of a myth or a symbolic healing ritual. In the present study, therapeutic emplotment is a broad concept encompassing something that one person can do for another (as in Mattingly's examples); something one can do for oneself, whether consciously or unconsciously (self-emplotment, which encompasses Freudian defensive distortions, as well as more creative refashionings); and something that *the structure of culture* can do for the members of a society (which I term *culturally embedded therapeutic emplotment*). Like the words *suffering* or *meaning*, *emplotment* is general term applicable to both personal and social levels of analysis and thus useful in a dialectical study of their interaction.

I thus expand the definition of therapeutic emplotment to encompass collective sociocultural processes in which therapeutic plot structures are built into shared meaning systems that are then transmitted across generations through socialization and are used to emplot individuals and groups. For me, then, therapeutic emplotment encompasses the dyadic interactional work that I do with my psychotherapy patients (similar to Mattingly's occupational therapists), as well as the intergenerationally transmitted belief that Christ's death and resurrection have enabled believers to attain life after death (or the intergenerationally transmitted symbolic structure of the Peyote Ceremony). This yields the following broader sort of definition of therapeutic emplotment:

Therapeutic emplotment is the interpretive activity or application of a preformed cultural narrative that places events into a story that is therapeutic, either in that it supports expectations of a positive outcome, makes illness or treatment comprehensible, discourages unhealthy behaviors, or otherwise supports health.

I will describe more fully why I think this expanded definition of therapeutic emplotment is useful. The most typical contrast drawn between modern Euro-American cultures and many traditional non-European cultures is the contrast between an individualist ideology and more communal or collectivist ideologies. The distinction is often overemphasized, as any society has its own individualistic elements and modern Euro-American culture has its own communal elements (Hollan 1992). However, this difference in cultural emphasis is helpful for understanding differences in therapeutic systems. When Euro-Americans think of psychotherapeutic intervention, what typically comes to mind is the therapeutic dyad: a patient, often reclining on a couch, and a therapist, often taking notes or probing with questions. The model is that of a conversation or cooperative relationship. Psychotherapeutic process, for most researchers, refers to elements of verbal behavior and interpersonal relationship between therapist and client in one-to-one interaction.

However, the form of psychotherapeutic intervention in many premodern traditions is not a dyadic conversation but rather a dramatic communal ritual. Rather than being excluded from the dyad for reasons of privacy (a value that is distinctively elaborated within more individualistic societies), the patient's significant others are present and participating. The British anthropologist Victor Turner even argued that healing among the Ndembu, an African tribe, was actually aimed more at the group than at the individual. Turner (1967, 392) writes that "The patient will not get better until all the tensions and aggressions in the group's interrelations have been brought to light." This observation resonates with the Native American Church rituals that I have studied, in which healing is not limited to the patient but is also aimed at relationships and is ultimately available to anyone attending the ritual. This is similar to some of the ideas of "family systems" approaches to psychotherapeutic intervention in modern psychology, though the central paradigm remains the individualistic/dyadic one.

Another difference between traditional and modern healing approaches has to do with the role of the healer. Many modern theories of psychotherapeutic efficacy focus on the personal properties of the therapist. The most familiar example is probably Carl Rogers's (1957) emphasis on the therapist's empathy, warmth, and genuineness. Even anthropological theories of therapeutic process such as the influential theory of James Dow (1986) are healer centered. In Dow's model, (1) the experiences of healers and healed are generalized with culture-specific symbols in cultural myth; (2) a suffering patient comes to a healer, who persuades the patient that the problem can be defined in terms of the myth; (3) the healer attaches the patient's emotions to transactional symbols particularized from the general myth; and (4) the healer manipulates the transactional symbols to help the patient transact his or her own emotions. Note that the healer is central to each of these stages. It is for this reason that Dow's model may still be too tied to Euro-American psychotherapeutic assumptions to be applicable across cultures. This is because, in many healing traditions, the healer's role may be minimal. For example, in the healing ritual of the Native American Church, the Road Man's actions do not play a dominant role. He is a role model, leads the ceremony, monitors the participants, prays for the patient with the other participants, and may administer specially blessed Medicine to the patient. But there is little verbal interaction during the ritual. It is often said that the patient is responsible for his or her own healing, that one does the ceremony for or on oneself, or that the real healer is the Peyote Spirit present in the sacramental Medicine. The most important therapeutic communications are those that come to the patient not from the healer but directly from God or the Peyote Spirit in the form of visions or other sacred experiences.

Our psychotherapy research approaches tend to have little to say about such healing experiences. Here, it seems that therapeutic messages are implicit in the symbolism of the ritual and have already been implanted in the mind of the patient through enculturation. The healing ceremony then "activates" these messages in an impressive way that, in combination with other ritual alterations of consciousness and the supportive presence of the community, may lead to cognitive and behavioral change in the patient. My argument is as follows: not only do clinicians and patients emplot illness and suffering in the treatment situation, but also culture provides emplotments that are preformed and imbued with power and positive expectations by socialization. These are the "culturally embedded therapeutic emplotments." Euro-American societies, in which healing is prototypically a one-to-one relationship between doctor and patient, as in the dominant focus of clinical psychology on individual therapy, rely more heavily on therapeutic emplotment as an interpretive activity of individuals (as described by Mattingly). But the process of healing we encounter in many other societies is communal and ritual based rather than individualistic. In these sorts of societies, therapeutic emplotment is often accomplished by immersing patients in symbol-laden communal rituals, with the meaning of ritual symbols and their contribution to an overall healing narrative already having been transmitted and reinforced during enculturation.

A good modern psychotherapist is typically characterized as nondirective. He or she tends to elicit the significant narratives of the patient or at least works collaboratively to fashion a therapeutic story through conversation. In contrast, traditional ritual-based healing approaches more often embed the patient in preformed narrative structures that are implicit in myths and ritual symbolism. Emplotment in this context can be described as a "laying on of narratives." In fact, in traditional Navajo healing ceremonies, a sand painting depicting mythic characters and stories is created, upon which the patient is placed during the ritual. This may be considered "laying the patient on the narrative." Some common therapeutic plot structures found throughout the ethnographic literature include a journey to retrieve a lost soul, the sucking out of a malevolent object or similar purifying rituals, ingestion of a medicinal and/or magical substance, reenactment of a mythic healing, and the sequence of death and rebirth (as in the symbolism of the Peyote Ceremony I will describe and also at the heart of the symbolism of Christianity).

Another mode of therapeutic emplotment combines elements of the culturally embedded therapeutic emplotment I have described and the situationally improvised emplotment that Mattingly describes. In this mode, characteristic of twelve-step groups, the person follows a stereotypical formula for ritualistically telling his or her own story according to a predetermined cultural template. Consider the personal narratives repeated by members of Alcoholics Anonymous and other self-help groups: the speaker begins with a statement like, "Hi. I'm Bob and I'm an alcoholic," after which the crowd says "Hi, Bob" and Bob launches into a description of his disease (alcoholism) and then moves to a description of his recovery. The resulting narrative resembles the very common death/rebirth narrative structure. The actively drinking self is shifted into the past tense, and thus rhetorically nullified, and the narrative of a new, recovered Bob is fashioned in the present tense: a revised self. Those who have converted to the Native American Church or have had a life-changing vision tell similarly structured stories, as do "born again" Christians, members of the mental health mutual help organization GROW (Corrigan et al. 2002), and others. The actual narrative is constructed by the individual and has elements specific to the individual's life, but it follows a preformed cultural pattern very closely.

In this section, I have argued for a broader understanding of therapeutic emplotment that encompasses both (1) therapeutic plot structures that are situationally improvised and (2) therapeutic plot structures that are preformed, embedded in culture, and applied to the particular case without significant modification. My argument is that we need to acknowledge both types of approaches rather than reduce our understanding of therapeutic emplotment to one or the other. In this book, I also make a parallel argument about ritual. Critics of meaning-centered approaches to ritual, such as symbolic analysis, have argued that they reduce a ritual to a text to be read (Schieffelin 1985). This has led to performance and practice approaches that have emphasized ritual meanings as extemporized, arising from social interaction (Schieffelin 1985) in a manner that resonates with Mattingly's approach to therapeutic emplotment, or that analytically separates what ritual does from its meanings, de-emphasizing the importance of the latter (Bloch 1974). The result has often been an unnecessary dichotomization of meaning-centered approaches and practice-centered approaches and a mischaracterization of symbolic anthropologists as ignoring dramatic elements and treating the efficacy of symbols as "a rather rational, intellectual business" (Schieffelin 1985, 708, though, to his credit, Schieffelin even admits that he overstates his case). When we consider the typical examples targeted by critics of symbolic analysis (Claude Lévi-Strauss, Victor Turner, and Clifford Geertz), we find that Lévi-Strauss (1963) actually emphasized the dramatic temporality of the Cuna healing song for difficult childbirth and how it was linked to bodily experiences, Turner (1985) championed the study of social dramas and what rituals do, and Geertz (1973) argued that rituals reflect society but also shape it, providing models *of* how things are but also models *for* how things should be.

Scholars who dichotomize meaning and practice also tend to mischaracterize the extent to which the meanings of symbols can be ignored in an ethnographic approach focused on embodied practice (see my critical reading of Desjarlais in the next chapter). My argument is that, in approaching ritual, we need to keep one eye on meanings and one eye on embodied practice rather than simplistically reducing our approach to one or the other. We must also be open to the possibility that the most important aspect of a ritual may actually be the dialectical relationship between meaning and embodied practice (and this is exactly what I argue in the case of the Native American Church). At the very least, we should acknowledge that some rituals, such as the Kaluli séances described by Schieffelin, are more interactive and improvised than others, such as the highly formalized Peyote Ceremony.

The Influence of the Cultural on the Clinical

Cultural structures and practices influence clinical realities in many ways. The human mind develops in an interpersonal and culture-historical matrix that deeply influences its very structure. This is apparent in ontogeny (the development of the individual life), as well as phylogeny (the development of the human species). Human ontogeny is distinguished by a prolonged period of immaturity. This reflects the time needed for humans to acquire local structures of cultural knowledge, including complex languages, classification systems, and systems of values. At birth, the human brain is only a quarter of its eventual adult weight (Shore 1996, 3). Three quarters of human brain mass is thus gained in social interaction and in relation to local cultures. Rather than human nature being completely "hardwired" by a fixed brain structure, the human brain is designed to be flexible and programmable in response to particular environmental and social conditions:

> So an important part of the evolutionary heritage of the sapient hominid is a nervous system that has evolved under the sway of culture (in general) and which develops in each individual under the sway of *a* culture (in particular). The human nervous system appears to be dependent on external models or programs for normal operation, and this notion of models has significant importance for anthropologists and psychologists alike. (Shore 1996, 4)

As Geertz (1973, 46) stated, "man is, in physical terms, an incomplete, unfinished animal.... [W]hat sets him off most graphically from nonmen is less his sheer ability to learn (great as that is) than how much and what particular sorts of things he has to learn before he is able to function at all."

Studies of human phylogeny also reveal that human biological evolution took place in tandem with the development of cultures. Theory in this area has progressed beyond a sequential view that the expansion of the human brain preceded symbolic communication and culture. Today, it can be convincingly argued that brain expansion was not the cause of symbolic communication but was instead a consequence of it, given a Baldwinian view of natural selection (Deacon 1997). Given the dialectical view advocated here, biological, psychological, and social systems are more properly understood as forming a heterarchy rather than a hierarchy (Averill 1990).

> [Culture,] rather than being added on, so to speak, to a finished or virtually finished animal, was ingredient, and centrally ingredient, in the production of that animal itself....Between the cultural pattern, the body, and the brain, a positive feedback system was created in which each shaped the progress of the other, a system in which the interaction among increasing tool use, the changing anatomy of the hand, and the expanding representation of the thumb on the cortex is only one of the more graphic examples. (Geertz 1973, 48)

Human consciousness is culturally mediated, having arisen in connection with the use of tools or artifacts. These tools included not only stone axes and flint knives but also systems of symbolic reference (Dewey 1916; Cole 1996). Chief among the latter sort of tools are languages, through which humans create complex representations of reality that, in turn, shape or construct perception and interpretation of the environment (Whorf 1941; Lucy 1992). Compared to other animals, the human is uniquely dependent upon these extragenetically transmitted sources of information (culture as opposed to instinctual mechanisms) for ordering behavior on the individual and social levels.

The realization that mind and culture codevelop and influence each other has been spreading across the social sciences, but there have been barriers to its acceptance in certain disciplines and by the general population. It is likely that the very cultural nature of human thought blocks many from realizing this aspect of human experience. Human socialization and enculturation processes typically result in individuals who see the world through a lens of unexamined cultural assumptions. There is a tendency toward naive realism: one's perceptions are naively assumed to be direct reflections of "reality" rather than interpretations mediated or constructed by cultural artifacts or templates. Just as a fish may be oblivious to its ever-present medium (water), it is often very difficult for humans to become aware of their own culture: the semiotic medium in

which they live. This is why the discipline of anthropology has traditionally institutionalized a period of immersion in another society for at least
one year: it is felt that over this period, the different cultural medium will
become obvious. In addition to naive realism, there is also typically the
ethnocentric assumption that one's own social group is somehow the best,
exclusively designated by God, or the only culture that is truly rational or
human. These positions derive from naive realism, deep emotional needs
(implicating the local cultural psychiatry and its emplotments), or simple
arrogance.

In addition to the overlapping situations of naive realism and ethnocentrism, within anthropology there is the doctrine of the psychic unity of
mankind: the conviction that the human mind is the same wherever you
go. This doctrine, which Stocking (1982, 115) identified as "the major prem-
ise of the comparative method in ethnology," is an article of faith for many
anthropologists, psychologists, and well-intentioned relativists generally.
Geertz (1973, 62) contended that the doctrine had not been seriously ques-
tioned by any reputable anthropologist he was aware of. Psychic unity is a
cherished disciplinary doctrine (rather than a hypothesis) because it represents an emotional and a disciplinary negation of the primitive mentality
arguments and racist evolutionist schemes that dominated earlier anthropological theories. In the latter half of the twentieth century, it became scientifically unacceptable (quite correctly) to argue that people in nonliterate
societies were mentally inferior and the doctrine of psychic unity arose
to deny any significant differences in mental processes between cultural
groups. The psychic unity doctrine played an important role in countering
these ethnically and sociopolitically self-serving theories in that it emphasized a common human kinship among diverse societies. But, given its
seemingly dichotomous assumptions (that our only alternative to racism
is an assumption of complete psychological uniformity), it may be a concept that has outlived its usefulness, at least in its current nebulous form
(Jahoda 1993).

The main problem with the concept is that it is ill defined. What exactly
does "psychic unity" mean? Like cultural relativism or functionalism, psychic unity may be stated in such a strong form that it is untenable, such
as stating that human minds are everywhere "so similar that they necessarily react...in identical fashion to the same stimuli" (Stocking 1982, 123;
paraphrasing Brinton). This view is refuted by several decades of cognitive
anthropology field experiments (D'Andrade 1995). Psychic unity may also
be stated in an acceptable form, such as, "All humans are members of the

same species, and thus possess a similar nervous system to other humans, resulting in certain uniformities in mental life." This statement of psychic unity is accurate but does not tell us much about actual human minds. The real challenge is to understand all the complexities of the relationship between general aspects of human nature and the diversity of local socio-cultural environments. We need an anthropology (and a psychology and a psychiatry) that encompasses the mind's biological, social, and semiotic roots in dialectical interrelationship at local and global levels.

Another problem with psychic unity is that it tends to view human mental life through a positivist and bio-reductionist lens. If people think alike wherever you go, it is assumed that it must be because a universal human biology more or less determines thought. The doctrine, in fact, has roots in Enlightenment philosophers who tended to have a mechanistic "natural science" view of humans (Jahoda 1993). But what if human thought is creatively constructed meaning at the local level rather than biologically hardwired stimulus response? What if mental health is, as I have suggested elsewhere (Calabrese 1997), a creative narrative emplotment rather than a biological given? Then we cannot simply make assumptions based on biology; we have to enter into human sociocultural contexts and become familiar with their unique narrative structures. We have to practice clinical ethnography to understand the multiplicity of the normal and the local culturally-embedded therapeutic emplotments.

Finally, though the doctrine of psychic unity was a reaction against ethnocentric evolutionist ideas, it may, paradoxically, reinforce ethnocentrism. If we believe that everyone thinks the same way we do, how do we interpret really different ways of thinking, including the radically divergent constructions of personhood across cultures that Fogelson (1979) highlights or that we find in the Native American Church? They are often interpreted as psychopathology, immorality, criminality, or another form of deviance. The psychic unity doctrine may thus result in a tendency to interpret difference from one's own cultural ways of thinking, feeling, and behaving as a departure from a universal normality rather than as a local variation. Difference becomes deficiency. From this perspective, the very need for an extreme knee-jerk psychic unity position itself reveals an inability to value difference. "The normal," it is assumed, must be a singular rather than plural.

This critique of the effects of the psychic unity ideology on the social sciences leads us to an important epistemological point related to the cultural nature of thought more generally: in human cultures, systems of psychological/clinical knowledge and systems of ideological and meta-physical assumption are not distinct but tend to interrelate and structure one another (B. Good 1992, 1994). This is most apparent in the domain of mental health. Systems of clinical knowledge typically contain tacit cultural commitments (e.g., to individualism, to particular religious understandings, to what is locally considered "normal" sexuality, to tolerance of only culturally familiar intoxicants, to the primacy of the male sex, to particular cultural views of childrearing or health care, etc.). Examples of these commitments to cultural ideology in clinical sciences include the former classification of homosexuality as a mental illness (Cohler 1999), pseudoscientific rationalizations of the War on Drugs (Cohen 2003), the individualist emphasis on intrapsychic causal explanations of distress, and the equally individualist assumption that autonomy or individuation is the ultimate goal of development.

As society changes, cultural psychiatric "knowledge" changes with it. Consider the cultural values encoded in the *Diagnostic and Statistical Manual of Mental Disorders*, third edition (DSM-III), diagnostic criteria for antisocial personality disorder, which includes "repeated sexual intercourse in a casual relationship" (American Psychiatric Association 1980). Whoever wrote these criteria obviously had a cultural value system that identified sex outside of marriage as diagnostic of an antisocial personality. But today, repeated sexual intercourse in a relationship outside marriage has become more of a norm than a real deviance, and, as such, the criterion was dropped from the fourth edition of the DSM (DSM-IV). One wonders how consensual sexual intercourse could medically be considered antisocial behavior in the first place, when it is so obviously the opposite! Here we clearly see the influence of moral ideologies on medical diagnoses that pretend to be indices of psychic unity.

This relatedness of clinical understanding and cultural ideology becomes problematic because of the fact of human cultural diversity. The societies of the world do not agree on fundamental issues of personhood, sexuality, health, consciousness alteration, religion, or childrearing. Instead, human societies have developed unique ways of understanding and adapting to their local environments, maintaining their relationships, and sustaining mental health. These diverse adaptations have included a variety of therapeutic practices, including ritual practices and unique psychopharmacological traditions that cannot be reduced to "drug use," resulting in a variety of divergent pathways to normal human development.

Psychiatric normality is thus, to some extent, a cultural construction: a particular equilibrium of consciousness and activity that developed within, and in response to, a particular sociohistorical context. The job of sociocultural research is thus not to measure other cultures against the particular adaptations and assumptions of European and Euro-American cultures; it is to understand the complexities of local clinical realities in context and explore the complete range of human normality. An essential research question for this approach is: "Which configurations of cultural practice are viable (in other words, which can support healthy outcomes in context) and which are not?" But the answer to this question must not simply equate deviation from dominant cultural understandings and moral sensibilities with deficiency or psychopathology. It must be open to the possibility of multiple ways of being "normal," including some that radically contrast with our own. In assessing mental health across cultures, we need to separate that which is scientifically known from that which is merely culturally valued or expected.

The Influence of the Clinical on the Cultural

The influence of the cultural on the clinical is only one half of the dialectic of cultural psychiatry: the clinical realities of human life also influence the structuring of culture and its restructuring, as in revitalization movements like the Native American Church. The development of collective meaning systems is responsive to the psychological and psychiatric needs of individuals (Spiro 1982; Obeyesekere 1990). Malinowski seems to have known this, though his view of person-related cultural functions, useful despite its problems, was relatively neglected by mainstream anthropology in favor of Radcliffe-Brown's Durkheimian separation of the social and the personal and insistence that only social factors can influence social phenomena. In the latter view, a superorganic, but nevertheless anthropomorphized, entity "society" needs integration and follows its own laws independent of biology and of the temporary placeholders that are its members. The dialectical view taken here is that Malinowski and Radcliffe-Brown were both correct in certain ways (though Radcliffe-Brown was arguably more "wrong" given his dichotomization of the social and the personal). Both person-related needs and society-level needs are reflected in the ongoing construction and reconstruction of culture. We do not need to choose one or the other, as Durkheim and Radcliffe-Brown seemed to assume.

Humans are uniquely self-reflective and uniquely dependent on the cultural meaning systems that we create. As self-reflective creatures, we are aware of ourselves, our histories and possible futures, and the temporal limits of our corporeal existence. This awareness of ourselves and our temporality gives rise to narrative emplotments (Ricoeur 1984; B. Good 1994) that lend order not only to our perceptions of external events but also to the often stormy inner lives of finite beings. These emplotments are given the added psychological legitimacy of common knowledge when they are built into the shared systems of meaning we call cultures. I refer to these aspects of culture as culturally embedded therapeutic emplotments. A common form of culturally embedded therapeutic emplotment is the conviction that accepting a particular religious affiliation or living in a certain way ensures one's survival in an afterlife. Another is the narrative that the world will soon be remade and our own place in it will be greatly improved. These culturally embedded structures of therapeutic meaning are prone to provoke fierce clashes of cultural paradigms. They are often tacit or taken for granted, though based in metaphysical speculation, and are imbued with deep emotion. We may use the term *therapeutic emplotment clash* to refer to the situations in which different therapeutic plot structures come into conflict.

In spite of the current popularity of information-processing approaches to human mental life, the brain is fundamentally a health maintenance organ (Ornstein and Sobel 1999). The biological need for psychological adjustment gives rise to a very basic process that we can call "meaning therapy" (Calabrese 1997). Autonomous intrapsychic processes (though, of course, utilizing cultural resources) color perception and interpretation to help manage anxiety and aid mental adjustment. Sometimes meaning therapy manifests itself in a therapeutic self-emplotment: a narrative structure that one comes up with that supports mental health, such as an inspiring dream, song, prayer, vision, or story. But in addition to this sort of self-emplotment, "meaning therapy" also encompasses other processes, such as the defensive filtering of reality.

Meaning therapy provides a shielding lens for the human. For our social adaptation, we sometimes must, using both cultural and personal resources, filter our own pain and anxiety enough to be able to function. The concept of meaning therapy thus encompasses the psychoanalytic concept of an "ego armor" of "defense mechanisms." But this psychoanalytic terminology is somewhat out of date because it is extremely mechanistic and positivistic. It certainly emphasizes denial and repression rather than meaning transformation and creation. In addition to self-emplotment and filtering of reality, meaning therapy may include other processes, perhaps psychological processes that predispose humans to accept the meaning-therapeutic stories (emplotments) they are offered by society. The latter sort of process would overlap with the hypnotic concept of "suggestibility" and leads us into the area of consciousness modification.

The Social Modification and Orchestration of Consciousness States

In line with the holistic, dialectical approach I advocate more generally, the theoretical approach to human psychology I want to develop in this study deals with holistic consciousness states rather than only one aspect of them, such as cognitive schemas or states of nervous system arousal viewed in isolation from meanings. It is important to simultaneously include consideration not only of cognition, behavior, and culture but also of psychophysiology, including health status, emotional status, and consciousness state. Has the population been traumatized by recent events or situations of injustice? Are they starving or do they have specific nutritional deficiencies? What behavioral effects does this have? What psychoactive substances are being used and for what purposes? Is their use tolerated or punished? Does this social decision contribute to or jeopardize public health? All these questions become relevant.

Such an approach constitutes a third, more dialectical and more clinically based approach to the interrelationship of culture and mind to supplement the semiotic/cognitive approach (Stigler, Shweder, and Herdt 1990; Shore 1996) and the somewhat more dialectical culturally mediated activity approach (Cole 1996; Vygotsky 1978; Dewey 1916). Important work in this third area, focused on experiential states, has been done by Kleinman (1974, 1977, 1988), Byron Good (1977, 1992, 1994), Fogelson (1965, 1979, 1980, 1985), LeVine (1982), Herdt (1987, 1990), Kracke (1987, 1994), Littlewood (1996, 2001), Csordas (1995, 2002), Kirmayer (1989, 1994), Young (1982, 1995), Dobkin de Rios (1972), and many others. This approach often has more in common with psychiatry than psychology and is thus variously called psychiatric anthropology, ethnopsychiatry, or cultural psychiatry. The term *psychiatry* describes a domain of mental health research and practice focused on the body, as well as on mind and meaning: embodied emotions, chemically or behaviorally induced consciousness states, and so forth. We need a psychiatry that seriously incorporates cultural/semiotic understanding, and we need an anthropology that takes the body and embodied experiential states seriously.

An important substantive focus of this approach is the existence of diversity in consciousness states (James 1958 [1902]) and how society and its clinical sciences deal with people who experience them. This includes a concern with cultural minority traditions of consciousness alteration and psychopharmacology, as well as concern with the consciousness states of persons with psychotic and other major mental disorders. In terms of how society deals with these people, both groups are often met with stigma, misunderstanding, and unfair treatment by the criminal justice system, which results in alienation and powerlessness. The approach proposed here problematizes the ethnocentric/naive realist view that "normal consciousness" is unmediated by studying consciousness states as locally variable cultural constructions. What we call "normal consciousness" is not simply normal; it is cultural, shot through with social conditioning, power relations, metaphysical assumptions, and habitual conventional responses.

The influence of culture on the human mind is nowhere clearer than in a society's culturally patterned use of rituals, psychoactive plants, and other technologies to modify the consciousness states of its members. For this reason, both psychiatric disciplines and general anthropological theory benefit from interdisciplinary study of how consciousness states are produced, emplotted, and manipulated to support societal goals, such as healing, socialization, and the coordination of stress-prone nervous systems in interaction. Though there has been a bias toward seeing pharmacologically or behaviorally modified consciousness states as completely intrapsychic, hedonistic, or unstructured (see Calabrese 1994), these experiences are culturally structured just like the Alcoholics Anonymous narrative is. Clinical studies indicate that these states are very sensitive to such things as cultural and personal expectations, environment, and behavior (Zinberg 1984). Ethnographic studies show that societies utilizing consciousness modification do not merely respond to the experiences but develop consciousness modification–related strategies, beliefs, and utilization methods.

Cultural Psychopharmacologies

Within the domain of the social modification of consciousness states, no topic is as central, contentious, and saturated by cultural ideology as the topic of psychopharmacology. The centrality of this issue is obvious when we consider that Western psychiatry has become virtually synonymous with the use of lab-created psychoactive chemicals marketed as consumer products by pharmaceutical companies motivated primarily by corporate profit. At the same time, psychoactive plants that have been used safely and therapeutically in other societies, sometimes for millennia, have been summarily and ethnocentrically labeled "drugs of abuse," with this label having devastating effects for the people who use them. Hundreds of thousands of nonviolent people who prefer other substances than the dominant culture's alcohol, tobacco, and psychiatric medicines, more often than not ethnic minorities, have been incarcerated (Human Rights Watch 2003; International Centre for Prison Studies 2010; Justice Policy Institute 1999). From an anthropological perspective, however, substance-induced consciousness alteration is a ubiquitous human activity across cultural space and historic time—not a "deviance."

The use of psychoactive plants is an extremely ancient part of human history. Some scholars, like the American anthropologist Weston LaBarre (1972a), even hypothesize that experiences deriving from the use of psychedelic plants may explain the development of religious beliefs in humans. Sacramental use of psychedelic mushrooms among the Maya is suggested by 3,000-year-old stone effigies in the form of mushrooms with human or animal faces. We find evidence of Peyote use going back to around 3000 BC in Texas (Bruhn et al. 2002). Many of the other drugs that are outlawed in the United States today have a history of controlled, prosocial use in other contexts (Schultes and Hofmann 1992).

Psychedelic plants are the psychoactive substances most associated with healing rituals across cultures. Why? Well of course, they lead to impressive experiential states, often with modified perceptions of reality that are interpreted in a religious context. But there may be other reasons. Psychedelic plants contain chemicals that are structurally very similar to neurotransmitters, the chemicals in our brain that regulate its function. Modern psychiatric medicines have a similar structure, operating by modifying the functioning of neurotransmitters, and it makes sense to see psychedelics as having analogous effects. Peyote, like Prozac and other psychiatric medicines, is a serotonergic substance: a substance that acts on the serotonin system. To be specific, the active ingredient in Peyote, mescaline, acts as an agonist at the 5-HT2A receptor. In any case, it is fascinating, from an anthropological perspective, that throughout history,

humans found and utilized plants containing naturally occurring ana-
logues of brain chemicals.

This is an area that is in desperate need of depathologization and
nonjudgmental scientific understanding. We must learn to distinguish
normative, though perhaps culturally divergent, use of psychoactive substances from damaging abuse. It is no longer acceptable simply to distinguish culturally familiar Euro-American substances from substances of
cultural Others and to assume that those substances culturally familiar to
Euro-Americans are rational to use and the cultural Others' are irrational
or evil. This is one of the last bastions of unreflective ethnocentrism,
and it has resulted in massive violations of human rights in the War on
Drugs. To be scientifically honest and ethically responsible, we must
adopt an anthropological viewpoint in distinguishing those substances
that are actually too dangerous for use from those substances that have
the potential for safe and controlled use (or even therapeutic and prosocial use).

In this ideology-laden domain of study, for the clarity and honesty of
the debate, we should first demand terms that do not already, in their very
structure, specify a particular ethnocentric metaphysical view as to the cultural practices and experiences in question. Consider the term *hallucinogen*. *Hallucinogen* is an ideologically biased term in that, in its very wording,
it already reduces a complex psychological reaction encompassing diverse
cognitive, emotional, perceptual, and motivational alterations (some of
which have long-term or life-changing impact) to a short-term perceptual
alteration called a "hallucination." It also treats as "unreal" some very real
and self-relevant experiences. The new term *entheogen* (translated as "giving birth to the god within") is, in my opinion, similarly biased toward a
particular New Age "god within" metaphysics that does not apply to all
of the cultures involved. *Psychedelic* (literally "mind revealing" or "spirit
revealing") is actually a much less biased term that reflects the complexity and self-reflective depth of this sort of experience. Psychedelic is more
accurate psychological terminology, as the self-reflective effects of these
substances are often much more prominent than hallucinations. And even
hallucinations revealing important information about the self should be
seen as primarily "self-communicative" rather than "hallucinatory." The
term *psychedelic*, though it has been given negative cultural connotations
after Timothy Leary and the 1960s, more accurately reflects the inward
quest of Native American Church members: a path of self-understanding
rather than reveling in hallucinations.

The Ideological Domination of the Clinical Sciences

As Gaines (1982, 1992) has stated, many people in modern industrial societies assume that their medical knowledge and practice "are 'scientific,' neutral, and set apart from the conventional beliefs and practices of the society in which they are found." This view is fueled by the hegemony of Euro-American medicine. For example, as we have already critically discussed earlier, psychiatry has adopted a biological position that too often assumes that the human mind is everywhere the same because the biology is the same. This ignores not only the central role of human cultures but also the very plasticity of the human brain. The vast majority of medical and psychiatric studies and norming of diagnostic instruments use subjects in European and Euro-American cities. In doing this, they have often simply taken the mentality they know best (Euro-American mentality) as a universal standard reflecting the generic human mind. This is as inadequate as Freud's taking his own self-analysis, firmly rooted in his c. 1900 Viennese culture, and applying the idiosyncratic results to all human societies. There are local/cultural and personal/idiosyncratic elements in subjectivity—not just universal human elements.

As Foucault, Good, and others argue, clinical reasoning is not simply an objective mapping of clinical realities; it is shot through with particular cultural interpretations, political positions, and moral commitments based on metaphysical assumptions. An important corollary to this argument is that the health care system of a society is typically also a mechanism of social control. Often, as Kleinman argues, it is the primary mechanism (Kleinman 1981). For this reason, in a multicultural democracy, the health care system should be critically examined for ethnocentric bias just as the government and its laws and punishments should be so examined.

Given the divergent cultural ideologies underlying psychotherapeutic practice, we must develop an understanding of diagnosis as a culturally situated process. From which particular cultural perspective is the diagnosis coming? What are its cultural and historic roots? We tend to focus exclusively on the pathological mind and ignore analysis of the minds and cultural perspectives that perceive pathology in others. In some cases, the one who perceives pathology is more problematic than the one who is supposed to have the pathology. I am interested in approaches that problematize the cognition and behaviors of the diagnostician in addition to examining those of the patient. In doing so, we should keep in mind the automaticity, naive realism, and ethnocentrism of cultural psychiatries. The word *ethnocentrism* is not a synonym for prejudice or racism. Ethnocentrism is a natural tendency for people to see the world in terms of their own cultural lenses. And cultural study can help us take a step back and see our lens and how it distorts our views of others.

The ideological underpinnings of cultural psychiatries, combined with the automaticity and naive realism of cultural cognition generally, yield pathologizing diagnoses that simply seem to be common sense but that are actually deeply ethnocentric. Cultural difference becomes pathology. We can summarize this process with the term *ethnocentric diagnosis.* Examples that come to mind include several items on the intelligence tests that are currently standard (tests that I have administered many times in clinical work). I often felt silly asking several of the items on these tests to an immigrant from a non-European country. To my amazement, the subject's IQ score decreases if he or she does not know the author of a particular centuries-old German or English novel. The questions that supposedly measure general biological intelligence across cultures include "Who wrote Hamlet?" and "Who wrote Faust?" One's "intelligence" decreases if one cannot identify the main theme of a particular chapter of the Judeo-Christian bible, or the meaning of narrowly local colloquial (and outdated) English language expressions, or the flying distance between a particular large American city and a particular large European city. In addition, the whole activity of completing geometric puzzles as quickly as possible is probably unique to a narrow group of cultures and assumes a particular level of motivation in the subject. People who grew up in the societies that invented the jigsaw puzzle and the Rubik's cube are bound to be found more intelligent on these puzzle-based subtests than people who did not grow up playing with, and perhaps competitively racing to complete, these puzzles. Yet IQ, as revealed in these tests, is typically interpreted as a measure of inherited biological potential or neuropsychiatric integrity. Those who score low on these tests for cultural reasons are made to feel biologically inferior.

The cure to this situation is a greater reflexivity and a willingness to depathologize cultural difference. In particular, members of multicultural societies that claim to accept diversity should limit pathologization only to those patterns of action that have clear negative consequences—not simply consequences to the dominant cultural group's mores or cultural system of metaphysics. Otherwise, diagnostic and therapeutic systems will continue to be a tool in the colonial imposition of distinctly European and Euro-American cultural and moral commitments (Gone 2008; Duran and Duran 1995). For this reason, we should do serious research on practices that contrast with European and Euro-American cultural sensibilities, as well as on those that match them, to arrive at an honest scientific understanding of the entire range of healthy and developmentally viable behaviors in their various cultural contexts. This is an important goal of this book.

Toward Culturally Relevant Therapeutic Interventions and Therapeutic Pluralism

In its general discussion of cultural psychiatric diversity, this chapter has described a contrasting form of cultural psychiatric intervention that is a prominent part of many traditional societies: alteration of the neurochemical substrate of experience paired with therapeutic emplotment in the context of a healing ritual. We can refer to this form of intervention as *psychobiologically assisted therapeutic emplotment,* a term that nicely summarizes my understanding of the ritual process of the Peyote Ceremony and many other healing rituals. This form of psychiatric intervention contrasts with the approach of Euro-American psychiatry, which does not use consciousness-modifying drugs specifically to facilitate emplotment and which more broadly segregates meaning and consciousness modification into separate clinical disciplines (clinical psychology and psychiatry). But the approach of psychobiologically assisted therapeutic emplotment may be uniquely suited to the ways that members of certain human groups have been socialized to think, behave, and respond to treatment.

There is a growing debate in the mental health disciplines around the issue of pluralism versus standardization of psychotherapeutic intervention. Much of this debate centers on the so-called empirically validated treatments, which frequently follow a how-to manual that facilitates research. It is often assumed that if a particular treatment has empirical support, typically derived from studies with mainstream Euro-American populations, then it should work for anyone anywhere. This completely ignores the issue of cultural difference in what works therapeutically. Because patients are not homogeneous, psychotherapeutic intervention should not be reduced to a "one size fits all" scientistic manual. Human diversity includes deep cultural psychiatric differences, requiring diversity rather than standardization of therapeutic options. Our anthropological imperative is to understand the diverse range of human approaches to health and healing. Our clinical and ethical imperative should be to understand and support rather than undermine local efforts at self-healing and social control. Both imperatives call for careful studies of illness and healing in a diversity of local contexts.

3
_____

Clinical Ethnography

CLINICALLY INFORMED SELF-REFLECTIVE
IMMERSION IN LOCAL WORLDS OF SUFFERING,
HEALING, AND WELL-BEING

My first experience of the Navajo reservation. I arrived at the Canyon de Chelly after nightfall. I was traveling with another student of the Navajo, Carolyn Epple. After we set up camp, I set off for the nearby town of Chinle. It had been a long day but I wasn't sleepy. I was eager to see the reservation. As I neared the limits of the town, I met an unlikely gatekeeper: an old Navajo man sitting on a stump by the side of the road. He was obviously drunk. In fact, it looked like he had been drunk for days, or months, or years. He had a huge bump on the front of his head. But he seemed happy to see me. He took my hand and started leading me down the road. I was perplexed. He didn't respond to my use of English. Maybe he had fallen down or was assaulted and he was confused. I didn't feel in any immediate danger, so I played along, though it all felt pretty crazy: he and I walking down the road hand in hand into this dusty Navajo town. We finally arrived at a hogan and he motioned for me to wait. I imagined him announcing to his family "Come see what I've found...a White Man!" Some time passed and I decided not to stay. I went back to camp. Thus my introduction to contemporary Native American communities, hand in hand with this old man, challenged any romantic views I held about Native Americans and foregrounded the devastating impact of alcohol on Native American lives (extract from author's field notes).

THE METHODOLOGICAL DIALECTIC of this study is clinical ethnography, a research approach that seeks to combine and balance the anthropological method of participant observation with clinical understanding and evaluation of self and others, derived from years of clinical training and practice. I define clinical ethnography as culturally and clinically informed self-reflective immersion in local worlds of suffering, healing, and well-being to produce data that are of clinical, as well as anthropological, value. Empathic skills and self-awareness are emphasized in this approach because they are understood as indispensable to both clinical understanding and intercultural understanding. My approach to clinical ethnography is influenced by my studies with Gilbert Herdt (Herdt and Stoller 1990), Waud Kracke (1987, 1994), Byron Good (1977, 1994; Good et al. 1985), and Bertram Cohler (1992; Cohler and Calabrese 1996), as well as by the writings of Robert LeVine (1982), Katherine Ewing (1987, 1992), and many others.

The term *clinical ethnography* emphasizes the clinical utility of ethnographic data. As Byron Good and colleagues (1982, 282) state, in a clinical ethnography approach, ethnographic observations can be considered "a central component of the therapeutic work" rather than of exclusively anthropological interest. Clinical ethnography also implies that the ethnography will be informed by a competent understanding of the clinical domain in question and may even involve the use of clinical methods or clinical practice in the field. Examples of the use of clinical methods in ethnography include Herdt and Stoller's (1990) use of psychoanalytic modes of reflexivity in interviews with the Sambia of New Guinea and my own application of local clinical practice as a mode of participant observation in Native American communities. This method does not require full clinical training, but the ethnographer must not be completely naive about the standard clinical understandings of a particular domain of health. For example, an ethnographer studying mental illness should be familiar with the major categories of symptoms that may be experienced in these disorders (e.g., psychotic auditory hallucinations, intense anxiety, or suicidal thoughts).

Though having relevant clinical knowledge is crucial, the clinical ethnographer usefully adopts an open-minded self-reflective approach, accepting that the clinical wisdom of the ethnographer's home society may be seen as deriving from that society's particular cultural orientations and norms (which may be irrelevant to other societies) and that the society studied may have clinical wisdom of a different kind. Just as clinical ethnographers must avoid being naive about clinical matters, they should also avoid being naive about the social and cultural diversity of the human species. The ethnographer should have some idea of the range of variation in human responses to illness, healing, and "the normal." When interviewing culturally diverse patients, for example, they should be aware that illness may be explained in terms of soul loss, spirit possession, witchcraft, punishment by a deity, or an imbalance of hotness and coldness in the body. These are all common explanations for illness cross-culturally.

Clinical ethnography, in this study, involves clinically informed use of the ethnographic techniques of observation, interviewing, cultural participation, and thick description. It also incorporates clinical skills such as an ability to present as nonthreatening and build trust, sensitivity to and control over one's own psychological reactions, and training in clinical interpretation and evaluation of psychological states. These were especially useful in the present study given the sensitive, intimate nature of the research topic and the tendency for many Native Americans to distrust Euro-Americans (for very valid historical reasons). As Herdt and Stoller (1990, 30) argue, "Most issues with great meaning are revealed only to those one trusts, someone who will not harm you." I believe this is foundational. Inability to achieve an adequate level of trust can taint even the most carefully designed field projects, resulting in questionable data. In my fieldwork, I spent several summers building field relationships until I was trusted enough in the community to be given a clinical position treating the community's at-risk adolescents.

As envisioned here, clinical ethnography encompasses Geertz's (1973) interpretive focus on public, shared meanings. But it also goes beyond this level to incorporate study of embodied experience, emotions, suffering, psychological and social dysfunction, and cultural systems of normality, diagnosis, and healing. This approach studies the dialectic between the public and the private rather than attempting to study one in isolation from the other (as if this is even possible). As Ewing (1992, 252) so convincingly argues, subsequent to Geertz's claims that meaning is public, many anthropologists began to assume that "psychological" meant private and they thus rejected as irrelevant anything psychological, creating an impenetrable barrier between the study of culture and the study of the mind. This was based on a simplistic and inappropriately dichotomous mode of understanding:

Geertz's strategy of equating symbols, culture, the public arena, and communication has become a central paradigm in anthropology....[A]nthropologists have gradually moved toward the analysis of increasingly psychological-looking phenomena, while continuing to declare that what they were looking at was purely "cultural" and had nothing to do with psychology. Subsequent researchers are moving to claim some of what Geertz ruled out of bounds in his establishment of the appropriate object of anthropological study. In particular, Geertz firmly, if casually, ruled out the relevance of the fieldworker and his or her relationship with the informant for the effort of grasping the informant's subjective experience. (Ewing 1992, 254)

This view of reality, which tends to reduce human life to the public performance of a shared script (Geertz referred to culture as an "acted document"), allows the ethnographer to create the illusion of objectivity while simultaneously avoiding deep involvement in field relationships (Herdt and Stoller 1990, 24–25; Crapanzano 1986). Personal relationships with people in the field seem less relevant when the ethnographer assumes that the essentials of a culture are unproblematically understood through observation of public events. Culture becomes "like a text in the hands of a literary critic. No need to worry over subjectivity…because what you see— public social action—is seemingly all there is" (Herdt and Stoller 1990, 24). We can see how this approach reinforces passive public observation at ethnographic sites rather than real immersion in field relationships. It also tends to take as its goal a misleading pseudo-objectivity rather than the disciplined exploration of the subjectivity of the ethnographer, as well as the people studied.

Dissatisfaction with the Geertzian interpretive approach has led to attempts by some ethnographers to abandon the meaning-centered approach altogether. In his writings on the Yolmo wa of Nepal, Robert Desjarlais (1992) argues for an approach to the ethnography of ritual healing experiences that is based in bodily sensations rather than language or symbolism. He argues for the importance of the bodily, the tactile, the emotional, and that which is not verbally expressed as focus areas for anthropology. Here he shows the influence of a phenomenological approach to ethnography, similar to Thomas Csordas (1990, 1995).

One of Desjarlais's key concepts is "sensibility." He seeks to study the "local sensibilities" of the Yolmo through observation and imitation of their everyday actions, which he sees in terms of an "embodied aesthetics." The central concern of his work is to analyze "how an ethnographer might go about developing felt understandings in living with a people, and how he or she might try to convey this knowledge in writing" (1992, 247). His approach is to experience the local sensibilities and embodied aesthetics as much as he can in the field and then write as evocatively as he can, to develop what James Fernandez has called "an argument of images." Desjarlais's experimental approach is interesting and useful. However, I will read it critically, in terms of the dialectical perspective developed in this book, and argue that it is not entirely successful in its rejection of symbolic analysis.

Desjarlais usefully problematizes the extent to which his experiences mirror the experiences of Yolmo. He generally concludes that he did not have authentic Yolmo experiences, but his own experiences of autonomous imagination, which may have contained insights about the local context. He provides good critiques of anthropologists who have too unproblematically presented their own trance experiences in the field as mirroring native experiences. For example, Maya Deren (1970) wrote of a "white darkness" she experienced in Haitian Vodou rituals, suggesting she experienced possession trance as a Haitian would. As someone who has spent time in Haiti and attended many Vodou ceremonies myself, I share Desjarlais's doubts about Deren's claims to insider experiences. Desjarlais also criticizes Michael Harner's (1980) shamanic visions as more related to the Christian Book of Revelation than to the local mythology of the Jivaro Indians he studied.

Desjarlais shares his field experiences of shamanic trance as an apprentice shaman, which he treats as necessarily different from what Yolmo shamans must experience in trance but nevertheless useful in the ways they present what he calls "crystallized embodied forms of knowledge." "Meaning, patterned within the body," he writes, takes form "through images, which [are] then absorbed anew by the body" (1992, 26). To his credit, Desjarlais admits that his initial visualizations were dismissed by his shamanic master as irrelevant: "you only see lightning flashes in the dark." But he thinks that his experiences got closer to Yolmo experiences as his fieldwork progressed, presumably due only to his mirroring of local bodily sensibilities. It is here that we see that the symbolic anthropologist's focus on meanings is far from unimportant, as Desjarlais sometimes suggests, because his images only became more similar to Yolmo images (if they did) when they began to focus more on the local system of symbolic and metaphorical connections. He frames his experiences as useful attempts to feel his way into the bodily sensibilities of Yolmos. But what are we to make of Desjarlais's conclusions about his visionary experience on page 23, which he describes as a "divination" of Yeshi's troubles? Desjarlais writes, "The 'revelatory' quality of these visions intrigues me." He interprets that

> a handful of images presaged much of what I later learned in other
> ways....The mute woman and blind family embody the Yolmo
> ethos, Mingma's fibrous body portrays the aesthetics of illness and

healing, healers see what laymen cannot, the imbalances in Yeshi's hearth reflect culturally patterned tensions between men and women, and the irreparable nature of these imbalances suggests that healing is often more salve than solution.

However, Desjarlais writes that the meanings of these images only became clear after living in Helambu for over a year, attending further healing ceremonies, talking in depth with patients and healers, translating shamanic divinations, and, upon returning to the United States, studying his field notes. So were these trance experiences really "divinations" sensed only through the body or were they Rorschach inkblots to which he attached relevant meanings after the fact (and after full exposure to the Yolmo symbolic world)? Desjarlais does not seem to consider that any meaning that he "realized" a year or more later could have been projected onto the trance experiences rather than present in them in the first place. I am also a bit critical of his rejection of the study of symbolism and meanings in favor of embodiment as yet another dichotomization of human realities. As one critic (Gellner 1994) has stated, this approach may have the effect of unnecessarily imposing a mind/body dualism. It is also obvious throughout the book that Desjarlais needs to comprehend the local context in terms of its meanings and metaphors. As I have stated, if his trance experiences began to more closely approximate local experiences, it was as a result of him learning more about metaphorical linkages between altars, bodies, and geography in the Yolmo symbolic world.

Very different from Desjarlais's account, James Fernandez (1972) took an exclusively interpretive or symbolic approach and positioned himself as very external to the eboka (psychedelic shrub)-induced experiences of the Bwiti cult he studied. He laments in the Conclusions section of his chapter that he ate only modest amounts of eboka, never experienced any soaring ecstasies or weighty meanings, and found the plant too bitter and nausea inducing to be of interest to him. He admits that his resistance to eboka was the result of a commitment to objective observation and the subjective revelations promised seemed irrelevant to his task. At the time he wrote this chapter, he realized that science itself required that he explore the properties of the plant in every possible way. The dilemma, however, is that taking the drug in the spirit of professional inquiry is a radically different intention from the intentions of insiders, and, given the importance of set and setting in the formation of psychedelic experiences (Zinberg 1984), this sort of ingestion can never produce the same experience that a *banzie* (initiate) achieves. So Fernandez's chapter confines itself to study of the ritual experiences of Bwiti initiates and study of ritual practices and shared structures of meaning. He characterizes the types of descriptions of initiation experiences he collects and is able to provide some interesting symbolic analyses of these visions based on his understanding of the broader culture and social history. For example, his knowledge of Fang migration legends allows him to realize that a particular category of vision experiences mirror these legends in their crossing various rivers, though in reverse order. His knowledge that white is considered the color of the dead made sense of the references to one's ancestors being white or clothed in white in the visions.

My general philosophical framework is dialectical, so I stress that the completely externalist interpretive approach of Fernandez and the completely internalist embodiment approach of Desjarlais are both, by themselves, incomplete. I tend to say "both/and" rather than "either/or" and to take a stand against the dichotomization of experiential studies of embodied practice and the analysis of meanings. I tend to think that the synthesis of these perspectives (the interaction of cultural meaning and embodied experience) is where the action is. So my approach to studying religious experiences in the Native American Church was to self-reflectively participate in some rituals in which I ingested Peyote, to observe others without ingesting Peyote, to craft an understanding of shared meanings, and to interview as many members as I could about their ritual experiences. I combined experiential with interpretive learning about the culture. I would never assume that my experiences would approximate those of Native American Church members, but I gained an important understanding of the potential of the ritual to shape embodied experience, as well as several other insights. Certain things became obvious when I participated in rituals, for example, the effort it takes to participate, in terms of the bitterness of the cactus; the discomfort of sitting cross-legged on the dirt floor all night; the intense introspection induced by Peyote; and the challenges of obeying all the ceremonial rules of the ritual while under the influence of the Medicine. Becoming a member of the treatment team at a Navajo clinical facility that incorporated rituals into the therapeutic process also enabled levels of experiential learning that went far beyond what I could have achieved through interviewing staff.

Reflexivity

The subjectivity of the ethnographer has become a central concern of contemporary anthropology, especially in response to the critiques of postmodernists. How do we obtain valid ethnographic understanding when the ethnographer's interpretations are no longer treated as scientifically objective but are instead seen as deriving from a particularly situated cultural and personal perspective? Contemporary anthropologists have typically dealt with this problem of the ethnographer's subjectivity by adopting a reflexive approach, striving to include descriptions of self in the epistemological equation. By problematizing the view that one's culture is the baseline truth and one's personality is a "blank screen," reflexivity has the potential to lead to greater world openness and thus a more "objective" understanding. However, the antipsychological stance of modern anthropology often results in a clinically naive reflexivity that never gets beyond self-critique or self-indulgent reminiscence. What we need is a reflexivity that facilitates accurate insight into the effects of the interviewer on research (Ewing 1992, 252).

> From a clinical psychoanalytic point of view, self-criticism is not the route to knowledge of self and other, but is rather a form of censorship that itself should be observed. The goal of the psychoanalyst in the psychoanalytic process is to be observant and non-critical of all reactions, because even the disvalued ones (especially the disvalued ones) can serve as guides for interpreting the interaction between anthropologist and informant. (Ewing 1992, 261–263)

Here, even though I take a stance against pseudo-objectivist rhetoric, I acknowledge the special vantage point offered by intensive clinical training, especially when approaching issues of illness and healing. As Herdt and Stoller (1990, 30) state, "The subjective connotes skills familiar to the psychiatrist, analyst, clinical psychologist, and social worker for collecting reliable information." I also acknowledge the special vantage point offered by a very broad anthropological training in the diversity of world cultures. Thus, the clinically and anthropologically trained ethnographer's interpretation, based on deep involvement in personal relationships in the field, is not simply another opinion in a world of equally valid opinions. It is rather an expert opinion based on an intimate knowledge of what is possible in the diverse range of human cultures, as well as what is possible in the human mind, including the mind of the ethnographer.

An earlier generation of ethnographers seemed aware of the importance of "disciplined subjectivity," as Margaret Mead once referred to it (Herdt and Stoller 1990, 30). Lévi-Strauss (cited in Babcock 1980) wrote that, in ethnographic experience, "the observer apprehends himself as his own instrument of observation. Clearly, he must learn to know himself, to obtain from a self who reveals himself as another to the I who uses him, an evaluation which will become an integral part of the observation of other selves." As Babcock (1980, 10) states, "Contrary to popular opinion, it is necessary to be reflexive if one is to be scientific.... The only cure for subjectivity is reflexivity." Margaret Mead also spoke of reflexivity as an ethical imperative, arguing that it is important "to include as far as possible our own disciplined self-awareness to observations on other lives and other cultures" (cited in Babcock 1980).

In my ethnographic research, I have used reflexivity in many ways that are influenced by my clinical and anthropological training. I find it useful to think in terms of different traditions of reflexivity. The first tradition of reflexivity I used may be referred to as "psychological or clinical reflexivity," which involves self-consciousness of one's personal identity, relationship history, dreams, and emotional responses and the way they clash or resonate with personal relationships and immersion in the field. Following Devereux (1967) and Kracke (1987, 1994), I have used awareness of my emotions in the field as a guide to understanding cultural differences, interactions, and the viewpoints of others. I paid close attention to the experiential bases for empathy in my own experiences. For example, I was always aware of my fears of investigation, arrest, and prosecution by the dominant culture for being interested in Native American Peyote use (even though I had research approval from the University of Chicago institutional review board and local cooperation). These anxieties gave me insight into the fears that Native American Church members live with. In addition, my intimate knowledge of several functional Peyotist families exposed the mismatch between this fear and the loving and harmonious family contexts in which Peyote is actually used, exposing the ignorance and bias of the dominant culture and its destructive drug laws.

The second tradition of reflexivity I have used can be called "sociocultural reflexivity," which involves self-consciousness of one's cultural background and sociopolitical positioning as they influence ethnographic observation and description. Throughout this project, I closely examined the assumptions of my own culture, including derogatory, as well as romanticized, views of Native Americans. I was also aware (sometimes painfully aware) of my status as a member of the politically dominant Euro-American society, with its history of violent conquest of Native American lands, broken treaties, and lingering racism.

When we combine these perspectives, we strive to understand ourselves in the field as products of particular sociocultural contexts and as
individual embodied persons with personal identities, histories, emotions,
anxieties, and fantasies. We can also add a third type of reflexivity implied
by the simultaneous use of the first two: "disciplinary reflexivity," involving self-consciousness of the ways in which the techniques, assumptions,
and ideologies of one's disciplines (in my case, anthropology and psychology) color and filter knowledge.

Dialectical Balancing

In addition to the reflexive approach to dealing with the problem of the
ethnographer's subjectivity, I have also used another approach based in
a dialectical philosophy. I call this approach "dialectical balancing." In
the previous chapters, I have described my dialectical approach to understanding social conflicts and theory in the human sciences. Conflicts and
contradictions, when approached dialectically, can pave the way for a more
encompassing understanding. Dialectical thinking represents a higher
mode of thinking that systematically attempts to recognize partial truths
(Clifford 1986). It also supports an interdisciplinary position, in line with
anthropology's traditional holistic focus, as illustrated in the "four fields"
model. At a disciplinary level, I aim for the dialectical balancing of anthropology's cultural relativism and communal focus with a clinical psychological understanding grounded in years of clinical training and practice
related to mental health and substance abuse problems.

This sort of interdisciplinary triangulation maps reality better than any
single discipline-bound perspective. Anthropologists are well aware of the
dangers of biological and psychological reductionism. We know that psychological categories are cultural constructions that traditionally derive
from more or less culturally homogenous samples and may only be valid
in relation to these samples. But anthropologists also sometimes go too
far in their relativistic arguments and demonstrate that they are clinically
naive. For example, I have encountered anthropology graduate students
who actually believe that all mental illness is a result of socialized perceptions, disorders of society, or social pathologization of bohemian noncon-
formists. There is thus the danger in anthropology of maximizing cultural
relativism into an extreme ideology or being absolutist about it, which
actually goes against the very spirit of relativism (see Calabrese 2003 for
a critique of extreme relativism). A true relativist would relativize even

relativism, adopting a meta-relativist approach that would accept some universals. An acceptable form of cultural relativism is the assumption that there can be different, yet equally true or rational or healthy, views of the world or ways of life. A lazy and unacceptable form of relativism is the assumption that, when faced with two different worldviews or ways of life, they must be equally true or rational or we must not judge one in comparison to others or to demonstrably universal standards of health or human rights.

In line with this approach of dialectical balancing, I tested my evolving understandings of my field situation not only by asking consultants if they felt my interpretations were valid, in the manner of a good clinician, but also by putting myself into positions in which my hypotheses could be experientially disconfirmed. For example, while I developed a relativistic understanding of Navajo Peyote use, I was also trained in the clinical treatment of substance abuse disorders and took a clinical position treating Native American adolescents with very real substance abuse problems. Thus, my relativistic view was more than a naive anthropological assumption. In fact, it was supported empirically by the fact that I witnessed no cases of Peyote abuse in the histories of the adolescents I treated. My positive conclusions regarding Peyote use had also survived challenges from other Navajos, given the fact that I had established friendships with and lived among traditional Navajos, many of whom were anti-Peyotists. A relativistic position arrived at through such a self-challenging dialectical process is much more valuable than one arrived at through blind allegiance to relativism as an ideology.

Immersive Fieldwork

The approach to research I have described requires deep community involvement and interviewing rather than detached observation of public events or handing out questionnaires. A highly structured approach to fieldwork yields data that are easily compared and summarized, but this approach limits data according to a predetermined scheme. Data gathering is often limited to one context (and a short period of time), and entire categories of people are eliminated if they do not fit the predetermined scheme. Whole human lives and whole societies are reduced to their easily measurable aspects rather than represented holistically. Important and relevant information may thus be left out. Devereux (1967) famously argued that methods could get in the way of this sort of self-reflective mode of study when they are used primarily as an anxiety defense mechanism.

A holistic, long-term participant-observational approach is more world open, is less limited by its predetermined structure, and encompasses many contexts. It includes all types of data in an attempt to create an inclusive, multifaceted account. The subjectivity of the researcher is often included and analyzed instead of hidden behind a cloak of objectivity. But the data are more heterogeneous and more difficult to compare. The process of data analysis requires more time and a more creative grasping at patterns and meanings—more like completing a puzzle than adding up numbers. The benefits include a greater breadth of coverage and data that are more suited to a holistic, empathic understanding, suitable to the goals of clinical understanding and the creation of empathy-facilitating texts. Lived reality is evoked in the writing to preserve the flavors of actual field relationships. Immersion goes beyond objectivist observation of public settings and insists that fieldwork be subjectivist and reflexive, and that "field contacts" be seen for what they are: real, complex human relationships. It can be compared to immersive language learning, in which a complex symbolic whole (a language) can be learned over a limited but intensive time period. But ethnographic immersion is more complex, as the symbolic languages to be learned include languages of practice, ritual, relationship, emotional experience and expression, and consciousness states.

Empathy and Reflexivity in the Psychoanalytic Tradition

Clinical training and practice ideally enhance the developing clinician's capacity to experience the client's pain, sadness, and anxiety without withdrawing from it. Instead, especially in psychodynamic forms of practice, the discomfort and anxiety that is evoked by the resonance of the patient's life experiences with those of the clinician is noticed, identified as important and useful data, and controlled so as not to disrupt the process of introspective, empathic listening. This enhanced capacity to listen allows a deeper analysis of the client's modes of thought and action and constitutes a distinct method of research in the human sciences:

> The role of the investigator's own anxiety as a source of "interference" in the study of lives and cultures has been well portrayed by Devereux (1969). Psychoanalysis (Fliess, 1942, 1953) offers a means

of studying this interference as the "natural" response of an observer to recoil from experiences founded on work with others which leads to increased personal distress. Recognition that this anxiety is itself a valuable source of information which is facilitated by the process of empathic listening, and the self-analytic function of understanding both for oneself and the other of this anxiety, makes possible the task of bearing and understanding the source of the personal pain which is observed without withdrawing from the situation or returning the experience of pain with interest through re-projection (projective identification) on the other. The task in both the clinical and the ethnographic situation is to be able to bear and to understand those factors leading to another's enhanced sense of distress; the analyst's own self-analysis and continuing self-inquiry across a life time is uniquely able to foster the capacity for informed and enhanced listening in the clinical or ethnographic situation. (Cohler and Calabrese 1996, 2)

The assumptions underlying the clinical method of psychoanalysis have been carefully explored by Kohut (1959, 1971, 1982) and Schafer (1959) in a series of papers focused on the place of empathy in psychoanalysis. Kohut (1959, 1971) defined two points of view in the study of lives: the experience-distant method of the natural sciences and an experience-near point of view founded on empathy. As elaborated by Kohut, empathy represents the capacity to vicariously experience, in a limited manner, the life world of another person, maintaining a state of intersubjectivity.

Ethnography and experience-near forms of psychoanalysis share a similar methodology involving holistic, naturalistic observation of meaning systems: cultural meaning systems in the case of anthropological ethnography and personal meaning systems in the case of psychoanalysis. There is a direct correspondence between aspects of the psychoanalytic interview and the ethnographic interview. As Kracke (1987), Ewing (1987), and other psychoanalytically trained ethnographers have noted, the same evenly hovering attention, vicarious introspection, and sensitivity to the process of enactment that characterize the clinical psychoanalytic interview also characterize many forms of ethnographic interview.

Psychoanalysis can be seen as participant observation in a single relationship: the same critical standards of length of analysis and development of trust apply in both ethnography and clinical psychoanalysis. As Kracke (1994, 196) writes, "Ethnographic fieldwork is, in the final analysis, a relationship between a person and other persons; it is a human relationship, and the anthropologist participates in it fully as a person....This view of the nature of ethnography is essentially psychoanalytic." Geertz (1973, 26) himself described ethnography as "clinical":

> To generalize within cases is usually called, at least in medicine and depth psychology, clinical inference....In the study of culture the signifiers are not symptoms or clusters of symptoms but symbolic acts or clusters of symbolic acts, and the aim is not therapy but the analysis of social discourse. But the way in which theory is used—to ferret out the unapparent import of things—is the same.

Because of the similarity in method, and their common holistic focus, both psychoanalysis and ethnography share the tension between a scientific and a humanistic/hermeneutic self-identification. The analytic payoff of the method in both disciplines is the decentering of our normal consciousness and assumptive world. Both approaches decenter what we view as normal consciousness, one focusing on the examination of ethnocentrism (rendering familiar the culturally exotic and exotic the culturally familiar), the other on defensive and transference-related distortion and the role of the unconscious.

Partly as a result of this crisis of disciplinary identity, there has been a growing self-consciousness in both fields. Countertransference has become a major issue for psychoanalysis. Gill (1994, 5), for example, has criticized the traditional view of the analyst as a blank screen as "exemplifying the fallacy that the analyst can be factored out, that is, that his observations and interpretations are free of any contribution from his own personhood." Recent anthropology has focused on reflexivity and self, learning about self "by detour of the comprehension of the other" (Ricoeur 1973). One cannot ignore the contributions of psychoanalytic theorists in this area. Though severely limited by the particularities of his Viennese context and many of his context-bound assumptions, Freud (especially early Freud), when properly contextualized, is a useful model of the self-reflective clinical ethnographer.

Clinical Training

In preparation for my clinical ethnographic research, I received training in fieldwork-based anthropology and in clinical psychology. On the clinical side, I have specialized in treatment of the most severe forms of mental illness and substance abuse. I completed my internship training at a busy state mental hospital in Chicago (the Chicago-Read Mental Health Center) after being trained in the treatment of severe mental illness and substance abuse at the University of Chicago Hospitals. I then went on to complete a postdoctoral clinical fellowship at Harvard Medical School, where I worked at the Cambridge Hospital's Behavioral Medicine Program and was trained in clinical hypnosis, biofeedback, and other mind/body modalities. Thus, my clinical training focused on anomalous consciousness states, pathologies of drug-induced consciousness alteration, relationships between mind and body, and the separation of delusion from valid interpretation, often with clients of diverse cultural and religious backgrounds. I also developed an intimate knowledge of how powerful psychotropic drugs are used in clinical contexts, sometimes with limited effectiveness and sometimes with significant and damaging side effects. These areas were all relevant preparations for the ethnographic study of the Native American Church and its form of intervention, within the context of Native American mental illness.

My approach to clinical training was itself self-consciously dialectical and integrative. I sought training in all the major approaches to psychotherapeutic intervention, assuming that each theoretical orientation had some important partial truth to contribute to my synthetic clinical understanding, as well as to my critical cultural analysis of European and Euro-American clinical paradigms. My mentors have included psychoanalysts like Bertram Cohler and Waud Kracke, behaviorists like Paul Holmes and Patrick Corrigan, cognitivists like Mark Reinecke, hypnotists like Peter McEntee and Jean Fain, humanistic psychologists like David Orlinsky, and mind/body researchers and clinicians like Benjamin Colby and Saul Rosenthal. Each had something valuable to teach. The dialectical approach was also a prominent aspect of my advanced training in dialectical behavior therapy, both at the University of Chicago Hospitals and from the Marsha Linehan (Linehan 1993) training group, with subsequent practice of this approach at the Cambridge Hospital.

Another clinical anchor for my ethnography was provided by clinical research involvement. For example, I worked on a multisite research project studying alternative therapeutic communities and interventions, focusing specifically at my site on the mutual help organization by and for persons with mental illness called GROW (Corrigan et al. 2002). This research, like my Native American Church research, took me beyond the standard dyadic model of clinical intervention and revealed the important role of support groups and other communal interventions within modern

Euro-American society. Other publications on the experiences of people with mental illnesses in the United States, including a reflexive study of patient experiences at the Harvard teaching hospitals (where I had treated patients during the year prior to the study), foregrounded experiences of stigma, discrimination, recovery efforts, and the dehumanization often experienced within modern psychiatric settings (Calabrese 2011; Calabrese and Corrigan 2005; Corrigan and Calabrese 2001, 2003, 2004)

Data Collection and Analysis

Data collected for this project consisted of ongoing field notes, including recording of my emotions and dreams, as well as transcribed interviews and documentation of my clinical work with Native American patients alongside Native American clinicians. I returned from the field with a duffle bag full of field notes and interview tapes. I transcribed the interviews and entered these texts and the field notes into a qualitative data analysis software package called NVivo.

I devised a coding scheme related to my areas of interest and my set of interview questions and coded all material in the NVivo database. Other codes were added as needed to represent new themes that were identified during coding. Next, various searches were run for different codes and keywords, enabling relevant data to be assembled and compared for various topics. I did not oversystematize these searches or emphasize their technical or scientific rhetorical value. Rather, these analyses allowed me to better understand my data in an empathic way and to better create an empathy-facilitating clinical ethnographic text. Again, it should be emphasized that empathic understanding cannot be generated from statistical number crunching. Instead, it derives from a process of wrestling with interpersonal experiences and communications, personal narratives, divergent systems of shared meaning, and modes of practice as observed in the field. My write-up sought to balance my own voice with the voices of my Peyotist consultants. The strategy was to present the dialogue that helped to produce my ethnographic understandings and thus let the text remain open to different readings and interpretations.

Clinical Immersion in the Field

As part of this study, I immersed myself in many Navajo contexts and activities. I lived with Peyotist families and non-Peyotist Navajo families;

interviewed Native American Church members in various Navajo communities; participated in Peyote Ceremonies, Sweat Lodges, and other rituals; met Road Men and attended official Native American Church business meetings; and became involved in clinical work with Native American clients at a treatment facility run by a Peyotist Road Man. In all these contexts, I attended not only to the words of my Native American consultants but also to their emotional experiences and I charted my own emotional reactions, anxieties, fantasies, and dreams during the fieldwork period to help me become more aware of my own psychological, cultural, and disciplinary baggage.

The fieldwork progressed through several phases. During my first summer on the reservation, I lived with a rural Native American Church family in an isolated area west of Chinle, herding their sheep in exchange for meals and a cot in the hogan (the circular log cabin that is the traditional Navajo dwelling). The grandfather of this family was an elderly Road Man who was also a Medicine Man in the traditional religion. I will refer to him in this study using the pseudonym *Mike. Following the style of anthropologist David Aberle (1991 [1966]), an asterisk before a name indicates use of a pseudonym. This technique has the benefit of clearly marking those areas of the book in which the voices of my Native American consultants are documented. I will refer to two of *Mike's grandchildren using the pseudonyms *Adam and *Ben. I will also refer to one of his daughters as *Emma. Subsequent summers spent on the reservation focused on building rapport in local communities.

The project culminated in a yearlong clinical placement at a clinical facility staffed by, and serving, the local Navajo community. This last phase constitutes a more intensive level of clinical ethnography involving observation of clinical cases and participation in health care. The facility was a residential treatment program for Native American adolescents with substance abuse and co-occurring mental health problems. It was accredited by the Joint Commission on Accreditation of Healthcare Organizations (JCAHO). The clinical director was a licensed clinical psychologist and was thus able to supervise my clinical work with patients. The CEO, Hoskie Benally, Jr., was a Road Man, the retired president of a local chapter of the Native American Church.

I met Hoskie in 1990 on my first summer visit to the Navajo reservation. At that time he was the president of the Four Corners Chapter of the Native American Church, which is a large chapter in the northern part of the reservation. As readers will learn, Hoskie went through a period of depression and alcohol abuse after he lost his eyesight in 1972. Anglo doctors explained his visual impairment as the result of retinitis pigmentosa, and traditional Navajo diagnosticians explained it as the result of his father's hunting a deer while Hoskie was still in the womb, creating a conflict between giving life and taking life. Hoskie shared this bit of information with us at a talk given to the University of Chicago's Committee on Human Development during a visit I arranged for him. Hoskie was healed from his depression in a Peyote Meeting during which he had an impressive vision. He went on to become a very influential Road Man. Hoskie was a key consultant for this study, and many of the Native American Church members interviewed for this book were patients of Hoskie's or were his clinical coworkers. In previous publications, I referred to Hoskie with the pseudonym "*Dan," but he asked to be identified by name in subsequent publications, and I consider him a professional colleague and supervisor on cultural treatment matters, as well as an ethnographic consultant.

Though the leadership of the clinical program was composed of members of the Native American Church, this facility used an interdisciplinary and multireligious structure of spiritual intervention. Depending on the background of the client and parental choices specified on the Consent Form for Spiritual Participation, a particular patient's treatment could incorporate traditional Navajo, intertribal/Lakota, Native American Church, and/or mainstream Christian spiritual interventions. In addition to conducting individual and group therapy sessions, I was expected to attend a weekly Sweat Lodge ritual with my clients and to include rituals in my treatment and aftercare plans where appropriate. The clinical placement thus allowed me to observe the role that Peyote Meetings play in bureaucratized clinical programs serving Native American communities.

As mentioned earlier, the placement also fit well with the dialectical approach of my research, as my anthropological relativism was continuously confronted with the clinical reality of severe substance abuse problems experienced by Native American adolescents and their families. The position allowed me to do participant observation in a role similar to that of Alfred Smith, the Peyotist substance abuse counselor whose termination triggered the *Oregon v. Smith* case. It also allowed me to work alongside Native American clinicians and to observe how the Peyote Ceremony is used in federally funded clinical settings as an intervention recognized and coded by the US Indian Health Service.

In addition to Hoskie, I did formal interviews with *Edgar and *Ruth, two other staff members of this facility who were members of the Native

American Church, and I had numerous informal interactions with staff and patients. I interviewed several Peyotist clinicians at other facilities in various sections of the Navajo Nation, including *Beatrice, *Mary, *Lucy, and *Henry. *Gladys is a Native American Church member in the southeastern section of the Navajo Nation; *Florence is her daughter, who attends a large university off the reservation; and *Leonard is an elderly Road Man I interviewed in the Canyon de Chelly area. I interviewed and interacted with many other Navajos informally, including Peyotists and non-Peyotists, and these interactions also helped form my understandings of the tradition. The reader should understand that the majority of Navajos are not Native American Church members, though a significant percentage are, and many traditionalist Navajos see the Native American Church as an unwelcome foreign influence from the Plains tribes within the Navajo Nation. The Navajo tribe has, in fact, outlawed the Native American Church in the past and jailed its members, including my elderly consultant *Mike.

Given my goals of experiential immersion and empathic understanding, and given the central belief of Peyotists that sacramental ingestion of Peyote is the catalyst for a major experiential shift and reorientation to life, I felt it was a methodological requirement that I ingest Peyote in ceremony. I did this during the earlier phases of my field project and later discontinued participation. Because of the legal issues created by the War on Drugs, this created a lot of anxiety, as revealed in my dreams during fieldwork. I had many dreams of being arrested. But this anxiety was itself very useful in understanding the perspective of Native American Church members, especially in the period immediately following the *Oregon v. Smith* decision. My anxiety pointed to the cultural paradigm clash involved, making it apparent in a deeply embodied manner. This demonstrates how the clinical ethnographer's stance of reflexive self-awareness, combined with immersive participation, can support empathic understanding of others and the challenges they face. These dreams also revealed the cultural shaping of my own superego, Foucault's panoptical normalizing gaze, and the internal control mechanisms instilled through my indoctrination into Euro-American cultural norms, all of which had to be understood and controlled for me to really grasp a culturally different way of life. Thus, participating in ritual ingestion of Peyote not only made the Peyote Meeting experientially salient but also illuminated an important aspect of socialization: the cultural shaping of the superego or, to use a term less bound to psychoanalytic metapsychology, the conscience.

My field project also conditioned anxious reactions in others. For example, a Euro-American anthropology student, who was also on the reservation during my first summer of fieldwork and who knew that I was interested in the Native American Church, told me of a dream she had in which I was a drug dealer who was somehow victimizing her. Here we see how deep and powerful Euro-American assumptions and stigmas surrounding drug use in another culture (of the "drug pimp" variety) are unconsciously applied to cases for which they are entirely inappropriate. They become automatically activated semantic networks (B. Good 1977) for intercultural misunderstanding unless our reflexivity exposes them.

Various anxieties over cultural clash were also present in another dream that was stimulated by my visit to Washington, DC for the American Anthropological Association meetings. Specifically, the stimulus for this dream was a blasphemous (from the perspective of the Native American Church) advertisement in a local newspaper for "Late Night Happy Hour" at a place called the "Peyote Cafe" in the Adams Morgan neighborhood. The night following my discovery of this advertisement, I dreamt I was at the Peyote Cafe. But what was on the menu was not the "1/2 Price Draft, Rail Drinks & Margaritas" mentioned in the advertisement. Instead, each table in the large, dimly lit cafe had a bowl of Peyote cacti on it. Seated next to me at my table was one of my younger male relatives. Next to him, surprisingly, was the character Shaft (or Richard Roundtree, the African American actor who played Shaft in the classic black exploitation film). We were all ingesting Peyote and things were peaceful until my younger relative began to get agitated and started causing a scene. This upset Shaft, and it seemed as if he might get violent. My interpretation of this dream was that Shaft was a symbol of cultural difference, specifically of other cultures with traditions of controlled use of psychedelics. My younger relative was a symbol of the reckless, uncontrolled (because unsupervised) use of these same substances in Euro-American society. Thus, this dream again dramatized the cultural paradigm clash connected with Peyote use, as well as the importance of realizing that use is likely to be safer when embedded in a cultural framework that supports controlled use.

Another dream recorded in my field notes reveals my concerns over Anglo disrespect of Native American sacred traditions. I am not sure if this dream took place during a Peyote Meeting or the night after one. I reproduce it as it is recounted in my field notes:

I dreamt of being a child playing with other children of different colors in the presence of benevolent Indian people. Into the scene suddenly drove a Mercedes carrying business suit-wearing white men. They got out and demanded the Indians give them all of their sacred eagle feathers. The Indians protested that this was their very life but the businessmen were unbendable and like machines. They seemed for an instant to regret what they did but were suddenly snapped back into a hard stare as the material rationalization for the venture came back into mind: the feathers were needed because they worked so well in a particular industrial filtration system. The eagle feathers were piled on the ground as all watched. The whites were "truly sorry" for these people but thinking about it too much would be counterproductive. After all, they explained, there would be no room in the New World for old "superstitions" or for more than one way of thinking. That would yield the nasty problem of incompatibility: like Betamax and VHS videotape formats. They left after a last meeting of the eyes that made their faces turn both afraid and threatening (extract from author's field notes).

This dream reveals some embarrassing remnants of a romanticized view of Native Americans, as well as my critical attitudes toward a Euro-American culture fixated on the economic bottom line of the capitalist business model and intolerant of differences. It may reveal some of my "guilt by association" but also a desire to locate myself in a culturally diverse alternate camp. My status as a child may provide support for Caudill's regression-resocialization model of the ethnographer's field experience, in which the ethnographer enters a stage of childlike dependence on people more familiar with the society and progressively "grows up" in the culture (Caudill 1961; Kracke 1987). However, the threatening nature of the dependency supposed to be typical for American ethnographers seems absent, possibly because Italian Americans like myself do not mind dependency as much as other subgroups of Americans (possibly being a bit more sociocentric than Northern Europeans).

One final dream, which occurred after the death of my father in 1997, gave me a feel for the personal importance and therapeutic potential that Peyotist dreams and visions in ritual must have. This dream is an example of the generation, within an alternate state of consciousness, of a reflexive narrative containing an important death/rebirth transformation theme (thus a basis for my empathic understanding of the emotional salience of Peyotist ritual symbolism and experiences). It had a life-summarizing form that is similar to the phenomenon of having one's life flash before one's eyes: another sort of mysterious and emotion-laden reflexive experience. It is important to note that, before my father died, I had to rush him to the hospital several times in the middle of the night when he was having congestive heart failure and could not breathe. These trips resonated with the many times in my childhood that he had to rush me to the hospital when I suffered from severe childhood asthma.

> The dream begins as I am at a shopping mall playing video games in an arcade [this section is a symbol of my childhood]. I realize I am separated from whomever I am with (I assume my family). I realize that they are in the mall on the floor below. My attention was then drawn from the arcade to a room with all sorts of fantastic guitars for sale, including a bizarre electric guitar shaped like a Christmas tree. [I see this as representing the next phase of my life: an adolescence dominated by an interest in music. The transition from computers (in the arcade) to musical instruments mirrors the two phases of my undergraduate education: first I was a computer science major and then switched to the music school].

> Before I can try any of the fantastic instruments, my attention is drawn away by something else. I noticed a huge glass tank at the other end of this floor of the mall that is full to the top with water and that amazingly contains a giant whale who, unable to surface, was thrashing about, drowning. [I know that this represents my father's death and the congestive heart failure he suffered]. The whale was bucking violently as I approached. I look up at the tank as I used to look up at my father. [His size no doubt represents the greatness my father had in my eyes as well as his actual height, which was well above 6 feet]. There was no air available to him in the tank—only a few small bubbles at the top. I was powerless to help. I was angry at whoever was responsible for putting an air-breathing mammal in a giant fish tank.

> Suddenly the tank broke and the whale slid out onto the floor, dead. I thought the enormous amount of water that had been released might drown us. Then I was suddenly concerned for the safety of my family members on the floor below. [I see in this part of the dream a death/rebirth symbol: release from life but with a birth symbol of amniotic fluid rupturing. I interpret the fear of drowning as the fear that my family and I would be emotionally overwhelmed by the loss].

I tried to find a way downstairs but the only way I could find was a creepy back room that looked like a mausoleum with lots of white marble. I returned here and left several times. I think there was a barrier I was afraid to cross. I finally did and as I was walking through I sensed a presence in the room and I became nervous. I glimpsed a skeleton's hand as it quickly pulled back behind a large white marble column. As I rounded the column, I walked into what I thought were two ghouls who were about to attack me. I screamed—but then I began to notice that they were not attacking and they were not ghouls—just two old people: a man and a woman (like man and wife). The old man gave me a reassuring nod and we stared at each other for a moment in silence. I somehow knew he represented my father reborn into a new form—or communicating a message to me in an alternate form. [Here my initial horror possibly refers to seeing my father's corpse at the hospital. The final reunion promises our relationship will continue after death and was thus understood as a therapeutic resolution arrived at unconsciously]. The dream ended as my wife woke me up after my scream woke her.

My reflexive analysis of this dream is relevant to my clinical ethnographic study of the Native American Church because it is the main experience of an autonomous therapeutic self-emplotment that I draw on in my empathic understanding of the dreams, visions, and other alternative states of consciousness described by Peyotists as having intense personal meaning and as being therapeutic for them. Both themes in my analysis of Peyotist symbolism (Calabrese 1994) are present: reflection on one's life course and a therapeutic transformation of viewpoint symbolized as a death and rebirth experience. The metaphysics of whether these sorts of dreams reflect an unconscious resolution of grief or a message from the Divine is not as important from my perspective as the meaningful form of the experience and its resonance with the person's psychological needs.

The Creation of Empathy-Facilitating Texts

The goal of the methodology discussed in this chapter is not the testing of a particular hypothesis but rather the construction of a holistic empathic understanding of the contexts and meanings of Peyote use that can be communicated to readers through the creation of what I have called an "empathy-facilitating text." A rich, multifaceted understanding of the people met in the field and what various cultural practices mean to them can be transferred to the reader through narrative evocation of unique personal, emotional, and sensory worlds. Such texts evoke the ethnographer's field relationships and experiences of cultural immersion and can facilitate an interaction of imaginations leading to a more empathic understanding by the reader of the human realities described. This empathic understanding can then guide future interaction with members of a particular group, as well as increase empathic and self-reflective capacities generally.

Empathy-facilitating texts go beyond survey results or statistical abstractions because these are not the types of data from which humans construct empathic understandings. Instead, empathic understandings develop out of concrete sensory experience of interpersonal interactions, conversations, narratives, and other behaviors and also from reflection on one's own reactions, thoughts, emotional experiences, working hypotheses, and so forth. These studies record naturally occurring events witnessed by the participant observer, rather than staged for the experimenter, and study people in the multiple contexts that they inhabit rather than in a single context (e.g., laboratory or clinical session).

Such clinical ethnographic texts represent particular encounters with other worlds of lived experience that can help create bridges of understanding across extremely dissimilar cultural traditions. In the context of the present study, it is particularly hoped that these textual bridges of understanding will increase the competence of clinicians working with Native Americans and other cultural minority clients, as well as the competence of those who create, adjudicate, and enforce laws. There is an almost complete absence in American public discourse of discussion of the functional lives of actual people who use psychedelics and certain other Schedule I substances in a controlled, prosocial way. This book documents functional Peyotist lives and coherent Peyotist voices. It seeks to extend the possibilities for empathic understanding across cultures and to advance scientific understanding of human cultural diversity and psychocultural adaptation.

PART TWO

Cultural and Personal Healing in the Native American Church

4

The Unfolding Cultural Paradigm Clash

RITUAL PEYOTE USE AND THE STRUGGLE FOR
POSTCOLONIAL HEALING IN NORTH AMERICA

Inasmuch as the use of the herb called Peyote has been introduced into these Provinces for the purpose of detecting thefts, of divining other happenings, and of foretelling future events, it is an act of superstition condemned as opposed to the purity and integrity of our Holy Catholic Faith....As our duty imposes upon us the obligation to put a stop to this vice...[w]e order that henceforth no person of whatever rank or social condition can or may make use of the said herb, Peyote....[D]isobedience to these decrees shall cause us...to take action against such disobedient and recalcitrant persons as we would against those suspected of heresy to our Holy Catholic Faith....Given in the Hall of our Court on the 29th day of June, 1620, Licenciado D. Pedro Nabarre.

—LEONARD *(1942)*

OUR BEST SOURCES of information, synthesizing archaeological and genetic studies, suggest that the first human inhabitants of the Americas were Asian nomads who crossed the Bering land bridge connecting Alaska and Siberia between 20,000 and 15,000 years ago during the last glacial period (Schurr and Sherry 2004; Tamm et al. 2007). These people spread across the Americas, reaching southern Chile by approximately 14,000 years ago (Dillehay 1989), eventually creating a diverse array of cultures, languages, and local adaptations. With the end of the last glacial period, around 12,000 years ago, ice melted and the sea levels rose, separating the Old World from the New World. These two worlds then followed their own separate paths of development for the next eleven and a half millennia, each completely unaware of the other's existence.

Needless to say, the adaptations and practices developed by the Native Americans in the New World were not identical to those developed in the

Old World. One difference between the two regions was the relatively greater elaboration, in New World cultures, of the use of psychedelic plants for social, medical, and spiritual purposes (LaBarre 1972a; Schultes 1972). These include the Banisteriopsis vine and Virola snuff used in South America, Datura (jimson weed) used in male initiation among the Algonquian and other North American peoples, and tobacco, which, as used in Native American contexts, is frequently characterized as a psychedelic. When the Spaniards entered Mexico, they discovered widespread use of psilocybin-bearing mushrooms referred to as *teonanacatl* or "flesh of the gods." This psychedelic plant, described shortly after the conquest by a friar named Sahagun (1969 [c. 1570]), was reportedly served at the coronation feast of Moctezuma in 1502. The Spaniards also encountered *ololiuqui*, which is made from the seeds of certain plants in the *Convolvulaceae* or Morning Glory family that contain the psychedelic D-lysergic acid amide (Schultes 1972). Ancient use of the psychedelic—but highly toxic—mescal bean (*Sophora secundiflora*) has been identified at numerous archaeological sites in the lower Pecos region of southwestern Texas and northeastern Mexico. Radiocarbon dating shows that these sites span the period from 7000 BC through 1000 AD (Adovasio and Fry 1976).

Pre-Columbian use of the Peyote cactus in the area now occupied by the United States extends back six millennia. Radiocarbon dating of Peyote buttons from the Shumla Cave excavation in Texas shows a mean age of 5,700 years (Bruhn et al. 2002). Mescaline, the main psychoactive ingredient in Peyote, was identified in this sample using thin-layer chromatography and gas chromatography/mass spectrometry. Another 3,000-year-old specimen was found in the context of a multiple interment burial cave, part of the Mayran mortuary complex, in Coahuila, Mexico (Bruhn, Lindgren, and Holmstedt 1978). Purposeful human use of Peyote is indicated by the fact that the specimens are identified as "buttons" (dried slices off the top of the Peyote cactus), were brought into caves, and, in the case of the Coahuila find, were strung together on a cord like a necklace.

Peyote grows in the Mexico/Texas borderland area, and its use has been reported among many Native American groups, including the Aztecs, Zacateco, Tarascan, Cazcan, Guachichil, Huichol, Lagunero, Tepehuan, Tepecano, Cora, Acaxee, Tamaulipeco, Coahuilteco, Tarahumara, Opata, Pima Bajo, Jumano, Julimeno, Lipan Apache, Carrizo, Tonkawa, Karankawa, Mescalero Apache, Caddo, Otomi, and Tlascalan (Stewart 1987, 17). Peyote use is still a central aspect of life in such Mexican tribes as the Huichol and Tarahumara. The practice among tribes in the region now occupied by the

United States and Canada, usually associated with an organization called the "Native American Church," diffused directly from the older Mexican forms and retains many Mexican traits, such as the belief that Peyote can reveal hidden information or can see and punish evil deeds.

With European conquest, traditional Native American patterns of life were disrupted. Native communities were decimated through genocidal wars and by European diseases for which they had no immunity. In addition to these assaults on Native American bodies, Europeans also set their sights on the conquest of Native American minds and souls. In Mexico, this began with the outlawing of Native American cultural practices and forced conversion to Christianity using the bloody methods of the Inquisition. The Spanish Inquisitors, in fact, can be credited with the creation of the first Euro-American antidrug law when, in 1620, they declared use of Peyote to be the work of the Devil and equivalent to heresy (Leonard 1942). An excerpt from this decree opens this chapter. Records of an anti-Peyotist Inquisition hearing held in Santa Fe in 1632 reveal the antiquity of this culture clash in the area now occupied by the United States (Stewart 1987, 22–24).

The centrality of Peyote use as a target of the Inquisition and subsequent Catholic missionary efforts is revealed in the confessional of the Spanish missionary Padre Nicolas de Leon. This confessional contains the following questions for the Catholic priest to ask the Indian penitent:

> "Art thou a sooth-sayer? Dost thou foretell events by reading omens, interpreting dreams or by tracing circles and figures on water? Dost thou garnish with flower garlands the places where idols are kept? Dost thou suck the blood of others? Dost thou wander about at night, calling upon demons to help thee? Hast thou drunk Peyote, or given it to others to drink, in order to discover secrets or to discover where stolen or lost articles were?" (Schultes and Hoffman 1992, 147).

This policy of cultural destruction and assimilation continued in the practices of the United States government. Spiritual practices that reinforced traditional cultures and thus hindered the spread of Christianity were outlawed. Policies of removal from traditional lands and dispersion through allotment were used to disintegrate native populations and enforce an individualist ethic. Native American children were removed from their families to non-reservation boarding schools that had as their explicit goal the destruction of Native American ways of life. As Richard Pratt, the founder of the Carlisle Indian School, explained it, the goal was to "kill the Indian and save the man." These children, who also no doubt served as hostages to control their parents at home (Slotkin 1975[1956], 11), were forced to cut their hair and wear European clothes. They were also punished for speaking their own languages (Adams 1995).

The result of this program of cultural destruction was not the happy Christianized Indians for which the missionaries had hoped. Today, the suicide rates among Native Americans are significantly higher, and are characterized by younger people engaging in suicidal behaviors, than the general United States population. For example, the suicide rate for Native American youth aged 15 to 24 is 3.3 times higher than the national average and makes up 40 percent of all suicides in Indian Country (Surgeon General 2005). In addition, deaths from alcoholism are over six times the national average, deaths from tuberculosis are four times the national average, deaths from diabetes mellitus are nearly three times the national average, deaths from unintentional injuries are over twice the national average, and deaths from homicide are 81 percent greater than the national average (Indian Health Service 2004). Many of these rates are improvements from prior years. Regarding alcoholism, the biological/genetic explanations of Indian drinking may be found to have some basis in truth. But they too conveniently absolve Europeans of the responsibility for inflicting catastrophic trauma on Native American communities. We cannot reduce alcohol abuse to a purely biological problem, thus ignoring colonialism.

It is in the chaotic, post-Conquest situation that the Native American Church arose as a revitalization movement that focused on personal healing, rebuilding community, harmonious family relationships, connection with the Divine, and avoidance of alcohol. According to University of Chicago anthropologist James Sydney Slotkin (1975 [1956], 34–35), the present form of the Peyote Ceremony was developed around 1885 among the tribes of the Kiowa, Comanche, and Wichita Agency, and from this reservation it diffused to tribes across the United States and Canada.

The Spread of the Native American Church across North America

This section will explore scholarly explanations for the spread of the Native American Church to tribes across the United States and Canada. These scholarly explanations, and the practice of ethnographic description and interpretation, have been influenced by dominant cultural narratives. One essay that makes this clear in the context of studies of Native American societies is "Ethnography as Narrative" by Edward Bruner (1986). In this piece, Bruner argues that "ethnographies are guided by an implicit narrative structure, by a story we tell about the peoples we study" (1986, 139). Bruner focuses on ethnographic stories about Native Americans, isolating two dominant narratives:

> In the 1930s and 1940s the dominant story constructed about Native American culture change saw the present as disorganization, the past as glorious, and the future as assimilation. Now, however, we have a new narrative: the present is viewed as a resistance movement, the past as exploitation, and the future as ethnic resurgence. What is so striking is that the transition from one narrative structure to another occurred rapidly, within a decade after World War II. Equally striking is that there is so little historical continuity between the two dominant stories: one story simply became discredited and the new narrative took over. (E. Bruner 1986, 139)

These two narratives of the Native American situation, two temporal mappings or emplotments assuming a different ending of the story, have led to different processes of ethnography with Native Americans: one focused on reconstructing the Native American past and seeing the present in terms of "progressive breakdown, pathology, and disintegration" (E. Bruner 1986, 140) and the other focused on documenting resistance and anticipating or even supporting cultural revitalization. These narratives have produced divergent strands of scholarly interpretation of the spread of the Native American Church.

The early literature on the Native American Church was dominated by the controversy over why the religion spread and how the Native American Church was related to the experience of conquest. One popular view saw Peyote use as a "flight from reality" that represented residual symptomatology derived from the trauma of conquest. Roland Wagner (1975, 203) has commented on the use of words such as *escape, passivity, resignation,* or *withdrawal* to describe the Native American Church, such as in Kluckhohn's book *Navaho Witchcraft*. Kluckhohn commented that one substitute for aggression is to "leave the field" altogether:

> This may take the form of social withdrawal or that of flight from reality through the use of narcotics. Both of these types of response

are employed by the Navaho, but there are circumstances which prevent their bringing large scale relief. Within the last five years peyote suddenly became very popular in restricted areas of the Navaho country. However, conflict with the native religion and the vigorous opposition of the Indian Service have sharply curtailed this practice. The use of alcohol is much more widespread. The compulsive (and apparently increasing) propensity of Navahos for drinking must, in part, be understood as a response which produces adjustment by deadening certain sensations and by granting release from some of the specific enactments of the culture. (Kluckhohn 1944, 90–91)

Similarly, Bromberg and Tranter, in the *Journal of Nervous and Mental Disease,* reduce the effects of Peyote to a painkiller, though this is a pharmacologically inaccurate characterization:

[P]eyote acts... to ease the pain of conflict which the clash of cultures engenders. In this sense, Peyotism as spiritual therapy implies a negative attitude towards emotional problems. To seek to gain permanence for a culture by the repression of conflicts through narcotics and mysticism is not a "constructive" way of life! (Bromberg and Tranter 1943, 527)

Wagner understands these views of Peyote use in terms of Euro-American ethnocentric views and misunderstandings of culturally unfamiliar psychoactive substances, stating that Kluckhohn equated the ingestion of Peyote with the use of alcohol and then implied that they are "functional alternatives," both offering a "flight from reality":

A clear negative value judgment is made in assessing the quality of response which Peyotism represents to situations of difficulty; by extending the analogy with alcohol, it is stigmatized as producing adjustment only by deadening sensations. (Wagner 1975, 198)

Here, we see the reduction of Peyote's effects to psychological numbing, though Peyote is not analogous in its effects to alcohol and definitely not an opiate. In fact, it tends to increase the intensity of sensations rather than deaden them. This attribution has less to do with Peyote than it has to do with Euro-American misunderstandings and assumptions about "drugs," with the prototype of "drug use" in the Euro-American imagination perpetually reduced to the figure of the socially dysfunctional heroin addict or drunk escaping from reality. We can compare this sort of inappropriate reductionist view of Peyote's effects to the other misinformed view that Peyote ingestion only produces short-term perceptual alterations that are "unreal" (hallucinations). Actually, Peyote's effects are cognitive and emotional, as well as perceptual; Peyote experiences often take the form of revelations regarding real features of the participant's life; and the effects are both long term and short term. In fact, life-changing realizations and reorientations occur under its effects.

Less pathologizing explanations for the spread of the Native American Church included adjustment, accommodation, and acculturation perspectives. In Slotkin's (1975 [1956], 34–35) view, the widespread acceptance of the Native American Church among various tribes was due to the fact that "the religion provides adequate adjustment to the external and internal environmental conditions confronting the Indians; and also acts as an effective transition." The Native American Church, in this view, was popular because it contained a program of accommodation: "Peyotism socially is an example of accommodation rather than militancy; culturally...it is a case of Pan-Indian nativism" (Slotkin 1975 [1956], 7). This view makes sense especially when the Native American Church is seen in the context of the violent suppression of the Ghost Dance, which sought to rid the land of the European invaders through ritual dances.

David Aberle offered an influential explanation for why the Native American Church became popular among the Navajos specifically: relative deprivation. According to Aberle, Navajos suffered relative deprivation primarily from the forced reduction of their livestock by the US government, which, he argues, led them to join the Native American Church. Comparing his explanation to the acculturation explanation, Aberle (1991 [1966], xxvii) argued that the subordination of a smaller society by a larger society that is culturally different can be considered one type of relative deprivation situation. For this reason, he argued, relative deprivation provided a more general explanation than acculturation.

A significant weakness of Aberle's explanation is that it seems to rely too heavily on a clearly delineated historical event (forced Navajo livestock reduction by the US government) and seems to de-emphasize the larger context of conquest and colonial domination. In addition, it is unclear why relative deprivation consequent to livestock reduction would lead Navajos to join a particular religion, unless the "escape from reality" scenario was assumed. Barkun (1974) supplemented Aberle's "deprivation" with "catastrophe" as a more general reason behind social movements like the Native American Church. LaBarre also criticized Aberle by stating that his argument changes a psychological explanation into an economic one, with all the issues surrounding acculturation becoming reduced to a disguised Marxian class conflict (LaBarre, 1972b, 287–288). Wagner (1975, 200) convincingly argued that reactive reasons have unfairly over-shadowed the pragmatic, agentic reasons for Native American Church involvement:

> Peyotism is not an attempt to flee from reality, but rather an attempt to deal with it in another form. Both through the manipulation of supernatural power and the manipulation of social networks opened up through membership, Peyotism is an attempt by American Indians not only to cope with contemporary social and economic conditions, but also to master and ultimately to transform them. (Wagner 1975, 204)

In a similar vein, Voget (1968) makes an excellent point in his argument that Aberle tended to ignore the explicit explanation given by his informants: that Peyote was used because it was effective in healing:

> In proposing economic deprivation, rather than curing, as the real motive for acceptance of Peyote by some Navajo, an implicit "scientific" interpretation is opposed to the explicit explanation of informants.... When release from anxiety due to economic deprivation fails to register as a "good" expected by the majority deriving satisfactions from a novel religious activity, as in this case, then there may be cause to suspect the scientific interpretation and the data. (Voget, 1968, 119)

To this, Aberle responded that his discussion of the effects of livestock reduction included not only deprivation of possessions but also damage to Navajo ethical standards and perceptions of the supernatural and social order (Aberle 1991 [1966], xxxi).

Thus far, we have discussed the tension in the scholarly literature on the Native American Church between the view that Peyote use was a "flight from reality" and the view that it reflected adaptation and agency. We have also discussed the tension between "scientific" explanations and a sensitivity to the reasons that Peyotists themselves give for their use. The insider's view of members of the Native American Church tends to emphasize the importance of the therapeutic efficacy of Peyote and the ability of Peyote to link the worshipper with the realm of the Divine.

There is yet another tension in the classic literature on the spread of the Native American Church that concerns therapeutic efficacy and religious belief and that would benefit from a dialectical reexamination: the disagreement between LaBarre and Schultes on the question of why Native Americans categorize Peyote as "Medicine" and the relation of this categorization to the physiological effects of Peyote. The famous Harvard botanist Richard Evans Schultes (1938) called attention to reported cures as the key to Peyote's widespread therapeutic reputation. The anthropologist Weston LaBarre (1939), seemingly discounting any actual therapeutic efficacy, maintained that Native Americans had instead been impressed by the visions brought on by Peyote, which they took to be evidence of its "medicine power."

A dialectical approach might suggest that both Schultes and LaBarre were partially correct. LaBarre (1939) was correct to emphasize Peyote's ability to produce impressive ritual experiences. But in defining this ability almost exclusively in terms of "visions," LaBarre overlooked many other important aspects of ritual experiences in the Native American Church, including experiences of healing and revelations or realizations about one's life. Schultes (1938, 704) was correct in arguing that "the peyote vision has been incidental while the medicinal reputation of peyote has been fundamental" in the spread of the Native American Church. However, we do not need to dichotomize therapeutic reputation and the ability to produce impressive ritual experiences as Schultes seems to. The present study argues that, in the cultural context of the Native American Church and of particular tribal understandings of illness and therapeutic intervention, and in view of the informational content of ritual experiences that provide insights to the participants about their own lives, healing may occur *as the result of* a vision or another impressive ritual experience.

The interpretation of the Native American Church that I adopt in this book strives to be dialectical and encompassing. I find Barkun's (1974) catastrophe thesis very useful for its historically encompassing perspective and its refusal to theoretically repress the role of Euro-American conquest and colonial domination. Aberle's deprivation focus might illustrate the way in which an aspect of the larger catastrophe (conquest and colonial domination) may have been experienced at a particular local site (the Navajo reservation) and at a particular time (during forced livestock reduction). However, the broad context of European conquest and subsequent colonial rule of the Americas cannot be ignored in our understanding of the Native American Church and other (post)colonial revitalization movements. I also stand with Voget and Schultes in attaching importance to what Native American Church members actually say are their reasons for using Peyote (mainly healing) and with Wagner in his focus on the pragmatic aspects of the Native American Church.

Misunderstandings and Anti-Peyotist Efforts in the United States

The spread of the Native American Church met with opposition from both anti-Peyotist Europeans and anti-Peyotist Native Americans, both traditionalist and Christian. The cultural paradigm clash and related misunderstandings of Native American Peyote use resulted in many legal attacks and other forms of attack on Native American Church members. As Slotkin (1975 [1956], 52) points out, the earliest official who reported on the use of Peyote in the United States, J. Lee Hall, suggested that it be prohibited because it "is evidently injurious" (Hall 1886, 130). Incidentally, Hall was dismissed from his position as Agent of the Kiowa, Comanche, and Wichita Agency a year later for drunkenness (Stewart 1987, 128). Regulations outlawing Peyote use began two years later, beginning with the Kiowa, Comanche, and Wichita Agency, and were implemented on other reservations. Offenders would have their annuity goods and rations cut off at a time when starvation was a real and ongoing fear. This was done based on no investigation of Peyote's effects and with no concern for the constitutional guarantee of freedom of religion. In fact, the Bureau of Indian Affairs ignored the findings of Smithsonian investigators that Peyote helped rather than hurt Native Americans, and it had the ethnographer James Mooney expelled from the Kiowa reservation in 1918, preventing the completion of his ethnographic study (Slotkin 1975 [1956], 55).

As with the Inquisition, attacks on the use of Peyote were often claimed to be in the Indian's best interests. However, the cultural imperialist intentions were apparent, for example, in the 1896 letter of Indian Bureau Commissioner Browning to Agent Baldwin that Peyote use among the Kiowa was "interfering quite seriously with the work of missionaries among them" or in the 1903 letter to the Comanche-Kiowa Agent Randlett from a missionary who complained that the Saturday night Peyote Ceremonies left Indians "in such a state of stupefaction that it is utterly impossible to teach them anything from the word of God" on Sunday morning (Stewart 1987, 130, 132). Reports of medicinal benefits for Indians were ethnocentrically dismissed then as they are now, though Peyote was offered for sale as a medicine to whites by such pharmaceutical companies as Parke, Davis, and Company and was listed in the *United States Dispensatory* (Stewart 1987, 131).

One of the many fascinating stories in Omer Stewart's excellent history of the Native American Church is the story of Charles E. Shell, the superintendent for the Cheyenne and Arapaho Agency. Shell worked closely with prohibitionist W. E. "Pussyfoot" Johnson to attack Peyote use vigorously wherever it took place. But Shell eventually decided for some reason to actually experience Peyote for himself, and he consumed a rather large amount under medical observation. Shell reported that he experienced thoughts "along the line of honor, integrity, and brotherly love" and wrote, "I seemed incapable of having base thoughts.... I do not believe that any person under the influence of this drug could possibly be induced to commit a crime" (quoted in Stewart 1987, 142).

Histories of opposition could be recounted for many other reservations to which the Native American Church spread. Among the Navajos, the main barrier was not the Bureau of Indian Affairs but rather the Navajo Tribal Council and anti-Peyotist Navajos acting independently. After arrests of Peyotist priests in 1938, the Tribal Council met to discuss Peyote in 1940. David Aberle (1991 [1966], 111–112) summarized the Navajo misrepresentations and concerns as follows:

> Peyotism was regarded as foreign, as leading to extravagant expenditures for peyote, as accompanied by gross sexual misbehavior (especially since peyote was said to enlarge the prostate gland), as a cause of insanity and death, as similar to the dangerous mind medicines, and as a danger to traditional Navaho religion. For some Christian Navahos, it was a threat to Christianity. The character of some peyote priests was castigated. Claims of the curative value of peyote were ridiculed, as were claims that it stopped people from drinking. There was also concern over rumors that schoolchildren were being given peyote and that Navaho employees of the schools were cult members.

The resolution agreed upon by the council and, ironically, drafted by a Christian missionary specified that Peyote was not connected with

Navajo religion and was to be "stamped out." Any person caught with Peyote would be sentenced to up to nine months of labor or a fine of $100 or both. When the head of the Bureau of Indian Affairs, John Collier, took an anti-enforcement stand on Peyote use, anti-Peyotist Navajos began taking matters into their own hands. Night raids on Peyote Meetings began. Anti-Peyotist individuals would break into an ongoing meeting and attempt to destroy the altar, steal ritual objects, and grab jewelry from the participants. In one case, however, Peyotists fought back nonviolently. They were prepared, and when the raiders came, the Peyotists tied them up for the night and continued the meeting (Aberle 1991 [1966], 115).

The old Navajo Road Man I am calling *Mike, whose rural family I lived with in the Chinle area, was jailed during these years when the Native American Church was banned by the Navajo tribe. However, he said he never thought that his use of Peyote was a mistake, even when they arrested him and put him in jail. It had worked for him and he had seen it help his family:

> When I first joined the Native American Church, there were a lot of people saying that when you use this herb, your life will only last— from the time you start using it—maybe 4 or 5 or 6 years and that was it. That's what people were saying at that time. And that was 40 years ago. (*Mike)

Another old Navajo Road Man told a similar story about his brother being jailed and having been told that Peyote use would shorten his life:

> That's what happened to one of my brothers—he's in his 80s now, close to 90. He's the one that way back started. Some of the old people, they went on already. They're not here. And they treated them kind of rough, you know. Put them in jail and took their instruments and Medicine. That happened years ago. After that, they come down and have this regulation and all that. Take it back to Washington and talk about that. Now it's officers here and there. At that time, they told one guy I know—they called it dope, you know—if you're using this Peyote, you're not gonna last long. You're gonna go crazy. That's what they told him. But the one that said that is not here. He gone away [died]. And the one that really told him off, he got burned. His house burned down. And here he's [the man's Peyotist brother] still going. (*Leonard)

Anti-Peyotist feelings were spread by the usual sorts of misguided pro-paganda found in the American media, such as a 1922 headline in the *Washington, D.C. Evening Star* that read "Peyote Eating New Drug Craze among Indians of South Dakota" (Stewart 1987, 230). There were many legal efforts to outlaw Peyote. In these legal attacks against the Native American Church, there was typically no Native American representation, or the Native American perspective was represented by carefully selected anti-Peyotist Indians. Many states passed laws against Peyote. However, thanks largely to its incorporation as a church (which began in Oklahoma in 1918), the Native American Church survived and has struggled to defend the religious freedom of its members.

The current situation for Native American Church members in the United States is a situation in which their history and spiritual traditions are still misunderstood and they are once again menaced by an increas-ingly punitive and damaging War on Drugs. The lingering misunder-standing was revealed in my interview with a college student raised in the Native American Church, who felt unable to discuss her tradition even in a university course on Native American history:

I took a Native American history course and there was a section where they talked about religion and Native American Church was part of that section. Most of this class was maybe 75 percent white students and the rest were minorities. And when it came about there was a lot of questions they had—their curiosity was around Peyote as a substance, like what it does to the body. It was inter-esting because I was just sitting there and listening. I guess just from listening to them talk, I could see that they didn't understand the way it is—its spirituality. They didn't think of it the way as you would think of the Catholic religion, how they have spirits. They just thought of it basically as a drug. They didn't think of what it means to the Native American people or what it does for them as a reli-gious belief. I think my professor did her best to explain, although she wasn't part of the Native American Church. She tried to basi-cally stay in the middle instead of jumping on one side. I would say it was a class of 40 and I would say there were less than 10 Native Americans. I didn't say anything because I didn't want to bring any-thing upon me or people ask me questions and stuff because that class could get real intense. There was one time when we were talk-ing just around the Boarding School time when Native Americans were taken away from their homes. There was this one time where these guys argued like "White people never did that." Just totally being ignorant. And I never really wanted to voice that opinion after that class. (*Florence)

In the wake of the psychedelic-supported intergenerational conflicts of the 1960s, which can be seen as aspects of a positive revitalization movement among American youth, and with the rise of not only a significant drug abuse problem in American cities but also an imperialist pharmaceutical industry, the ethnocentric and ideology-driven War on Drugs was born. It subsequently developed into a transnational militarized crusade. Consciousness alteration, and who controls it, has become one of the most focal and divisive issues of the modern world. After several decades of relative acceptance, members of the Native American Church again became targets in one of the most significant religious freedom cases in the history of the United States.

The *Smith* Case: An Overview and Critique

Held: The Free Exercise Clause permits the State to prohibit sacramental Peyote use and thus to deny unemployment benefits to persons discharged for such use.

—U.S. Supreme Court Opinion in *Employment Division of Oregon* v. SMITH, 494 U.S. 872 (1990)

Alfred Smith, a member of the Klamath tribe, was born on the Klamath reservation in Oregon but was removed from his family at eight years old and placed in a boarding school. As was stated earlier, these schools were set up by Euro-Americans for Native Americans with the purpose of stripping Native American children of their own cultures, languages, and identities so they could be more easily trained to act and think like a Euro-American (Adams 1995). The goal was thus the destruction of Native American cultures. Given this developmental history, it is not surprising that Mr. Smith became an alcoholic as a young adult. At the age of thirty-six, however, with the help of Alcoholics Anonymous, Mr. Smith was able to stop drinking and begin a new path that would lead to rediscovery of his Native American identity, including participation in Sweat Lodge and Native American Church ceremonies. Smith eventually found a new purpose: helping other Native Americans who were suffering from alcoholism as he had (Botsford and Echo-Hawk 1996).

In 1984, Mr. Smith was employed by a substance abuse treatment facility in Roseburg, Oregon, to help develop services that were suited to Native American clients. In light of this goal, it is ironic that, when the director of the facility (a service provider who ethically should have educated himself about the practices of his Native American patients) learned that Mr. Smith was a member of the Native American Church, a tradition that explicitly supports recovery and abstinence from drugs of abuse for hundreds of thousands of Native Americans, he ordered Smith to stop attending church meetings:

> One Friday afternoon my supervisor called me into his office and asked if I was a member of the Native American Church. I said I was, and he asked if I used the drug, Peyote. I said, "No, but I do take the holy sacrament." He told me not to, that it was illegal, and then checked up on me on Monday, asking if I had taken the drug during the Saturday night ceremony. Again I said no, but that I had partaken of the sacrament. So he said I left him no alternative but to fire me. (A. Smith 1996, 68)

A coworker, Galen Black, who had also attended the ceremony, was also fired. Smith and Black filed claims for unemployment compensation, and this began six years of litigation. A long line of Supreme Court cases holds that states must pay unemployment compensation to employees who lose their jobs because of their religious beliefs. The Oregon Employment Appeals Board ruled that Smith and Black were not entitled to benefits, but the Oregon Court of Appeals ruled that they were entitled to benefits. The state's attorney general challenged this opinion, but the Oregon Supreme Court upheld it. The attorney general then referred the case to the US Supreme Court. The US Supreme Court vacated the judgment, deciding, in seeming ignorance of the First Amendment and established jurisprudence regarding Native Americans, that Peyote is illegal and if Oregon could send Smith and Black to prison for using Peyote, it could surely refuse to pay them unemployment compensation.

The Supreme Court's case was a significant blow to religious freedom and many other rights in the United States, especially for those from minority cultures. Prior to this ruling, the burden of proof had rested with the government to demonstrate a "compelling government interest" in denying religious freedom. The benefit of the doubt was on the side of religious freedom and personal liberty. But to the majority justices, this freedom became, in the words of Justice Scalia, who wrote the majority opinion, a "luxury" we can no longer afford in an increasingly diverse society. The Native American Church member who ingested Peyote, and whose right to do so was previously upheld, could now be considered "guilty of a Class B felony" (*Employment Division of Oregon v. Smith*, 494 U.S. 872 [1990]). In order to rationalize this finding, the majority justices invented a strange "two constitutional rights is better than one" hybrid test: it was argued that religious freedom can be protected against generally applicable laws only when the case involves other constitutional protections, such as free speech or the right of parents to direct the education of their children.

This decision could only be reached by ignoring a century's worth of ethnographic research findings on the Native American Church. In his dissent to the *Smith* opinion, Justice Blackmun eloquently described the Court's deliberate ignoring of evidence contradicting the view that sacramental use of Peyote is dangerous:

> [T]his Court's prior decisions have not allowed a government to rely on mere speculation about potential harms, but have demanded evidentiary support for a refusal to allow a religious exception.... In this case, the State's justification for refusing to recognize an exception to its criminal laws for religious Peyote use is entirely speculative.... [T]here was no opportunity for factfinding concerning the alleged dangers of Peyote use. What has now become the State's principal argument for its view that the criminal prohibition is enforceable against religious use of Peyote rests on no evidentiary foundation at all.

The attorney general of Oregon, in arguing against the view that Peyote use by Native Americans does no harm, claimed that the scholarly literature "provides us no security...no real information as to how the underlying danger of the substance or harm is, in fact, avoided" (Frohnmayer 1989). This statement ignores much relevant research, as a large portion of the literature on the Native American Church does address the question of how danger is avoided (e.g., Bergman 1971; Albaugh and Anderson 1974; Aberle 1991 [1966]). Specific protective factors include the positive expectations that derive from cultural beliefs about Peyote, the controlled nature of the ritual environment, cultural explanations for adverse effects, and self-limiting dosage because the bitter-tasting natural plant form is used. But the most relevant piece of information that is side-stepped by the attorney general's framing of his question concerns not how harm is avoided (a complex question for any harmless activity), but the very fact that harm is, invariably, avoided.

Though the Court merely invoked Peyote's Schedule I status to support its opinion that Peyote is a dangerous drug of abuse, there are several research studies that have found Peyote to be harmless when used properly. The alleged safety concerns in this area have to do with emotional or behavioral disturbance, psychotic reactions, and chromosome damage. Oscar Janiger, a physician at the University of California-Irvine Medical School, and his colleagues (Dorrance, Janiger, and Tepliz 1975) investigated the question of chromosome damage among Native Americans who use Peyote ceremonially. They compared a group of Huichol Indians who used Peyote from childhood to old age with another group of Huichol who did not use Peyote. They found that there was no difference in chromosome damage between the Peyotist group and the non-Peyotist group.[1]

As for psychological or behavioral disturbance, Dr. Robert Bergman (1971), a psychiatrist working for the Indian Health Service on the Navajo reservation, tracked every report of an adverse reaction to Peyote for a period of four years. Bergman concluded that there was "almost no acute or chronic emotional disturbance arising from Peyote use." He only observed five cases of reported disturbance, all of which subsided soon after. Based on his observations, Bergman made some estimates about the actual incidence of adverse reactions to Peyote:

> The Native American Church of Navajoland estimates its membership at 40,000. This estimate may be high and there may be inactive members, so we will use a population base of 30,000. Our informants report attending meetings with an average frequency of about twice a month. Since this may be exaggerated, we will assume an average attendance of only once every two months. This would result in a total of 180,000 ingestions of Peyote per year by the population we serve. Assuming that all five of our cases represent true reactions to Peyote and that we hear about only half of the cases occurring, the resulting (probably overestimated) rate would be approximately one bad reaction per 70,000 ingestions. (Bergman 1971, 697)

In relation to psychosis, given what we know about the distribution of schizophrenia spectrum disorders across human populations, we would expect that at least 1 percent of Bergman's subject population would have had a biological vulnerability to psychotic symptoms. It is also widely believed that hallucinogen use will precipitate an acute psychotic reaction in biologically vulnerable individuals. Given the numbers and the fact that Peyote is believed to be good for all members of the family (especially troubled individuals), this means that it is likely that many persons with schizophrenia are taking Peyote regularly with no adverse reactions. Given these findings, it appears that Peyote is extremely safe when used in this sort of context.

As was stated, Schedule I substances are believed to have no therapeutic uses. But the primary reason Native Americans take Peyote is for "healing." In fact, Peyote is typically referred to using the English word *Medicine*. The Navajo word commonly used by Navajo members of the Native American Church to refer to the Peyote cactus is *azéé*, which translates as "Medicine." The belief in Peyote's therapeutic efficacy is not limited to Native Americans; reports from several Euro-American psychiatrists, psychologists, and ethnographers have noted that Native American use of Peyote does not produce pathology and, in fact, seems to benefit many Native American communities. The distinguished psychiatrist Karl Menninger, for example, wrote:

> Peyote is not harmful to these people; it is beneficial, comforting, inspiring, and appears to be spiritually nourishing. It is a better antidote to alcohol than anything the missionaries, the white man, the American Medical Association, and the public health services have come up with. (Menninger 1971, 699)

Twenty years earlier, in 1951, five scholars who had observed and studied the Native American Church, Weston LaBarre, David McAllester, J. S. Slotkin, Omer Stewart, and Sol Tax, published a "Statement on Peyote" in the journal *Science* supporting Peyote use by Native Americans (LaBarre et al. 1951). This protectionist stance was recently reaffirmed in a public statement by the American Anthropological Association (1993, 47) supporting the legitimacy of the Native American Church. As for the Navajo tribe specifically, David Aberle (1991 [1966], 212), doing long-term participant observation among the Navajos, verified Peyotist abstinence. He wrote that he had made careful observations at public events, such as "squaw dances" and rodeos, in which there would typically be a lot of public drinking to the point of drunkenness. He observed that, on these occasions, very few Native American Church members showed any signs of drinking.

There are many ways to understand this therapeutic effect, any or all of which may play a role in positive outcomes from Peyote use. In my analysis of the symbolism and larger cultural meaning of the Peyote Ceremony (Calabrese 1994), I found that the Peyote Ceremony has the symbolic structure of a death and rebirth mediated by the Peyote Spirit present in the meeting. Another important factor in the symbolism, revealed in the many testimonies of recovery narrated by Peyotists, is reflexivity or self-awareness, as embodied in the crescent moon altar as a symbol of one's life course. Many Native American Church members state that the Peyote experience made visible to them the maladaptive behaviors they had been habitually engaging in and the need for change.

The symbolism of the Peyote Meeting may very likely support the therapeutic goals of the ritual by symbolically depicting the human life course and by embedding this depiction of a human life in a symbolic context that emphasizes natural transformative processes (gestation and birth, the changing of the moon, etc.). The Peyotists themselves are embedded in a powerfully symbolic natural transformative process, as the ritual begins at night and culminates in the dawning of a new day. Peyote is well equipped to facilitate the mind's openness to these cultural messages by altering suggestibility and inducing a spiritually oriented state of self-reflection. This enables culturally valued, therapeutic cognitive and affective restructuring.

In addition to this symbolic sort of understanding of efficacy, we should not ignore the fact that pharmacological research is being done on psychedelics because of the potential they show in treating addiction (Halpern 1996). Much of this research focuses on the hallucinogen ibogaine, the psychoactive component of a shrub used ritually in the African Bwiti religion (Fernandez 1982), but it has been suggested that the effects may generalize across all major hallucinogens. Ibogaine is being used therapeutically by addict self-help groups in the United States and Europe to treat cocaine and heroin addiction, and it is claimed that ibogaine allows people to quit these addictive drugs without experiencing withdrawal symptoms. This addiction therapy follows a different paradigm from the agonist/antagonist paradigm that informs methadone maintenance programs. The director of one of these self-help groups, based in New York, calls it an "interrupter" approach (Sisko 1994). This terminology follows findings of Dutch pharmacologists (Cappendijk and Dzoljic 1993, 261), in experimental studies with addicted rats, that "ibogaine or its metabolite(s) is a long-lasting interrupter of cocaine dependence." Amazingly, when the psychedelic ibogaine is given to lab rats that have been hooked on heroin and cocaine by investigators, the rats stop self-administering the addictive drugs and subsequently show no signs of withdrawal.

The therapeutic potential of psychedelic agents for addiction treatment and other clinical applications is credible enough for the US Food and Drug Administration (FDA), National Institutes of Health (NIH), and National Institute on Drug Abuse (NIDA) to support further research on various psychedelics using human subjects. FDA-approved safety trials on ibogaine have been conducted by Professor of Neurology Deborah Mash and colleagues (2000) at the University of Miami School of Medicine. Dr. Charles Grob, director of the Division of Child and Adolescent Psychiatry at Harbor-UCLA Medical Center, is conducting research, funded by the NIH, on the safety and efficacy of psilocybin in patients with advanced-stage cancer and reactive anxiety. A pilot study (Grob et al. 2011) found that there were no clinically significant adverse events with psilocybin; the State-Trait Anxiety Inventory trait anxiety subscale demonstrated a significant reduction in anxiety at one and three months after treatment. In addition, the Beck Depression Inventory revealed an improvement of mood that reached significance at six months. Another study of psilocybin, completed by researchers at the Johns Hopkins University School of Medicine (MacLean, Johnson, and Griffiths 2011, 1453), found that, in participants who had mystical experiences during their psilocybin session, the personality trait of Openness, which encompasses sensitivity, imagination, and tolerance of others' viewpoints and values, "remained significantly higher than baseline more than 1 year after the session. The findings suggest a specific role for psilocybin and mystical-type experiences in adult personality change." In another study, supported by NIDA, researchers at the University of Chicago's Human Behavioral Pharmacology Laboratory (Bedi, Hyman, and de Wit 2010, 1134) examined empathy and prosocial feelings among subjects using MDMA and found that socioemotional processing alterations "might underlie possible psychotherapeutic benefits of this drug." Several similar studies have been completed or are in process. The "interrupter" approach to the pharmacological treatment of addiction and other effects described earlier may also be exemplified by the Native American Church, though I would argue that therapeutic emplotment and self-reflection are crucial factors that we cannot ignore. I thus argue for a more contextualized and experiential "semiotic/reflexive paradigm" of psychopharmacology (beyond "interruption") when considering intervention in the Native American Church.

Whether we understand Peyote's therapeutic efficacy in terms of traditional anthropological understandings of ritual process and symbolism or in terms of psychopharmacological effects (or a combination of both), the ethnographer of the Native American Church invariably encounters testimonies of a substance abuse problem or other problem that has been changed by participation in the Native American Church, leading to recovery and abstinence from alcohol and drugs of abuse. I got to know several people who are leading very functional lives as members of the Native American Church, including several clinicians, counselors, and nurses; a CEO of a residential treatment program; a district prosecutor; and many others. Clinicians working with Native American populations also acknowledge the efficacy of Peyote. Albaugh and Anderson (1974, 1249) note for their Native American patients a "carry-over period" lasting seven to ten days after attending a Peyote Meeting that is marked by "increased openness and willingness to communicate." And, as Kunitz and Levy (1994) have documented, therapeutic use of Peyote even has its own accepted Indian Health Service "client service code."

Justice Scalia claimed that the Supreme Court has "never held that an individual's religious beliefs excuse him from compliance with an otherwise valid law prohibiting conduct that the State is free to regulate." He also claimed that religious freedom is protected against generally applicable laws only in conjunction with other constitutional protections, like the right of parents to direct the education of their children (*Pierce v. Society of Sisters*, 268 U.S. 510 [1925]; *Wisconsin v. Yoder*, 406 U.S. 205 [1972]). According to Scalia, "The present case does not present such a hybrid situation, but a free exercise claim unconnected with any communicative activity or parental right." This line of argumentation is an imaginative distortion of both legal precedents and the realities of the Native American Church. Outlawing Peyote does interfere with the established right of parents to raise their children in their own religious tradition, and the continued existence of their cultural tradition is what Smith and others were, in effect, arguing for.

Scalia's ethnocentrism is apparent: he states that Oregon law does not preclude "communication of religious beliefs or the raising of one's children in those beliefs," but this claim rests on Eurocentric views of "religion" as a matter of belief or faith. As Scalia writes, "The free exercise of religion means, first and foremost, the right to believe and profess whatever religious doctrine one desires" (*Employment Division of Oregon v. Smith*, 494 U.S. 872 [1990]). It is well known that other cultural traditions place much more emphasis on ritual practice (even looking at Catholicism versus Protestantism), and in many societies the socialization and education of children relies on traditional ritual-based modes that often involve altered states of consciousness (e.g., Grob and Dobkin de Rios 1994). The First Amendment itself does not distinguish between religious belief and religious conduct. In addition, when Scalia states that the Court has "never held that an individual's religious beliefs excuse him from compliance with an otherwise valid law prohibiting conduct that the State is free to regulate," he is ignoring statements of his own court such as that in *Wisconsin v. Yoder*: "A regulation neutral on its face may, in its application, nonetheless offend the constitutional requirement for government neutrality if it unduly burdens the free exercise of religion" (*Wisconsin v. Yoder*, 406 U.S. 205 [1972]).

In the Native American Church, beliefs are not simply transmitted from one member to another verbally; rather, it is believed that one must come upon one's beliefs independently through the sacramental experience of Peyote consumption (Calabrese 1994). This was the essential difference between Native American religions and Christian religions identified by the Native American leader and Road Man Quanah Parker. According to Parker, when the White Man goes into his church he talks about Jesus, whereas the Indian goes into his tipi and talks *to* Jesus. As the elderly Road Man *Mike explained to me, "When you ask me, 'what do you see?', 'how does it work?'—really you yourself have to be the judge of that when you partake of this Medicine—when you go into a ceremony. You have to partake of it yourself" (*Mike).

Thus, Peyote use is even implicated in the transmission of religious beliefs and knowledge. According to the Supreme Court in *Wisconsin v. Yoder*, "The Court's holding in Pierce stands as a charter of the rights of parents to direct the religious upbringing of their children." But that right was not honored in the case of the Native American Church, no doubt primarily because the majority justices are more ethnocentric in relation to Native Americans than they are in relation to the more culturally familiar Amish, who educate their children verbally rather than with communal rituals involving consciousness alteration.

Peyote is central to parenting in connection with its status as an omniscient spirit functioning as a teacher, healer, protector, and guide for life (see the seventh chapter of this book). Peyote is referred to as "Mother Peyote" or "Father Peyote," and it acts as a sort of parental figure, enforcing moral prohibitions, especially against alcohol consumption, when parents are not present. Because "nothing is hidden from it from horizon to horizon" (Aberle 1991 [1966], 377), it is believed that Peyote knows when children are misbehaving (e.g., drinking or using drugs of abuse) no matter where they are. It is, at first impression, similar to what some tell their children about the supernatural figure called Santa Claus: "He knows if you've been bad or good, so be good for goodness sake." But Peyote has a much more sacred quality and is sincerely believed in by parents and children alike. Peyote is often associated with Christ by Peyotists (deity made flesh), and sacramental ingestion of Peyote is required for a true communion with the spirit. This omniscient spirit obviously has a role in raising children in an alcohol-free lifestyle. LaBarre (1989 [1938], 97) suggests that this belief that Peyote "sees and punishes evil deeds" may go all the way back to the Huichol and Tarahumara tribes of Mexico, making it one of the most important Mexican influences on the Native American Church and thus one of the oldest features of the religion.

A Perennially Misunderstood Medicine

From an anthropological perspective, the misunderstanding of the Native American Church is symptomatic of a much broader Euro-American ignorance concerning the role of consciousness modification in human history. Shamanic and other forms of spirituality and ritual healing that utilize various techniques of consciousness modification are, in fact, among the oldest and most widespread forms of religious practice of which anthropologists and historians are aware (Schultes 1998). As Schultes and Hofmann (1992) state, use of psychedelic plants "goes back so far into prehistory that it has been postulated that perhaps the whole idea of deity could have arisen as a result of the other-worldly effects of these agents." Use of psychedelic plants in traditional societies was marked not by abuse but by controlled therapeutic and spiritual use. Nevertheless, the traditions of our earliest ancestors and all these millennia of human cultural history have been reduced, in the contemporary United States and in many other countries, to "criminal drug abuse." The War on Drugs is, in effect, a war on plant medicines that compete with the pharmaceutical industry (and the tobacco and alcohol industries).[2] More importantly, it is a war on the typically nonviolent users of these plant medicines, who become slave laborers of an expanding for-profit prison industry in an insane inversion of a free society (Marion 2009; Gilmore 2000; Wacquant

2001). The very existence of a tradition like the Native American Church in such a War on Drugs–dominated country as the United States is something of a miracle.

Centuries after the Inquisition, the ethnocentrism continues, though its rationalization has shifted from the eradication of sinful activity within an explicitly Christian framework to a pseudoscientific (and demonstrably false) claim that Peyote is a dangerous drug with no medical application. Today, the majority of contemporary Euro-Americans either seem completely ignorant of the tradition or hold an inaccurate, stigmatizing view of it, such as the stereotype of the "Peyote smoking Indian" (a common racial slur that misunderstands the way Peyote is physically ingested) or the label of "addict" (which misses the fact that Peyote is not an addictive substance). The persistence of this lack of understanding is surprising given the fact that ritual Peyote use, in the context of the intertribal revitalization movement called the Native American Church, is the most widespread Native American spiritual/religious tradition in North America, having members in tribes across the United States and Canada.

Even the highest court of the land, the US Supreme Court, demonstrated its inability, or, more to the point, its unwillingness, to understand the purposes and outcomes of Native American use of Peyote. In its ruling against two therapists fired from their jobs for attending a ceremony of the Native American Church (*Employment Division of Oregon v. Smith, 494 U.S. 872* [1990]), the Court ignored ethnographic evidence, policies of the US Indian Health Service, and legal precedent in its move to suspend the religious freedom clause of the Constitution and expand a destructive War on Drugs.

However, in spite of an unrelenting culture clash and continuous efforts to stamp it out, Native American Peyote use has persisted in the European-dominated Americas for five centuries. The following chapters will explore why this is the case as they look at the Native American Church today, paying special attention to the existence of multigenerational Native American Church families, human development and socialization in these families, and the use of the Peyote Ceremony in federally funded clinical programs serving Native American communities.

5

Medicine and Spirit

THE DUAL NATURE OF PEYOTE

PEYOTE IS CENTRAL to the Native American Church. It is central as a medicine, as a potent symbol, and as a spiritual entity. In approaching the topic of the Native American Church member's understanding of Peyote, we enter a domain at the intersection of ethnobotany and ethnopharmacology on the one hand, and anthropological studies of personhood on the other. This is because members of the Native American Church describe Peyote both as an herbal medicine and as an omniscient spiritual entity. Peyote is dried, ground, and consumed or applied as a poultice. It is also addressed and interacted with as a wise and benevolent being, usually called "Mother Peyote" or "Father Peyote," that monitors the Peyotist's thoughts and behavior and helps keep the person on the right path.

This double meaning of Peyote is not unusual in world cultures, especially given the findings of anthropological research on ritual symbols. Victor Turner (1967) found that ritual symbols tend to have certain properties in common. These properties include multivocality, in which a single symbol can link together many meanings. For example, Turner wrote about how the *mudyi* tree symbol of the girl's puberty ritual among the Ndembu of Zambia united sensory meanings, such as breast milk, with ideological meanings, such as matriliny and the unity of Ndembu society. Peyote can be seen, in Turner's terms, as a multivocal symbol uniting the ideological meaning of "omniscient spiritual entity" (as well as spiritual transformation and cultural revitalization) with the sensory meaning of "natural, medicinal herb."

One of the more intriguing findings of classic ethnographic research is that personhood is defined differently in different societies and is often not synonymous with the Euro-American category of "human." For example, the wooden "False Face" masks of the Iroquois are related to as social persons and need to be fed regularly (Fogelson 1979). Cheyenne children, lacking full responsibility for their actions, were considered only "potential persons" (Straus 1977), while Tallensi considered certain crocodiles to be persons (Fortes 1973). In the contemporary capitalist United States, certain entities such as corporations are treated legally as persons, which is as bizarre a cultural formulation of personhood as any of the others. Discussions of the Peyote Spirit should also be placed within the context of the diverse conceptualizations of the person in human cultures.

To get at the insider's understanding of Peyote, I began each of my ethnographic interviews with Native American Church members by eliciting a definition of Peyote. Their answers to this question form the primary data analyzed in this chapter. In line with my previous findings, I found that my consultants described Peyote in two ways: Peyote was identified as a medicinal herb with God-given properties and as a personality or spirit that is omniscient and that functions in various roles to help the Indian. Many mentioned both aspects in their definitions. Some Native American Church members emphasized one aspect over the other. The college student *Florence stated, "I think of it both ways: as an herb and as a spirit as well. But I think of it more as an herb than as a spirit." *Gladys answered as follows:

> I guess the physical description would be an herb. And as far as what I see Peyote as, it's a very powerful spirit, a holy being.... [I]t's the opportunity to have the ability to communicate with the creator, to ask him for the spiritual guidance that you need to solve a situation.

These two passages from the interviews with *Gladys and *Florence seem to differ in relative emphasis given to Peyote as a spirit, even though *Gladys and *Florence are mother and daughter. Another interesting finding, to be discussed later, was that some Navajo Peyotists have a more metaphorical understanding of the spirit of Peyote. These people seem to understand the personal ways of addressing Peyote mainly as a sign of respect for the sacred or as something tangible that the Peyotist can relate to. This demonstrates the diversity of metaphysical perspectives tolerated in the religion.

Peyote as Herb

Native American Church members typically define Peyote as an herb, and its use is sometimes described in the context of Navajo herbal medicine.

The Road Man I am calling *Mike simply stated, "I know Peyote as an herb. There are other herbs on this reservation and Peyote is another one of those that you can use." Slotkin (1975 [1956], 41) suggested that, in the postfrontier period, Peyote addressed two white disorders, tuberculosis and alcoholism, that were not curable by traditional means. However, among the Native American Church members I have interviewed, Peyote is most often seen as a spiritual panacea for many sorts of illnesses, curing primarily through its spiritual rather than pharmacological essence, but particularly useful against alcoholism: "It's everything. It's a teacher, a protector, it's a guidance. It's everything to us. The Creator...put this herb down for us. We look at it as an herb. And the Creator put certain properties within that herb" (Hoskie).

The pre-Peyote Navajo word for "Medicine," 'azee', has come to be used by Navajo Native American Church members to refer to Peyote. This follows a cross-tribal pattern. Thus, as Schultes (1938, 711) reported, the Delaware *biisung*, the Taos *walena*, the Comanche *puakit*, the Omaha *makan*, the Kickapoo *naw-tai-no-nee*, the Shawnee *o-jay-bee-kee*, and (possibly) the Aztec *ichpatl* are reported in the literature as terms formerly meaning "Medicine" but now also specifically meaning "Peyote" in these contexts. This terminology certainly supports Schultes's view of the medicinal appeal of Peyote.

In discussing "Medicine" in a Native American context, it is important to emphasize the inclusive, spiritual nature of the concept. The Navajo word for Medicine ('azee') can refer not only to herbal medicines but also to ceremonies and ceremonial paraphernalia. For both traditionalist and Peyotist Navajos, Medicine is something that sets right the person's disturbed state "by means of both spiritual and organic processes—difficult to separate in any case" (Aberle 1991 [1966], 178). My consultant *Edgar explained it as follows:

> Just like with any herbs that we use for healing, we call that Medicine. Just like with the mountain tobacco, it's an herb. That one we look at as tobacco, it works on your system as well. And then there's these other herbs that we have that we utilize for certain symptoms and we generalize that as Medicine but they have their own names—they all have their spiritual name, they have their ceremonial names, different ways to gather them and use them.

As an herbal preparation, Peyote is sometimes eaten fresh, but it is more often dried, and the dried button chewed, or dried and powdered. In powdered form, it can be eaten dry or water can be added to achieve an oatmeal-like consistency, which I found was the easiest way to consume Peyote. Alternatively, a Peyote tea can be made. One Peyotist told me, "We either have a liquid form or the one with the powder…I guess whatever is convenient at the time" (*Ruth). Peyotists do not smoke Peyote. This seems to be a common misconception among Euro-Americans (as "Peyote-smoking Indian" is a common racial epithet aimed at Native Americans generally). The taste of Peyote is notoriously bitter and often induces vomiting. This bitterness is given a spiritual meaning by Native American Church members, who say that Peyote is referred to in the following passage from the Bible: "And they shall eat the flesh in that night, roast with fire, and unleavened bread; and with bitter herbs they shall eat it" (Exodus 12:8).

Peyote as Spirit

The characterization of Peyote as a spiritual entity is a cross-tribal pattern within the Native American Church. This spirit may be identified with the Holy Spirit or with Christ but never loses its identity as Peyote. Writing about the Shawnee Peyotists, LaBarre (1989 [1938], 72) stated that some thought of Peyote as the messenger between God and humans and others called it "the interpreter" or "the Holy Ghost." LaBarre also reports that there is a Mexican folk-Catholic saint called El Santo Nino de Jesus Peyotes, whose attributes are a staff, gourd, feathered hat, and basket, similar to but distinct from El Santo Nino de Atoche, and another attribute is the crescent moon. He is depicted as a little boy and his statue is at the cathedral -in Rosales, Mexico (LaBarre 1989 [1938], 35).

Peyote is considered a benevolent guardian spirit or a messenger spirit allowing communication between humans and divinity (Slotkin 1975 [1956], 70; Aberle 1991 [1966], 178). Peyote is present in the ceremony in the form of the "Mother Peyote" or "Father Peyote," an especially large and perfectly formed cactus that is placed on the central crescent-shaped mound of earth. Prayers are sent through Peyote to the Creator or to Peyote itself, who has powers of its own. As Navajo Peyotist Wilson Aronilth (1981, 1) writes, "This Divine herb…has a mind; it can see, it can move, and it grows." In response to my query about Peyote as a spiritual being, my consultant *Henry replied, "Yes there is a spirit for me. And I look at that and I respect that spirit." Hoskie explained it as follows:

> This Peyote was put down with certain properties by the Holy
> Spirit. That's the mediator between you and the Creator. It's also

got properties and a spirit of its own. And so we call it "Mother Peyote," "Father Peyote.". . . We believe that we tell our problems to this Medicine here, then it's gonna help us to overcome whatever problems we're having.

An interesting manifestation of Peyote's spirit in the ethnographic literature is the existence of stories describing talking or singing cacti. This is a central part of the Peyotist origin myth. It is also said that one may find Peyote, in the desert fields where it grows, by listening for its beautiful singing. It continues to sing inside the bags in which it is stored after harvesting. Lumholtz, working among the Tarahumarah, wrote that one of the Tarahumarah men, who wanted to use his bag as a pillow, could not sleep because he said the plants made so much noise (Lumholtz, cited in LaBarre 1989 [1938], 13). D'Azevedo's Washoe consultants also reported the singing of Peyote:

Each one of Them little green Herbs is singing His own songs the Creator gave Him. Any Indian Member in good standing can hear Them all singing if he go on a run down there to get the Medicine. (Anonymous Washoe Peyotist in D'Azevedo 1985, 2)

When we get a load of Peyote I go through and pick out some of the biggest ones. They is the oldest. Them's the ones you can hear singing sometimes where they grow. (Anonymous Washoe Peyotist in D'Azevedo 1985, 9)

As with the inclusive Native American concept of "Medicine," personification is not limited to Peyote but is also applied to other aspects of ceremonial life. Aberle's consultant Mike Kiyaani stated, "Fire is a person who doctors. There is a fire in every home, and fire is like a person. We cannot live without it. And the poker, too, is like a person. Peyote is a woman; mother earth is a woman; and water is a woman" (Aberle 1991 [1966], 140). Another of Aberle's consultants, David Morton, states that the gourd, staff, and sage, which pass together around the meeting, "are like a person who talks to you" (Aberle 1991 [1966], 175). However, Peyote's personality is unique in its special guiding role in the lives of many Native American Church members. This special relationship is obvious in the following passage from *Gladys:

I guess maybe because my faith is so strong in this Medicine that even today's challenges I always think back to the Medicine. When I fall down, I make a mistake, I think back to the Medicine and think, "OK. What are you trying to teach me today?" or "Why did you put this in front of me?"

Omniscience

Omniscience is among the most typical characteristics attributed to the Peyote Spirit. Aberle reported that various terms are used in the ceremony that imply that Peyote is all-seeing, such as "nothing is hidden from it from horizon to horizon" (Aberle 1991 [1966], 377). The omniscience of Peyote is implied by Peyotist ritual experiences, such as dreams or visions, that are interpreted as communications from or through Peyote but which nevertheless refer to the Peyotist's deepest thoughts, guilt feelings, or memories. Because nothing is hidden from it, ingestion of Peyote reveals the nature of the problem and its resolution to the meeting's participants. They partake in the omniscience of Peyote. One of my consultants told me that the person for whom the meeting is called is asking the participants, "Think to the four directions for me. Think to Mother Earth for me. Help me." As a young Peyotist explained it to me, "If you pray to Grandpa Fire in that way, he can give you blessings in that way to have a spiritual vision. If you have faith, he can show you that. The Peyote will see all" (*Adam).

This educational guidance of Peyote extends beyond the ceremony. One of my consultants told me of a problem his young son was having in learning how to tie his shoes. His father gave him a single Peyote button to eat and, with the help of Peyote, he learned how to tie his shoes that day. The omniscient Peyote took the form of an authority figure for *Mike's grandsons, who were taught the familiar formula "it knows if you are bad or good." Because nothing is hidden from it, not only does use of Peyote reveal the nature of the problem and its solution to ceremonial participants, but also Peyote's omniscience functions to keep the Peyotist from committing moral infringements like consuming alcohol. As *Mike's young grandson *Ben told me, "It knows if you've smoked or drunk." When I asked him "Who?" he replied, "The Father Peyote."

As stated previously, LaBarre (1989 [1938], 97) suggested that the belief that Peyote "sees and punishes evil deeds" may go all the way back to the Huichol and Tarahumara tribes of Mexico, making it one of the most important Mexican influences on the Native American Church and thus one of the oldest features of the religion. Radin (1914, 5–6, 19) writes,

> If a person eats peyote and does not repent openly, he has a guilty conscience, which leaves him as soon as the public repentance has been made....If a peyote-user relapses into his old way of living, then the peyote causes him great suffering....The disagreeable effects of the peyote varied directly with a man's disbelief in it.

Peyote as Parental

Another typical way of characterizing the Peyote Spirit is as a parental figure. Native American Church members refer to Peyote as "Mother Peyote" or "Father Peyote." *Gladys simply stated, "The way I look at it, I look at it as both my Mom and Dad." When I asked *Edgar to explain this way of addressing Peyote, he stated:

> That's part of our clanship, the extended families of that clan, like my Mom's clan, if I meet an elder, a lady that's of the same clan, she can address me like her son. It's an opportunity to say that. And when we say Mother Peyote, to me, that's the same thing. You're saying on a spiritual level, you're saying mom and asking for help. And again, it takes it on a personal level where, it's like for us as human beings, the Peyote—Medicine—has its own characteristics.

We see from this passage that some Native American Church members use the parental form of address to invoke the aid of Peyote following the model of reciprocal relationships in traditional matrilineal Navajo clans. Native American Church members also appeal to God using parental forms of address. Aberle reported Navajo Peyotist references to God as "Our Father," or even "Our Father and Our Mother," and to the participants as "Your children" or "Your babies" (Aberle 1991 [1966], 153).

The question of the gender of Peyote is a topic that LaBarre addressed in a few places. We learn from LaBarre that the Zacatecas "say they are male and female," that the Huichol distinguish *Tzinouritehua-hicouri* ("Peyotl of the Gods") from the stronger and more bitter *Rhaitoumuanitarihua-hicouri* ("Peyotl of the Goddesses"), and that the Huichol have a tutelary goddess for Peyote called *Hatzimouika*, while the Peyote deity of the Tarahumari is male (LaBarre 1989 [1938], 12–13). The Winnebago are evidently influenced by an older tribal pattern in their use of two sacred Peyotes, one male and the other female (LaBarre 1989 [1938], 72).

I addressed this topic in my interviews with Native American Church members and opinion was divided, with some identifying Peyote as female and some saying that Peyote is both male and female. None said it was exclusively male. *Beatrice said, "Probably both.... [W]hen I think about it, I think of both." *Edgar responded as follows:

> Well my understanding is both male and female. Mainly what I was told, and I seen this before when I was under the influence, is that there's four females that are guarding this Peyote. They are all sisters. That's one of the stories that I've heard. And sometimes when that Medicine and the drumming and singing really gets moving spiritually, and then there's only about one or two women in there, if you concentrate, sometimes you can hear a whole bunch of ladies singing. And to me, that herb is by itself and then the fireplace and the altar where we pray is both male and female. And the way the herb grows, it has to be male and female as with anything—the same with the fire. They say that only one log cannot work as well as two. So they start with two, then they add more to it—just like a family, the more the family stays together, the fire gets stronger and stronger.

Many things in the Navajo universe are male or female, including ceremonies and even hogans, the traditional Navajo log dwelling. The rural Peyotist family I lived with had three female hogans and a male hogan. The female hogan is the more typical type with the flatter roof. The male hogan is conical like a tipi and is more rarely seen. A Peyotist consultant in another part of the reservation echoed this idea that Peyote is both male and female because everything is male and female:

> I think with that, it's like the concept there's always a male and a female.... So we talk about Grandpa and Grandma Fire too, there's both. And the same thing with that Medicine. In order for everything to be *k'e*, you always have to have a male and a female.... It's showing respect and there's a way of communicating too. It depends on where you're at when you go in that meeting. (*Henry)[1]

Other Native American Church members identified Peyote as primarily female, which is not surprising given that the Navajo tribe is matrilineal and given the importance of the female in the Peyote origin story and in Peyotist ritual symbolism. One elderly Road Man, referring to the origin story, answered this way: "Well, at the beginning they say the female is the mother Peyote. That's the way they called it. Not the male. Female. The reason why is from the beginning, way back, the story" (*Leonard). *Florence attributed her female identification of Peyote to her Navajo culture:

> I think of it more in the female sense, probably just because growing up and learning about the Navajo culture and tradition, everything seems to revolve around females—like Changing Woman. And just like from when I was small—learning from just watching my mom—she called it mother. I've never heard anybody call it father.

Identifications of Peyote as male are encountered more often in other tribal traditions of Peyotism. For example, Crashing Thunder used the terms "Grandfather," "Peyote Chief," and "Father Peyote" (LaBarre 1989 [1938], 72). My consultant *Mary explained that her father calls it "Mother Peyote," but on her husband's side of the family, they call it "Chief Peyote." She stated, "I guess it depends on which traditional teachings you have that pertain to it." One Menomini Peyotist interviewed by George Spindler (Spindler and Spindler 1984, 98) described a vision of Peyote as a powerful man with a police cap who was pounding the message into him.

More Metaphorical Understandings of Peyote's Spirit

Some Native American Church members seem to have a more metaphorical understanding of Peyote's spirit. For example, when I asked *Beatrice about her understanding of Peyote as a spirit, she placed this element of the church's teachings in the context of more general Native American patterns of personalizing the natural environment:

> I think as Navajos and as Native American people, one of the things that we do is we give those properties of entity, spirit, life to trees, rocks, the earth. We say there's a spiritual side too. We

also do the same with the Medicine…and even animals. Like when they say "All my relations" [a ritual phrase often used in the Sweat Lodge]…being a part of the earth.

In a similar way, *Henry discussed Peyote as a Medicine and a spirit but used "spirit" in more phenomenological/psychological terms:

It overlaps. I see it as a little of both. I guess Medicine is like phys-ically—you taste it and that's the Medicine. Spiritually, it's the spirit of that Medicine. I guess you could say it really has that energy in there….[I]t's like the spirit of alcohol—remember in Duran's book he talks about it? There's always a spirit there. We give it a name: Jack Daniels. And we actually can taste it because that's addiction. We have post-withdrawal. We actually can taste it, we dream about it, we can actually smell it. And that's the spirit of it. I guess that's the negative spirit of it. Same thing with Medicine too. We take the physical part of that Peyote. But the spirit part is another story too. I see as the spirit part like "Yeah, I took this Medicine and it's gonna make me better." But we're not looking at a placebo, we're looking at the spiritual side.

*Ruth described Peyote as sacramental messenger service. But she placed much less stress on personification:

JC: If somebody were to ask a definition of the Medicine, what would you say?
*RUTH: I think it's a sacrament—a sacrament that when you take it, that sacrament, if you really truly want to…you will be able to get your answers. It's like a messenger service to the Creator.
JC: Some people say it has a personality of its own. Do you see as male or female spirit?
*RUTH: I really don't, but I just address it in that fashion when I'm pray-ing about it. And I think it's something tangible that you are able to relate to. That's the way I think of it.

Cultural Psychiatry in the Peyote Origin Myth

In the second chapter, I described the theoretical focus of this study in terms of the dialectic of cultural psychiatry (the reciprocal influence of the cultural and the psychiatric). This focus has roots in the more general focus on the relationship of culture and personal experience (Stigler, Shweder, and Herdt 1990; Obeyesekere 1990; Jahoda 1993). This relationship between culture and personal experience is apparent in the stories Peyotists tell about how they first encountered Peyote. I will refer to this story as the "Peyote Origin Myth." There are many versions of this story, but most Navajo stories of which I am aware depict a helpless, lost Native American woman separated from her tribe and left to die. The woman hears the voice of Peyote speaking to her and telling her what to do and instructing her to eat the cactus. She then is strengthened and healed of her suffering and is able to reunite with her tribe. The following version of the story is by Wilson Aronilth (1981, 1):

> As the story goes, this woman was participating in a hunting trip with fellow hunters from her tribe....A group of warriors attacked these hunters and in the process many were unfortunate and others ran to safety. Among the unfortunate was this one woman. She was wounded from the war party, and was left behind by her people to die. Through all of her suffering she became lost and helpless in the desert. But, out of this desolation and terror this woman heard a voice speak to her first through a dream and after she woke from the dream. The Voice said "Eat the sacred plant that is growing beside you, that is life and all of the richest blessings for you and your Indian people." Weakly, this woman turned her head against the earth's surface and saw the herb. Its head was divided into five points. These five points are the symbol of man, his beliefs and his religion. She reached for the plant and it seemed to extend outward to meet her fingers. She pulled out the herb and partook of it. Through the partaking of this plant her strength returned and she was healed and cured from her sufferings.

This story may be interpreted as a symbolic representation of the experience of any Native American person who encounters Peyote and is healed from illness or social alienation. The story's main character and her tribe were attacked by a group of warriors. My interpretation of this feature of some versions of the story is that it is a symbolic reference to the conquest of Native American societies by Europeans. Next, the main character of the story is portrayed as being alone, wounded, separated from the group, perhaps abandoned and left to die. This portrayal is a potent symbol of the postconquest situation for many Native Americans: intergenerational trauma, community disruption, and alienation from mainstream Euro-American society, perhaps with the relative deprivation that Aberle wrote about. Next, the voice of Peyote is heard, first through a dream. This seems symbolic of the ritual experiences of Peyotists, which are often not visions but rather auditory experiences of the voice of Peyote warning or reassuring them. When the woman turns to look at the Peyote cactus, she sees "the symbol of man." This is reminiscent of the self symbolism of the moon altar that is contemplated during the ritual (see chapter VI). Finally, the woman is healed by ingesting Peyote, which is also what happens to many ritual participants. She is subsequently united with her tribe, which is perhaps symbolic of the social integration and supportive relationships that many individuals achieve through involvement with the Native American Church.

This narrative exemplifies the symbolic message "self in transformation" that, as I will argue in the next chapter, dominates the ritual symbolism of the Native American Church. The story has the characteristic structure of a healing narrative: the first half deals with the state of being ill and/or alienated from society and the second half deals with a healing renewal and reconnection to society. The narrative shape of this story is homologous to the death/rebirth symbolism of the Peyote Ceremony: the first half is dark and hopeless and the second is bright and hopeful. This structure is also encountered frequently in self-help groups (Corrigan et al. 2002) and may be a cultural universal of healing narratives. I elicited the following version of this story from a nice old Road Man in the Chinle area:

> Some of them got little bit different stories. But the way that I found out and I know, the first tribe that got this Peyote was the Mescalero Apache. They live right below Albuquerque, down south. Mescalero Apache. They say way back what happened was there was this young lady, she got really sick and there's no way to cure it so...they just left her behind. And it was just, nothin' to eat, thirsty, all the sickness. Just about to give up. And I guess she went to sleep. Then she heard someone talkin' to her. Then she feels somethin' on her hand...and heard somethin' talk—a voice. And then all of a sudden she feels somethin' by her hand. It was kind of soft...and they talked somethin'. Sure enough, it was the Medicine, the Peyote. It said [his voice becomes dramatic and raspy]: *"Take me. Take me and eat me. You'll get cured. Take me and eat me and you'll be well. You*

got a tribe and you got relatives over there. You're not going over here.
You go back to your tribe." So she done it; went back and reached
her tribe. That's how this Medicine helped her. And then it says,
"When you get back to your tribe, I want you to talk about me"—
the Medicine was talking to her. "I want you to take care of me
because you got well by me. This is gonna be the prayer—this is
gonna be the way the prayer is gonna go by. That'll be the songs,
all the teachings is gonna come about. So when you get there, tell
them…The man folks—they're the ones who are gonna take care
of this." (*Leonard)

This version has a greater emphasis on the pact made between Peyote
and the Peyotist, which will be discussed in greater depth in subsequent
chapters.

To summarize, not only does the Peyote Origin Myth explain how the
Peyote Ceremony came about and give a rationalization, in terms of mythic
history, for the use of Peyote, but also the story bears a structural resemblance to the experience of the individual Peyotist. On one level, it is proper
to interpret the story as *expressive* of the experience of individuals. However,
given our dialectical orientation to the interrelationship of culture and personal experience, it is also proper to interpret the story as aiming to support
these very experiences through its narrative structure. Here we can recall
Lévi-Strauss's (1963) argument about the Cuna healing song for difficult
childbirth: the shaman's song manipulated the patient's body through its
narrative shape, a shape that was homologous to the illness condition. This
homology not only enabled the patient to meaningfully grasp her situation
but also enabled a structural reorganization of physiology "by inducing the
patient intensively to live out a myth" (Lévi-Strauss 1963, 201). Following
Lévi-Strauss, I propose that the Peyote Origin Myth, properly "lived out"
by practicing Native American Church members, also enables Peyotists to
mentally grasp their experience of suffering, through identification with
the main character, and it helps them emplot themselves in a narrative of
transformation and relationship with the Peyote Spirit.

Peyote's Multiple Levels of Significance

This chapter has explored the centrality of Peyote to the Native American
Church on many levels. On a more material level, Peyote is a sacred

medicinal herb that is used as a panacea for various problems but that has shown itself especially effective against alcoholism. On a more ideological level, Peyote is understood as an omniscient and benevolent spiritual entity: a personlike presence in the culturally constituted behavioral environment of the Native American Church, to use Hallowell's (1955) terms. Characterizations of the spirit of Peyote by Native American Church members range from identifications with Christ to images of an authoritarian police officer (Spindler and Spindler 1984, 98). But the most typical characterization of Peyote is as a vigilant and protective parental figure ("Mother Peyote" or "Father Peyote"). Some Peyotists seem to have a metaphorical rather than literal understanding of Peyote's spirit, reflecting the pluralistic attitude toward belief in the religion.

These two understandings of Peyote (herb and spirit) come together in the concept of "sacrament," a term that Native American Church members use and which they share with Christians, as well as in the spiritually inclusive Native American concept of "Medicine" (*'azee'* in Navajo). Similarly, cultural meaning and personal experience reflect each other in the Peyote Origin Myth, in which Peyote communicates with and heals a lost Indian woman separated from her tribe.

Some would claim that referring to the Peyote cactus as an entity, as "Mother," for example, is irrational, because a plant has no brain and is thus not capable of conscious thought. But in its application as a feature of a cultural psychiatric system or an approach to socialization, seeing Peyote as an entity is part of a social intervention that is very rational in its goals. Belief in Peyote's spiritual presence may also be seen as a logical interpretation given the sorts of ritual experiences available in the Native American Church, such as actual perceptions of the voice of Peyote or visions of spiritual beings. And, even though it is true that the Peyote cactus does not have a brain, it is full of chemical substances that are structurally similar to neurotransmitter substances in the brain and that have unique psychological effects. These same psychological effects that Peyotists interpret as signs of a spiritual presence have had a much different meaning to the Europeans who invaded North America. To the Spaniards who conquered Mexico, the effects produced by Peyote were evidence that it was the vegetable incarnation of Satan. This view was an ethnocentric assumption based not on actual experience of the effects of Peyote but rather on culturally saturated judgments of the Native Americans who ingested Peyote. The culture clash has persisted and is still based on an inadequate, ethnocentric understanding of Peyote as used by Native Americans.

This chapter has addressed the lingering misunderstanding of Peyote by non-Peyotists, adopting an anthropological perspective based on long-term participant observation and interviews with members of the Native American Church. It is only by adopting such a perspective, grounded in an understanding of the diversity of world cultures rather than in a narrow ethnocentrism, that we can hope to understand and assess a complex cultural reality such as the Native American's understanding of Peyote.

6

The Peyote Ceremony

PSYCHOPHARMACOLOGY, RITUAL PROCESS,
AND EXPERIENCES OF HEALING

THE PEYOTE CEREMONY or "Peyote Meeting" of the Native American
Church is among the most misunderstood rituals within the contemporary United States. It has been mischaracterized as everything from an
invocation of the Devil to a sexual orgy to "drug use in the guise of religion" (Stewart 1987, 17–30, 128–147; see also Aberle 1991 [1966], 205–223).
But the Peyote Meeting is actually a very formal and controlled ritual with
a beautiful symbolic structure. It is also, as I will argue, a form of therapeutic intervention that can be analyzed using both anthropological and
clinical concepts. This may seem a controversial claim but, as a clinician
working on the Navajo reservation, I quickly discovered the accepted role
of the Native American Church in health care. The therapeutic reputation
of the Peyote Ceremony against alcoholism is reflected in the US Indian
Health Service's coding of the ritual as an intervention "for the purpose
of treating persons with alcohol and drug problems" (see Kunitz and Levy
1994, 202). The reputation is also supported by several anthropological and
medical observers of the Native American Church (Aberle 1991 [1966], xii,
212; Menninger 1971; Albaugh and Anderson 1974; Schultes 1938). In addition, I have had the personal experience of working in a federally funded
clinical program, accredited by the Joint Commission on Accreditation of
Healthcare Organizations, which utilized Native American Church and
other rituals as components of the treatment process.

In this chapter, I outline an interdisciplinary understanding of the symbolic structure of the Peyote Ceremony and its underlying therapeutic processes, drawing on the theoretical perspectives of medical anthropology,
ritual studies, clinical psychology, and the interdisciplinary study of cultural psychiatries. The Peyote Ceremony is a very adequate case for such

an interdisciplinary approach because, as I will argue, its ritual process involves a dialectical relationship between two practices often encountered in cultural psychiatries: *therapeutic emplotment* and *consciousness modification*. The term *therapeutic emplotment* concisely captures the ritual-based symbolic or rhetorical approach to shaping consciousness studied by anthropologists and often referred to as "symbolic healing" (Dow 1986) or "the effectiveness of symbols" (Lévi-Strauss 1963). Emplotment is a familiar term both in narrative studies and in medical anthropology (Ricoeur 1984; B. Good 1994, 144; Obeyesekere 1990, 267). Therapeutic emplotment, as defined in this study, refers to interpretive activity or application of a preformed cultural narrative placing events into a story that is therapeutic, in that it either supports expectations of a positive outcome, makes illness or treatment comprehensible, discourages unhealthy behaviors, or otherwise supports health.

In the Peyote Meeting, emplotment of the patient in a therapeutic narrative structure is aided by a technique of consciousness modification. The term *consciousness modification* refers to any cultural technology used to modify the consciousness state of self or others. This includes pharmacological techniques and behavioral techniques such as fasting, ritual ordeals, hypnotic induction, or prolonged dancing. A dialectic between a structure of meaning (e.g., a myth) and a technology of consciousness modification is found in many initiation rites and healing ceremonies in which society has an important message that it wants to implant in the mind of the individual. In initiation rites, these messages focus on a change of one's social status and the rights and responsibilities that go with it, for example, "you are now an adult" or "you are now a warrior" (see Van Gennep 1960 [1909]; Turner 1967; Herdt 1987). Secret or otherwise vital teaching is often presented after an exhausting ritual ordeal or after ingestion of a psychoactive substance. Healing ceremonies aim for a change in the health status of the person and are typically characterized by transformation symbolism and messages such as "you are now healed." The consciousness modification technology in such rituals makes the mind more malleable—in other words, more open to social messages— by altering the individual's attention and suggestibility. This is an effect noted for various hypnotic induction methods, as well as for certain psychoactive substances and painful or exhausting ritual ordeals.

The ability of mescaline, the main psychedelic substance in the Peyote cactus, to enhance suggestibility was confirmed in an infrequently cited experimental study completed by researchers at Stanford University and the Veterans Administration Hospital in Palo Alto, California (Sjoberg and Hollister 1965). These researchers found that suggestibility, as measured by the Stanford Suggestibility Scale, was enhanced by mescaline to a level comparable to that produced by the induction of a hypnotic trance. More recent studies of this phenomenon are unavailable due to a decades-long moratorium on such research that has only recently been lifted (see Winkelman and Roberts 2007).

This pattern of the delivery of a therapeutic message supported by consciousness modification is even to be found in the traditional multinight Navajo ceremonies called "sings," in which the consciousness modification technology seems to be based on repetition of the positive message in a musical form over an extended period of time. One Navajo woman, while attending a traditional Navajo healing ritual, told me: "The more I learn about Navajo religion, the more I think that it is like psychology. When the Medicine Man sings he keeps telling you that you are well and, after a while, you believe it. It's like he brainwashes you into being cured" (*Emma). Here we have a therapeutic emplotment (the message that "you are now well"), as well as a very basic sort of consciousness modification technology (repetition of the message over a certain span of time within a ceremonial context, combined with sleep deprivation and repetitive, rhythmic music).

The consciousness modification technology in the Native American Church ceremony includes ingestion of Peyote, which, like certain other psychedelics and in line with the Sjoberg and Hollister findings, can be expected to enhance suggestibility in relation to cultural messages, as well as introspection or reflexivity, allowing for life-changing insights. The goal of facilitating hypnotic suggestion is also implied by the rhythmic drum beating that occurs throughout the night, as well as the rule that participants should fix their attention on the symbol-laden central altar. Fixation of attention and repetition are basic techniques used by hypnotists (Brown and Fromm 1987). Notice how this rule of fixing attention on the altar also supports self-reflection behaviorally: if the participant's attention is focused on the central altar, the participant is not exchanging glances or giggles with friends or siblings. The person is also not exchanging tense glances with strangers, which could induce paranoid feelings and interpretations. Instead, the person introspects while gazing at Peyote (a specimen of which sits on the altar) and at the symbolic messages encoded in the altar (which, as described later, refer to the course of one's life and its healing transformation). The Peyotist consciousness modification technology thus helps pattern ritual experience in the desired directions: introspection and self-awareness, behavioral and mental self-control, emplotment of the person in ritual symbolism, and therapeutic self-transformation in line with the ritual symbolism.

The ritual symbolism of the Peyote Ceremony depicts the human self or life course in the arc of the crescent moon altar and symbolically embeds this depiction of the self in natural transformative processes of gestation, birth, and the dawning of a new day. The message is one of a natural transformation and renewal of the self to facilitate the goal of living harmoniously into old age (Calabrese 1994). This seems to be a very emotionally potent message for Navajo members of the Native American Church, and its form somewhat resembles the central mystical formula of the traditional Navajo religion *Są'ah naghái bik'eh hózhǫ́*. This Navajo term is not easily translated, and a full conceptualization of the term is beyond the scope of this study, but it has the sense of a beautiful, harmonious condition arising out of the natural completion of human life courses into old age (see Witherspoon 1974; for other readings of the phrase, see Farella 1984 and Lewton and Bydone 2000).

In view of this, it can be seen that study of Peyotist symbolism reveals the dialectical relationship between cultural meanings and personal experience (Stigler, Shweder, and Herdt 1990; Obeyesekere 1990; Kleinman 1988; B. Good 1994). The depiction of the human life course in Peyotist symbolism implies reflexivity, and contemplating this self symbolism reinforces and guides the self-reflection of the ritual participant. Peyotist transformation symbolism can be seen to represent the transformative experiences of Peyotists, both short term and long term, and can also be seen to help shape these very experiences.

To say that the Native American Peyote Ceremony deviates from standard Euro-American theories of psychotherapeutic intervention is quite an understatement—and not just because a psychedelic plant is involved. Euro-American theories of psychotherapeutic process typically focus on therapist behavior or aspects of the therapeutic relationship, conceived in dyadic terms. The cultural prototype of psychotherapeutic intervention is individualistic and rationalistic: a one-to-one conversation in which the patient is expected to disclose and discuss his or her innermost feelings with the therapist in regular office visits. This may (or may not) be the most appropriate approach for particular individuals within modern Euro-American society. However, ethnographic research finds that, in many other cultural psychiatric systems, psychotherapeutic intervention is typically communal, it utilizes dramatic ritual ordeals and altered states of consciousness rather than rational conversations, and the patient/ healer relationship may be of little importance. Therapeutic communication is often built into cultural narratives and practices rather than created anew by a therapist and a patient. I have been referring to this process as *culturally embedded therapeutic emplotment*.

In its combination of meaning-centered intervention and pharmacology, Peyotist cultural psychiatry parallels Euro-American psychiatry (Luhrmann 2000). The contrasts are apparent, however. In the Euro-American system, psychopharmacology and psychotherapy are institutionally separated rather than integrated. In the Peyote Ceremony, psychopharmacology and meaning are aspects of the same intervention. Psychopharmacology in the Euro-American context aims at correcting a malfunctioning biochemical mechanism, whereas psychopharmacology in the Native American Church aims at interrupting the addiction process, reawakening spirituality, and facilitating the patient's insight. The Peyote Ceremony is thus an excellent case for comparative research and the elucidation of a cultural psychopharmacology that radically diverges from mainstream scientific approaches but that nevertheless can be shown to have its own features that support a therapeutic process.

Anthropological Theories of Ritual and Therapeutic Emplotment

Early anthropological theories of ritual focused on functionalist theories in which rituals were seen as functioning to represent and maintain the existing social order (Durkheim 1965 [1912]; Radcliffe-Brown 1945). A later generation of anthropologists added to this orientation a more dynamic emphasis on rituals as supporting social change and personal transformation (Turner 1967; Gluckman 1954; Wallace 1956, 1966). In terms of this developmental trajectory of ritual studies, the French anthropologist Arnold Van Gennep (1960 [1909]) was far ahead of his time in describing the ways in which the "rites of passage" facilitate the transition from one social status (e.g., "child") to another (e.g., "adult"). This was accomplished, he argued, through a process composed of three stages: (1) separation, (2) margin (or limen), and (3) aggregation. In the first stage, ritual behaviors symbolically remove the person from his or her prior role in the society. The next stage is a sort of social limbo in which the ritual subject is treated as in transition, "betwixt and between" social catego- ries. This liminal stage is often symbolically associated with a return to the womb, with death, or with monstrous distortions. As Victor Turner (1969, 95) writes,

> Liminal entities, such as neophytes in initiation or puberty rites, may be represented as possessing nothing. They may be disguised as monsters, wear only a strip of clothing, or even go naked, to dem- onstrate that as liminal beings they have no status, property, insig- nia, secular clothing indicating rank or role, position in a kinship system—in short, nothing that may distinguish them from their fellow neophytes or initiands. It is as though they are being reduced or ground down to a uniform condition to be fashioned anew and endowed with additional powers to enable them to cope with their new station in life.

The final stage of the rite of passage involves social recognition of the individual's new status and his or her reincorporation into the group. Van Gennep understood the ordering of social transitions in rites of passage in a manner that did not dichotomize the social and the personal. He saw rites of passage as having implications for both individual psychological well-being and social order (Bell 2009, 37).

Lévi-Strauss (1963) was also ahead of his time in his development of the notion of symbolic efficacy. Examining the text of a Cuna shaman's healing song for difficult childbirth, Lévi-Strauss shows how the representations evoked by the song, which mirror and manipulate the pregnant woman's embodied experience, had the potential to bring about a modification in the organic functions of the woman giving birth. This chapter helps estab- lish the foundation for subsequent anthropological concepts of symbolic healing (Moerman 1979; Dow 1986). Dow (1986) proposed a universal structure of symbolic healing in which the healer helps the patient par- ticularize a mythic world and manipulate healing symbols in it. The works of these and other anthropologists have demonstrated that ritual symbols like the Peyotist crescent moon are not merely decorative but may serve an integral function in the ritual process. In both the Cuna shaman's song (Lévi-Strauss 1963) and the symbolism of the Peyote Ceremony (Calabrese 1994), culture provides what Wallace (1966, 140) referred to as a "model of the transformative process."

These cultural models of the transformative process or therapeutic plot structures take many forms in human societies. There are plots of death and rebirth (which are very widespread), plots of a journey to retrieve a lost soul, plots centered on the ingestion of a medicinal and/ or sacramental substance, plots of the sucking out of a malevolent object (or other purifying rituals), and the rite of passage structure. In addition, society may specify that the individual develop his or her own personal narrative according to a particular cultural template. A very widespread template is what may be called the "illness and recovery" narrative. Like death/rebirth symbolism, illness and recovery narratives tend to have two phases. First, there is an illness narrative, in which the person describes his or her problem. The second phase is the recovery narrative, which rhetorically creates a "recovered self" (either already existing or in process) that contrasts with the former self. The personally formed narrative of illness and recovery that results may then function in the same way as the "personal symbols" that Obeyesekere (1981) describes. It is interesting to find that this practice of developing a personal narrative of illness and recovery is explicitly encouraged by the community in such diverse traditions as the Native American Church, twelve-step addiction programs like Alcoholics Anonymous, "born again" Christianity, and the mutual help group for persons with mental illness called GROW (Corrigan et al. 2002).

An implication raised by the various cultural psychiatric processes described in this section is that mental health is a creative emplotment, a human construction rather than a biological given. Freud was very rationalist in his argument that mental health equals truth (i.e., the patient's insight into his or her own mind). But mental health may require going beyond mere rationality. It may require a creative, imaginative effort on the part of individuals and societies to make life meaningful: a creative emplotment. For this reason, it could be argued that a cultural psychiatry that does not address existential issues of meaning is far less effective than a cultural psychiatry that does. This is why traditional systems of cultural psychiatry are, from a modern secularized viewpoint, so often merged with religious domains of culture.

The Peyote Meeting

The ritual of the Native American Church is most typically referred to as a "Peyote Meeting," a "ceremony," or a "prayer service." One of my consultants prefers to call it a "church service." In addition, I have just referred to it as a "ritual," which is a basic anthropological term for a very basic aspect of human life across human societies. A Peyote Meeting takes place in a circular enclosure, usually a tipi but sometimes a hogan, which opens to the east. Inside the enclosure, a crescent mound of earth is constructed and a line drawn along the top to represent the "Peyote Road." There are four main officiants: the Road Man, who is the leader of the meeting; the Drummer Man, who is responsible for drumming; the Fire Man, who tends the central fire; and the Cedar Man, who sprinkles cedar incense on the fire.

The participants enter the tipi at sundown. The Road Man places an especially fine Peyote cactus, most often called "Mother Peyote" or "Father Peyote," on top of the moon altar. The Peyotist is taught to maintain focus on this Peyote, sending his or her prayers through it. After an opening prayer, which states the purpose of the meeting, Peyote is passed around and drumming and singing of Peyote songs begins. The ritual number four is very important, and each participant sings a set of four songs. The drum is passed in a clockwise direction and rounds of singing alternate with the passing of Peyote, which is also clockwise. Most of the participant's time is spent in silent prayer while others are singing.

At midnight, there is a ceremony in which more prayers are said and a bucket of water is passed around. At this time, the Road Man may exit the tipi and blow a whistle made from the wing bone of an eagle to the four directions. Rounds of singing and passing of Peyote resume and continue until near dawn, when morning water is brought in by a woman, usually a relative of the sponsor, who is often said to represent "Peyote Woman," the mythological character who first found Peyote. There is a ceremonial breakfast of corn, meat, fruit, and water. The meeting ends soon after dawn when the participants may go outside to "greet the sun." Later, toward noon, a larger meal is served.

Peyote Meetings are most often classified into two general types. The first type, often called a "doctoring meeting," is called to heal a particular person of a particular problem. The second type is usually called an "appreciation meeting" or, following the terminology of traditional Navajo ritual, a "Beautyway" meeting. This second type of meeting is more focused on continuing health and harmony, expressing thanks, or celebrating certain phases of the life course. These meetings are called to celebrate the birth of a new child, a wedding, and, with one Road Man I interviewed, funerals. Also included in this category are the "education meetings" that are held near the end of the summer when children are preparing to return to school, which may involve traveling and living away from home. Education meetings are held to pray for the success of the children and for their protection. A third possible type of meeting I heard about in the northern section of the Navajo reservation is a "ghostbusting meeting." My consultant *Beatrice explained that a ghostbusting meeting "is where the Medicine Man himself is the diagnostician able to tell you what spirit is bothering your body."

Though most of my consultants answered the question "What kinds of meetings are there?" by mentioning the two types described previously, one consultant, *Edgar, emphasized the unity of the Peyote Meeting: "I think the concept of meetings are all one, except the procedures and certain philosophies change and that kind of makes it different. But all of it is one: one Medicine, one fire, one water, one sage, one cedar."

Symbolism and Therapeutic Emplotment in the Peyote Meeting

> Interpretations of the moon symbolism are almost as numerous as individual users; for, given the physiological effects of peyote and the acceptance in Plains culture of the individual vision "authority," standardized meanings are not to be expected.
>
> —LABARRE (1989 [1938], 75)

Ethnographers of the Native American Church like LaBarre (1989 [1938], 75) and Aberle (1991 [1966], 174–182) often stressed the variety of idiosyncratic interpretations of Peyotist ritual symbols. In the previous statement of LaBarre, we can identify one of the assumptions that has supported this emphasis on idiosyncratic meanings: that the physiological effects of a psychedelic substance like Peyote must be unshaped by culture and result in experiences that only have personal, idiosyncratic meaning. However, though personal interpretations of symbolism are definitely encouraged in the Native American Church, there is a core therapeutic emplotment in terms of which the multiple meanings of Peyotist symbols can be understood. Though the structure of the ritual is theoretically subject to any changes suggested by a Road Man's visions, the Peyote Ceremony's narrative structure is nevertheless very uniform throughout North America.

In addition to the symbolic understanding of Peyote discussed in the previous chapter, two types of symbolism associated with the ritual process of the Peyote Meeting are revealed in the texts of my consultants:

what I will call "self symbolism" (symbols of the individual human life) and "transformation symbolism" (symbols that refer to the process of change). These designations refer to cultural trends in the activity of interpreting ritual symbols that may result in the generation of a variety of related interpretations. A significant number of the interpretations of Peyotist symbols recorded by ethnographers in the literature and by the present ethnographer seem to be variations on these two themes of self and transformation.

The focal symbols of the Native American Church include Peyote, the crescent moon (or "half moon"), the dawn, the tipi, the Peyote Bird or Water Bird, fire, the eagle feather, and the various ritual implements. The Native American Church has taken many elements of the symbolic languages of North American tribes and fused them into a new synthesis. It should be noted that these symbols function in a general way as symbols of an "Indian" identity, which can be considered a part of the "self symbolism" to be discussed later. Euro-American symbols are also seen in some groups and may include the Christian cross, the Bible, or the American flag.

Humans are distinguished by our ability to objectify ourselves. We may call this property "reflexivity" or self-reflection. Reflexivity is most apparent when humans create symbols referring to the self. Self symbols demonstrate the emergence of the self as an object in a world of other objects (Hallowell 1955). This depiction of the self is present in the iconography of the central moon-shaped altar of the Peyote Meeting and in the ritual behavior associated with this moon symbol. The moon altar seems to function as an aid to reflexivity, helping the individual to more objectively contemplate his or her own life and the nature of human life in the abstract. During the ritual, the Native American Church member is instructed to focus on the altar and to look inward, being receptive to the teachings of Peyote.

Aberle's description of Peyote's effect in terms of the feeling of "personal significance" suggests an awareness of the importance of reflexivity in the Native American Church. As Aberle states, "One's self, one's aims, one's relationships, and one's ethics have become matters for reflection" (1991 [1966], 8). But Peyotists stress corrective reflexivity, as well as contemplative reflexivity. As such, self-awareness is generated in connection with symbols of transformation.

One context in which transformation symbolism is prominent is well known to anthropology. This symbolism is associated with the liminal phase of a rite of passage between social roles (Van Gennep 1960 [1909]; Turner 1969). Though certain Peyote Meetings, such as Peyote weddings, do support sociostructural transition, the usual meaning of the term *rite of passage* does not adequately describe the central process of the Peyote Meeting. Perhaps a more general term such as *rite of transformation*, encompassing both sociostructural and nonstructural change, could be used. Both sociostructural and nonstructural rites of transformation have as their goal a transformation of the individual.

The all-night healing ceremony of the Navajo Native American Church is a good example of a nonstructural rite of transformation. The transformation here involves the restoration of spiritual harmony (Nav. *hózhǫ́*), which enables physical health and mental balance. The ritual process is, however, very similar to a rite of passage and exhibits symbolism typical of the liminal and postliminal phases. Through the symbols of the Peyote Ceremony, the healing process is linked to natural processes of physiological and astronomical transformation.

Peyote as Symbol

Peyote is not easily classified as a self symbol or a transformation symbol, but its significance to the transformative process will become apparent. Peyote may be seen as the "dominant symbol" of the Peyote Meeting in the same way that Turner (1967, 31) found *nfunda* (also a ritual "medicine") to be the dominant symbol in the Ndembu boy's circumcision ritual. We may also, following Dow, classify Peyote in terms of its role as a generalized symbolic medium. In this case it would be called a transactional symbol linking the individual to an omniscient spiritual power. In addition, Peyote is often understood to have a personality and omniscience of its own, as was described in the previous chapter.

The Moon Symbol

The Mother Peyote, symbolic of Peyote Spirit, sits upon the enigmatic moon symbol of the ceremonial altar (see Figure 6.1). Though Aberle (1991 [1966], 174) found *the* meaning of the moon impossible to pin down, he did not consider the possibility of a finite number of multiple meanings, such as are found in the multivocal symbols described by Turner. Individual interpretations in the texts of my consultants and in the literature seem to center on three main referents: the moon as a symbol of nature, as a symbol of gestation and birth, and as a symbol of the human life course.

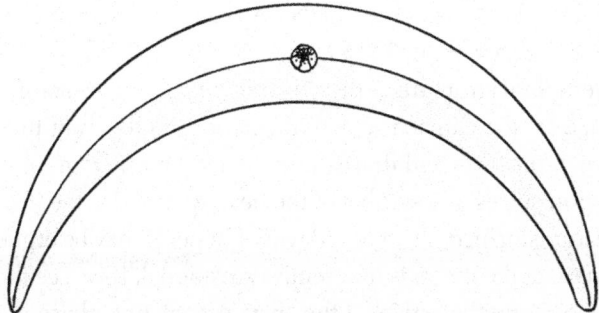

FIGURE 6.1 Crescent moon altar with Peyote Road and Mother or Father Peyote.

These three ideas are obviously closely related, all dealing with universal natural phenomena.

Transformation symbolism is present most significantly in the first two referents: astronomical transformation in the moon as nature symbol and physiological transformation in the moon as symbol of gestation and birth. In relation to the third referent, the moon is primarily a self symbol, although the transformation process is also apparent in the passage of the self from birth to death. We see here that the meanings of the moon are not random. Rather, the moon is a nexus of the major themes of the religion: self, transformation, astronomy, physiology, and nature. More specifically, the moon links the central idea of self with the central idea of transformation.

The Moon as a Symbol of Nature

The general relationship of the moon and the natural world is obvious. As the Peyote Meeting takes place at night, the moon is the governing celestial body. Aberle's consultant Mike Kiyaani describes it as a symbol of "the universe" (Aberle 1991 [1966], 174). In the meeting, the worshipper is brought face to face with the realities of nature with which he must come into accord. As Lamphere (1969) points out, Leach's dichotomy between nature and society does not accurately reflect Navajo beliefs. In Navajo ritual, nature becomes "an all-inclusive organizing device: a fusion of natural, supernatural, and human or social elements." Thus, it seems harmony with nature implies social cohesion as well. As my Navajo Peyotist consultant Hoskie stated, "What you're trying to do is to get in harmony with everything. Everything is there—you're part of it. As I said, you're part of the four elements of life, that's why you gotta respect it. You're part of nature, you're part of anything that lives."

In the temporal structure of the meeting, the all-night moon meditation sets the stage for the climactic dawn meditation. In this way, the ceremony symbolically represents and dramatizes the transition from night into day. This transition serves as a symbol of the healing process: the "dark night of the soul" is transformed into a new dawn of hope. It may be argued that the crescent phase of the moon is inherently transitional. If we see the arrival of the "full moon" and the arrival of the "new moon" (the phase in which the dark side of the moon is facing earth) as states, then the intervening periods of waxing and waning (growth and decline of the moon) are transitional periods between the states, what Turner referred to as "liminal" phases.

The Moon as a Symbol of the Human Life

The moon altar also functions as a self symbol. In the construction of the moon altar, a line is sketched along the top that is called the Peyote Road. This line symbolizes the ethical code of the religion: the proper path to be followed in life. Thus, the moon is a symbol of the path of a human life, "from birth (southern tip) to the crest of maturity and knowledge (at the place of the peyote) and thence downward again to the ground through old age to death (northern tip)" (LaBarre 1989 [1938], 46). The Mother Peyote is placed in the center of this line and Peyote is believed to guide the worshipper along this straight path. The Road Man also helps through his knowledge of the Road. According to Navajo Road Man Wilson Aronilth, "The Great Spirit can tell you good things of life through this herb. It can show you the right direction of life. It has life in itself. It will take you from childbirth to old age and into everlasting life" (Aronilth 1981).

The human life span is symbolically depicted in the context of nature, as the isomorphism of the crescent moon and the Peyote Road demonstrate. If the individual is in harmony with nature, he will avoid falling off the path:

On top of that moon there's a line drawn like that. This side of the moon on the south side, where it begins, that's the beginning of birth and you travel along the top of this road here. You go on down into old age. That's where you become elderly and old age overcomes you. Now, the moon is such that some people say that you stay on this road. If you go this way, you're gonna fall into the fire, you're gonna hurt yourself. If you go this way, you're gonna fall off the cliff. So if you stay on this road and live a good life, then you'll reach old age down on the other side. And that's the ultimate goal—that's what that represents. [JC: And in the middle of the road they put the Father Peyote?] Yeah. They say somewhere along the way you're gonna need help and you're gonna come up on that Peyote. And it's gonna help you out to continue on in life. That Peyote is there always to help you with your hardships. (Hoskie)

It is interesting to compare this metaphor of a path between extremes (the fire and the cliff) with the "middle way" of Buddhism or the "synthesis" in Hegelian/Fichtean dialectics. The ethical code of the Peyote Road has four basic rules: (1) brotherly love, (2) care of family, (3) self-reliance (especially economic self-reliance), and (4) avoidance of alcohol (Slotkin 1975 [1956], 71).

The Death/Rebirth Symbolism of the Moon/Tipi Symbolic Complex

The moon, particularly in conjunction with the tipi (see Figure 6.2), also represents the natural process of gestation and birth that produces the human life. One of Aberle's consultants states that the symbol of the crescent moon typifies "the female from which all things come; the mother earth; Navajo mothers; female rain" (Aberle 1991 [1966], 174). Native American ritual structures typically unite microcosm and womb symbolism. The process of gestation is referred to symbolically as the changing of the moon: "The sacred moon is right before us again. Through the changing of this moon is how we were born" (Aronilth and Ashley 1981, side 1, song 1). The development of the human takes place during the changing of nine moons. Hoskie explained it this way:

The moon itself represents when the female becomes pregnant, there's gonna be nine moons or nine months. So that moon, what it represents is life because after nine months, after nine moons you give birth....The tent in the Peyote Ceremony represents a female with a blanket facing east. The nine fastening pins on the front of the tipi represent the nine months that it takes for a human being to develop.

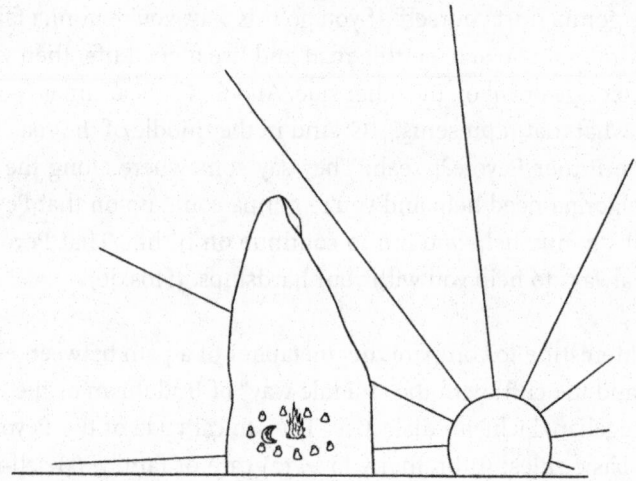

FIGURE 6.2 Tipi and dawn symbolism.

The ceremony is thus a symbolic gestation. The experience of death and rebirth is a central feature of shamanism, mysticism, conversion, and certain forms of psychotherapy (Grof 1976; Bean and Vane 1978, 122). Surely the most familiar example of this type of imagery for Euro-Americans is the newly converted Christian's experience of being "born again." Walsh (1990) offers a plausible psychological model to account for this widespread experiential structure. According to Walsh, the death/rebirth or dismemberment/reconstitution experience occurs when intense emotional arousal and stress overwhelm the mind's habitual patterning forces and the psyche's organization temporarily collapses. This destabilizing process "is projected, pictured, and experienced as images. These are so-called autosymbolic images, which symbolize one's own psychological state" (Walsh 1990, 63). Rebirth coincides with the reorganization of experience after the disruption of habitual thought patterns and self-image.

The visualization in the moon symbol of life as a finite road or arc suggests awareness of the impermanence of life. As Palgi and Abramovitch indicate (1984, 385), "death awareness is a natural sequel to the development of self-awareness—an intrinsic attribute of humankind." Just as the moon is born and dies in its cycle, contemplation of the nature of life may allow a realization of death and a new appreciation for a proper experience of life:

> When I eat it I feel happy and good and thank God for his many
> gifts. As we use peoti in our meetings we realize we have to die and

it aids us to do right, it helps us to live better lives and enjoy happier experiences. (Black Dog 1908, cited by Slotkin 1975 [1956])

Confrontation with the possibility of death can bring about a major behavioral change, as is exemplified by Hoskie's crucial ritual experience. The presence of the moon in the following passage may be significant consciously or unconsciously. Reflecting the spiritual nature of Navajo conceptions of self and healing, we see in this passage that, in many cases, "healing" refers less to a relief from physical symptoms than to an acceptance of one's life, a readjustment, and a new hope and courage:

> I went through some depression after I lost my vision in '72....I was teeter-tottering back and forth. Anyway, I was in a meeting and I ate some Medicine and I sat back. Something happened. I don't know if I went asleep or what. But I had a vision—or I don't know what it was—a dream. I was out somewhere with some friends and we were drinking. And I was carrying a can of beer and the moonlight was shining and I could see that can of beer open like this. And we stopped and parked the car. So, I walked away from them. And I could hear all the noise, laughing and guys having a good time, behind me, but I kind of walked away from it. All of a sudden I heard a shot. I heard two shots from a gun. Next thing I knew, where I live there's a graveyard up on a hill...and this voice told me, "If you don't make up your mind, this is where you're headed. If you don't decide one way or another, this is where you're headed. You can't play with this." And that turned my life completely around. I always remember that. And then I woke up and I was in that meeting. And that turned me completely around. (Hoskie)

This ability of Peyote to make the ritual a near-death experience for the participant seems to be a major reason for the use of Peyote in the Native American Church. The ritual has the character of an ordeal, and contemplation of the finite nature of life may, for some participants, combine with the fear that the altered state of consciousness one is experiencing may be fatal (this was a common charge of anti-Peyotist Navajos according to *Mike). It seems likely, in the latter case, that survival of the ritual, which inevitably occurs, would be attributed to the protection of God, Jesus, or Peyote.

Dawn Symbolism

As the crescent moon is a symbol of spiritual gestation, the dawn seems to be a symbol of spiritual rebirth and renewal to Native American Church members. The temporal focus of the ceremony is anticipation of the coming dawn. One old Road Man I interviewed described a Sioux fireplace in which the charcoal is shaped into the rays of the sun, creating a dawn symbol:

> When it comes to conclude the service, they want to put the straight charcoal with the straight half moon. Then they put seven marks: one in the middle and three on each side. That represents the dawn when the sun comes up, the light. (*Leonard)

According to LaBarre (1989 [1938], 20), the popular Peyote song "Heyowiniho" came to John Wilson in a synesthetic auditory hallucination that he interpreted to be the sound of the sun's rising. In a detailed study of Peyote songs, McAllester was struck by the large number of texts that refer to the coming of the dawn. Many songs simply repeat exclamations like "Dawn is coming, wake up!" or "It is day" (McAllester 1949, 29). Such texts probably not only refer to the end of the present ceremonial ordeal but also provide a more general symbol of optimism, which, in line with the ritual symbolism, may support the cognitive restructure. The potency of this dawn phase of the ritual is apparent in the following passage from one of my consultants: "I guess it's when they're doing the closing song, that's when everything seems like it's lifted and their songs and their prayers are really strong. And you can be there and experience that if you let yourself" (*Lucy).

The experience of the new dawn is transformed by the all-night ritual, and there are references to a renewed perception of the world in general, as in the following informant's memory of a Tonkawa meeting he attended in 1902:

> Dave said, "When you see that sun, you're going to see it come out on the best world you ever saw. It's going to make you feel young and good in every way."...Dave stayed there the next morning for a little to eat. I got up early and looked at the sun. It was very, very beautiful! The sun was coming out just as if it was before my face,

the rays spreading out every way. My heart surely felt good to see it, so good, such a beautiful world! I can't tell you how good I felt. (Opler 1939, 437)

The Underlying Metaphors of the Peyote Ceremony

To put into words more adequately the understanding of Peyotist symbolism outlined previously, we now turn to a feature of studies in symbolic anthropology that suggests a link with the field of cognitive anthropology (Colby, Fernandez, and Kronenfeld 1981): the interest in tropes, especially metaphor. Fernandez (1973) holds that metaphors, rather than symbols, should be considered the basic analytical units of a ritual because ritual and ritual symbols spring from metaphors. A metaphor is "the statement, explicit or implied, of a correspondence between some subject of thought in need of clarification and an object that brings some clarity to it" (Fernandez 1973). According to Lakoff and Johnson (1980, 3), our ordinary conceptual system "is fundamentally metaphorical in nature." The function of a metaphor is to give focus to an inchoate target domain through the use of a familiar source domain. As Quinn states, metaphorical source domains are "easy to think with in the sense that the thinker can readily conceptualize the relations among elements in such domains and changes in these relations that result when these elements are set in motion conceptually" (Quinn 1991, 80).

The use of the metaphor concept in the study of symbolic systems is valuable because, as Colby states, "symbolic representations form a web of meanings that jump across and link different domains of attention" (Colby 1991). Quinn, however, argues convincingly for the primacy of cultural models in generating metaphors. Quinn lists eight "classes of metaphor" that form the American cultural model of marriage. To Quinn, metaphor helps one to pursue a complex line of reasoning to its end without losing track of its logic. Quinn cites speakers who switch metaphors in midthought, demonstrating that speakers have in mind their desired reasoning independent of the metaphors in which they cast it. Quinn also finds that speakers prefer metaphors that map onto multiple elements of the cultural model targeted, allowing it to be "apprehended in its entirety, as an 'experiential gestalt'" (Quinn 1991, 80).

In the case of the Peyote Meeting, metaphor is useful for several reasons. First, the state of consciousness induced by a psychedelic substance is an inchoate experience par excellence. It is consistently characterized in the literature using the word *ineffable*, and subjects often report that it is impossible to describe using language. The human life is, of course, another notoriously inchoate subject. In the ritual symbolism of the Native American Church, familiar astronomical and physiological source domains provide models that are "easy to think with," allowing these inchoate experiences to be grasped. Ritual metaphors also provide a "road map" for the thought process in ritual, keeping the thoughts and emotions of the Peyotist, to use a native phrase, "straight."

It is important to note that the symbols and metaphors of the Native American Church serve the emotional and cognitive needs of the worshipper and are used to facilitate healing. Peyotist symbolism provides models *for* reality, as well as models *of* reality (Geertz 1973). This is an area in which meaning is very important. Having a positive model for the experience of an altered state of consciousness can mean the difference between experiencing oneself as having glimpsed Ultimate Reality or as having lost touch with reality altogether.

Peyotist life span metaphors are embodied primarily in the moon and dawn symbols. The most central metaphor of the Native American Church seems to be "Life Is a Road." This correspondence is apparent in the role of "Road Man" and in the ethical code of the "Peyote Road," which is symbolized in the line drawn along the top of the moon altar. The Peyotist is encouraged to walk the "straight path," and deviation from this path is believed to be dangerous. A second life span metaphor is "Life Is an Arc." In the crescent moon symbol, life is depicted as a parabolic curve—increasing in potency from birth until it reaches its peak, and then decreasing as it approaches death (this view of life corresponds to the traditional Navajo goal of a life lived into old age). To be more specific, it seems that "Life Is the Arc of the Sun across the Sky." The arc depicted in the moon is always identified as being "in the direction the sun travels," and one of the rules of the meeting is that participants and ceremonial objects move around the tipi in a clockwise (sunwise) direction. It seems that "The Human Life Is a Day," which has a sunrise, a noon, and a sunset. This interpretation would add significance to the arrival of the dawn after the meeting: the participants are placed at the beginning of a new day, a new life.

Transformation metaphors are embodied in the moon, dawn, and tipi symbols. The main metaphor here seems to be "The Ritual Process Is a Gestation and Birth." This metaphor may be broken down into two parts: "The All-Night Ritual Is a Gestation" and "The Dawn Is a Birth." Here again life is equated with day. The moon in this context refers to the realm of night and also to the process of gestation, which takes place in the waxing and waning of nine "moons."

To pursue this metaphor further, the view of day (or sun) as a state and night (or crescent moon) as transition suggests the equations "Sun = State of Waking Consciousness" and "Moon = the Unconscious or the Altered State of Consciousness." This hypothesis draws support from the fact that night is the time of dreams to the Navajos. This correspondence is, of course, prevalent in Euro-American usage, an example being Turner's contrast of "the brightness of conscious attention" with "the darker strata of the unconscious" (1985, 36).

The context of the transformation process discussed earlier seems to embody the metaphor "The Tipi Is a Womb." The tipi also has the character of a map of the Navajo cosmos, symbolically embedding the worshipper in nature at the crossroads of the four directions. The moon, and perhaps Peyote itself, point to nature via part–whole metonymy. As Quinn stated, speakers prefer utterances that map onto multiple elements of the cultural model simultaneously, allowing the model to be apprehended as an experiential gestalt. We may see the central crescent altar as such an experiential gestalt, simultaneously embodying metaphors of life, transformation, and nature. This representation of the Peyotist cultural model is completed when the Mother Peyote is placed on top of the altar, signifying that Peyote is present as spirit and medicine.

The Generativity of Symbolism

It is important to note how the generality of a central meaning, such as transformation, allows it to be referred to from various contexts simultaneously (astronomical events, physiology, flora and fauna, social structure, religion). This interpretive grammar is not transferred to the believer as a complete system. Its parts are referred to separately in educational interactions and synthesized by the individual member. Once the basic elements of this symbolic language are apprehended by members of the religion, they are applied freely in interpretation. One example of this reapplication of an interpretation to a different symbol is the Wichita gourd rattle described by LaBarre, the red tufts of which are said by an informant to represent the rays of the rising sun (LaBarre 1989 [1938], 68). Another application of death/rebirth symbolism is given by one of Aberle's consultants, who refers to the sitting place of the patients in the tipi as "the 'death chamber' from which people hope to emerge" (Aberle 1991 [1966], 176). A reapplication of self symbolism is Aronilth's (1981) statement that the five sections of a Peyote cactus are "the symbol of man." We see here how individual symbols and interpretations become detached from their original relationships to generate a variety of new symbolic understandings. Even the radical ritual innovations of John Wilson may be seen in terms of the reapplication of self symbolism and transformation symbolism: the face of an Indian represented in the "Moon Head" altar may work as a self symbol, enabling a "face to face" encounter; the empty grave of Christ may be a death/rebirth symbol; and so forth (LaBarre 1989 [1938], 154–156).

Aberle (1991 [1966], 174) mentions a Peyotist, Ambrose Lee, who said that man had "come from the moon." Aberle seems to treat this as a completely idiosyncratic interpretation. But given my symbolic analysis, which reveals that the central meanings of the moon include gestation, the womb, and the feminine, a statement that "man came from the moon" may plausibly be read as "man came from the womb or from the feminine." Natives stress the feminine principle when they speak about the moon, and Euro-Americans interpret the moon referred to in this statement in planetary/astronomical terms. In this connection, consider Aronilth's statement "through the changing of this moon is how we were born." Thus, when the symbolic structure and its social uses are better understood, what had seemed like a completely idiosyncratic interpretation may begin to seem less idiosyncratic and more cultural.

The Peyotist Consciousness Modification Technology

In the previous sections, I have discussed the cultural meanings of Peyotist ritual symbols, and I have argued that these meanings support a therapeutic emplotment of the "death/rebirth" type (a type that is very widespread in human cultures). Many anthropological analyses would end here at the level of meaning structure without exploring the social uses of this meaning structure, how society transmits this meaning structure through socialization, or how society activates it through ritual. However, as I have argued, the Peyote Ceremony, like many systems of cultural psychiatry, involves a dialectic between therapeutic emplotment and a technique of consciousness modification and embodied experience. The technique of consciousness modification, including the psychopharmacological agent and cultural rules for its use and for behavior while in the modified state of consciousness, supports the therapeutic emplotment by enhancing self-reflection, enhancing suggestibility, and focusing attention.

Pharmacologically, psychedelic substances are known to alter suggestibility and have been used clinically to loosen the old psychological set, suspending habitual patterns of consciousness and facilitating positive psychological restructuring (Grof 1976; Bravo and Grob 1989). Use of psychedelic plants in combination with therapeutic emplotment, a common method in healing and initiation rituals (Grob and Dobkin de Rios 1994), may thus render the mind more malleable and open to therapeutic messages. Psychedelic substances also appear to enhance self-awareness and insight into one's problems. The notion that psychedelics are "mind expanding" was ridiculed by LaBarre (1989 [1938], xv) but is supported by the findings of experimental research. For example, a study by Spitzer and colleagues (1996), published in the journal *Biological Psychiatry*, found that the psychedelic substance psilocybin increased indirect semantic priming in normal subjects and brought about "an increased availability of remote associations." This could very plausibly be described as an expansion of the mind beyond habitual, culturally structured associations, allowing one to "think outside the box."

It must be admitted that psychopharmacological intervention to facilitate creative shifts in perspective, therapeutic emplotment, or insight is not the standard usage of psychiatric medicines in Euro-American psychiatry. We may call this pattern of use a semiotic/reflexive paradigm of psychopharmacology in contrast to the rather limited agonist/antagonist (materialist) paradigm of Euro-American psychiatry, which focuses on fixing discrete neurochemical imbalances within a mechanistic medical model. In the absence of serious research on both traditions, it is not acceptable to assume that the Euro-American psychiatric paradigm is the only valid approach and that the semiotic/reflexive paradigm is ignorant or mistaken. The safest assumption is that this is a psychopharmacological paradigm clash and thus an interesting focus for cross-cultural research.

As described in the fourth chapter, serious clinical research is being done on psychedelics because of the potential they show in treating addiction and other conditions (Halpern 1996). In addition to the studies of ibogaine, the psychedelic substance used ceremonially in the Bwiti religion (Fernandez 1982) that has been found to interrupt the addiction process in experimental studies (Cappendijk and Dzoljic 1993), a variety of studies using psychedelic agents with human subjects have been supported by the US Food and Drug Administration (FDA), National Institutes of Health (NIH), and National Institute on Drug Abuse (NIDA). These include studies of psilocybin at the Johns Hopkins University School of Medicine (MacLean, Johnson, and Griffiths 2011) and UCLA (Grob et al. 2011); studies of MDMA at the University of Chicago (Bedi, Hyman, and de Wit 2010); and studies of ibogaine at the University of Miami School of Medicine (Mash et al. 2000). A two-volume overview of the new generation of research on the potential benefits of psychedelics as medicines has been assembled by Winkelman and Roberts (2007).

Cultural norms also help shape ritual experience, facilitating therapeutic emplotment. As a rule, the Peyotist's attention in the ritual is focused on the symbolically structured ceremonial environment, particularly the symbolic gestalt that is the moon altar, rather than lost in a completely personal visionary experience. When visions do occur, they usually reflect not only personal concerns but also the goals implicit in the structure of the ritual. The symbolic message of rebirth into a new day, implying a new beginning, is also supported by the temporal location of the ritual: it starts at the end of one day and ends at the beginning of a new day.

Other aspects of Peyotist socialization shape ritual experiences by cultivating positive expectations regarding outcomes and providing explanations for adverse experiences. For example, the Peyotist is taught that vomiting, which sometimes occurs due to Peyote's bitter taste, rids the body of evil. The following exchange with an elderly Road Man illustrates the cultural specification that one must believe in the ritual for it to heal you. This specification of belief undoubtedly conditions positive expectations going into a ritual and can be considered an aspect of the Peyotist consciousness modification technology:

*LEONARD: Sure enough, if they really believe in it, then they get cured.
JC: So their belief is important?
*LEONARD: That's what I say: number one, you have to believe in it. And the second, you have to do it right.

Another cultural imperative is an openness to reflexivity or self-examination:

When I go in, I go with an open heart and an open mind—so I can see what do I need to do so I can be a better person, so I can make changes in myself, so I can understand myself. When I go in with that frame of mind, seems that when I go in, then I learn something about myself and my situations. (*Beatrice)

The Peyotist maxim that one must learn about the religion directly from Peyote may force the Native American Church member to find his or her own meaning in ritual symbols, causing them to become what Obeyesekere (1981) calls "personal symbols," cultural symbols used with deep motivation. Thus, shared symbols have a role in structuring deeply personal ritual experiences.

Ritual Experiences in the Native American Church

Peyotist ritual experiences take a variety of forms. LaBarre (1989 [1938], 18) commented on the great variability of ritual experiences, pointing out that the Winnebago Indian Crashing Thunder experienced states of intense fear and deep depression, while a Taos Indian described euphoria and laughter. Some Native American Church members emphasize the importance of having a vision, and others do not. As Aberle (1991 [1966], 8) states, some members claim to have never seen a vision. Another of Aberle's consultants, Joe Sherwood, states that he sees visions in every meeting (Aberle 1991 [1966], 161). My consultant *Mike emphasized the visual modality and de-emphasized the auditory in his explanation, though the informational content in the visions is clearly what is important:

> When the Medicine is being used—you do not hear any audible connection—but it's mostly visual. You begin to see your answers or what knowledge you might be seeking or what questions you might have as you stand and have these visual interpretations brought on by the Medicine and prayers. (*Mike)

Though *Mike states there is no "audible connection," it should be stated that other Peyotists hear the voice of Peyote or another deity talking or singing or the sound of the ceremony becoming different. For example, *Edgar stated that "sometimes when that Medicine and the drumming and singing really gets moving spiritually, and then there's only about one or two women in there, if you concentrate, sometimes you can hear a whole bunch of ladies singing." LaBarre (1989 [1938], 13) writes that, in the Plains, when she is pleased with the singing, the peyote goddess "actually joins in with it....This auditory hallucination of hearing voices in peyote intoxication is most striking." *Mike's grandson also described visions as a desired part of the ritual, emphasizing the omniscience of the Peyote Spirit:

> If you pray to Grandpa Fire in that way, he can give you blessings in that way to have a spiritual vision. If you have faith, he can show you that. The Peyote will see all. What we use is nature, see. And through nature, we benefit off of it. (*Adam)

I asked the Peyotist college student *Florence what it means to have a vision. I asked her if it is an important part of the religion or if it would make the person feel part of the religion in a deeper way:

*FLORENCE: I don't know if I would consider it important or not important because I myself haven't seen anything like that. But I just like listening to everyone who's seen it. I'm like... I haven't seen it.

JC: In the Lakota Vision Quest, they seek visions. Do they seek them in NAC? Or is it that either it happens or it doesn't?

*FLORENCE: I think either it happens or it doesn't. I've never actually heard someone say this is important, you've got to have this. It wasn't really stressed as important. To the people it does happen to, it's important.

JC: How is it interpreted by the people who have a vision? What do they see it as?

*FLORENCE: To the people who I've heard have a vision, I think it's like an eye-opener. Something they've got to be more aware of. A message for them, a sign that maybe they're going the wrong way. Or maybe they're doing good and it's kind of maybe the higher spirit's way of saying thank you, you're going the right way.

JC: So it's not just that they're having a hallucination but it's that something is communicating with them?

*FLORENCE: Yeah. There's always a message behind it.

The dosage of Peyote taken is usually recognized as important. Aberle's (1991 [1966], 161) consultant Joe Sherwood stated that if he only takes two Peyote buttons, he has good feelings but sees nothing. However, if he takes twenty or more buttons, he can see and hear. If he is interrupted, he knows where he is and can respond, but to get back into the experience, he might have to consume more Medicine. Peyotists also recognize the influence of one's mindset on the experience. My consultant *Beatrice stated that, when she first used Peyote, she did not like its effects. But she later learned that the experience was affected by how she approached and interpreted it:

> I didn't like that feeling it gave me: that dizziness. So I'd just take a little bit of it. But when I got older, I found out that it was not really the Medicine, it's really me: how I affected it. And now I look at it differently. I look at it as a source of strength, a source of love, that it's not there to harm me, it's there to help and protect me. (*Beatrice)

Another female Native American Church member, a teacher, described a vision that was meaningful for her. Once again, the important aspect of the vision is the informational content, which she compared to "Aesop's fables," that she interpreted as a communication from the Creator:

*RUTH: You see these visions and sometimes it's almost like...they have a meaning to it. I can't really find the right word for it, but it's almost like Aesop's fables.

JC: So it kind of gives you a story that teaches a lesson?

*RUTH: Yes. And I remember when I graduated from college, I put up a Thank You Meeting, thanking my parents. And I got my degree and that morning I seen another vision. I seen a chef with a hat, dressed in white and he was carrying a silver platter. And he came up and he said what else do you want? And so I kind of knew it meant I could do a better job.

JC: When people have those kinds of experiences, where do you think they come from? Is it a mystery or is it your mind?

*RUTH: I think it is the Creator talking to you. Because none of us have ever seen the Creator. But I've seen angels of people that have left. I see their presence. And I see evil things that people try to do. And I've seen when you're trying to make a decision, you think about it and it comes to you. And I think it is the Creator that's speaking to you. How would I have figured it out to begin with? Because if I had the answer, I wouldn't even have gone.

Another woman did not mention visions but instead described experiencing a feeling or emotion in the ceremony that she found difficult to put into words:

> That morning, when I brought in the morning water it was something so different—it was very spiritual. I had never felt that in as

long as I've been going. And that morning I prayed and that fire-place and everything sitting there, it was so powerful. It was a good feeling. It was a real strong spirit that was there. A good spirit. And for days after that I kept crying because I tried to tell people how that was. It was a good feeling and it still gets to me to this day. And I tried telling my husband and my parents, "Why am I cry-ing? Why do I feel this way? Is it of a sadness?" And my Dad says I don't know. And then he says it should be of good stuff. And so he told me, "Take the Medicine, ask the Medicine why you're cry-ing." And I took it that night and I just kept crying and like "Why am I crying, what's this crying about? Why do I feel this feeling inside my heart and my chest?" And that night I could hear some-body saying, "You're crying 'cause of happiness. Our church gives you happiness. And it's the faith that your elders and people—your ancestors—have in this church. That's the faith you feel and that's what you feel. It's not a sadness, it's a happiness and joy." And it says, "Enjoy that feeling." And ever since then, I changed towards stuff. I used to stress out over work, over what people say, over bills. But now, why should I worry about that? The creator is going to take care of it. My prayers are going to take care of it. (*Mary)

Mary's comments show how ritual experiences can generate joy and hope for Native Americans in the postconquest situation. The following sec-tions will discuss several other specific ways that the Peyote Ceremony is personally and clinically useful. These include the reported ability of the ritual to facilitate decision making and problem solving, setting goals in a way that they become spiritually binding commitments, the expressive and communicative aspects of the ritual, and the community-building effects of a shared ordeal.

Decision Making and Problem Solving

Ritual experiences, for many Peyotists, act as the catalyst for important decisions and solutions to important problems. Native American Church members call ceremonies when they need to make a decision or solve a problem, and they approach the experience with these issues in mind. One Shawnee Peyotist told LaBarre that the place of the Peyote cactus on the moon altar represented "the space between Jesus Christ's eyes, just over the brain," and the horns of the crescent moon represent his arms as he lay face down on the cross: "If we eat the peyote which is on his brain, maybe it will make us think too" (LaBarre 1989 [1938], 75). In LaBarre's (1989 [1938], 97) opinion, it is the individual's total wishes that find expression in the course of action followed, but the consultation with Peyote gives a special authority to the decision, "which the 'unaided' individual might not have been able to summon" (LaBarre 1989 [1938], 97). My consultant *Mike explained it this way:

> When you ask me "what do you see?," "how does it work?"—really you yourself have to be the judge of that when you partake of this Medicine, when you go into a ceremony. You have to partake of it yourself to see how it works. But for me, the way I use it and the way I see things, when I say I see things, I use my head, my brain. I think about these things, any problems I may have. I take these things, I present these things when I'm on this Medicine and it shows me my answer. That's how I see it. It's just showing you the right way, the right decisions before you actually get into it and do it. For example, there's a lot of people my age that get into a lot of different things nowadays—especially wine. And they roll in the dirt and get drunk and nothing is happening in their lives. They can't understand why they can't get control of it. But ever since 40 years back when I started using the Medicine, my thinking has straightened out my ways. The decision making—that's where I use it. People see the two sides and get the answers in that way. And as far as I know, there's nothing but good comes out of using that herb. When you make these decisions, you see the good side. The way you live: you just want to live good. You see good, you decide to do good. That's what the Medicine does.

Goal Setting in Ritual

Once a decision is made in a ceremony, Native American Church members feel bound by their decision or prayers stating what they intend to do. Aberle's consultant Joe Sherwood described this situation as being "branded by your smoke." This refers to the use of tobacco rolled in corn husks during prayers:

> A man is to remember his prayer and what he said, and when he rolls his cigarette, lights it, and speaks to the Lord, and the Lord

knows every word and what kind of person he is and each person's mind and thought and feeling. So you are "branded" by your smoke. If you really tell the truth in your prayer, remember the prayer. A true believer should remember his prayer. (Aberle 1991 [1966])

Such prayers become part of the personal narrative of the Native American Church member and may continue to function to keep the person on the right path. This is likely an important mechanism in the continuing sobriety of members of the Native American Church: if they have pledged before God and the Peyote Spirit that they will not drink, then they are spiritually bound to that pledge and it takes on a metaphysical, as well as personal, significance. My consultant *Lucy explained it as follows:

> I think everything is connected—from as far as the thought you have at that moment in time that you want to have that ceremony done for you, that's when it becomes a ceremony. That's when it becomes your ceremony, because you go to the person and give them tobacco and you ask them would you please run a Peyote Meeting for me? And everything from all the experiences that I have had from that point—being at that moment in time in your thought—from that point to the point of the very end when they're singing the closing songs, that's all connected. And then after everything is said and done, then it becomes a prayer that you have to journey with. I guess you walk the talk as they say.

Expressive/Communicative Aspects of the Ritual

Learning how to give an account of oneself in an emotional way, sharing one's feelings and drawing lessons from one's life experiences, is generally important to my Navajo Peyotist consultants. This seems more characteristic of intertribalism and Christianity than it is of the traditional Navajo religion. As Hoskie stated, "Traditional ceremonies are more non-participatory as far as expressing meanings, whereas there's a lot of sharing in NAC and sweats—making that reconnection." LaBarre (1989 [1938], 99) writes that the Peyote Meeting has incorporated in it "a powerful mechanism for the liquidation of individual anxieties" in the practice of the public confession of sins, stating that it is difficult to overestimate the importance of confession before the Father Peyote and repentance before the group. LaBarre (1989 [1938], 99) writes: "More than ritual tears stream down the confessant's cheeks as he acknowledges his faults and asks aid to keep his promise to mend his ways." In this connection, I recall my discussion of weeping in ritual with a very nice old Road Man:

*LEONARD: Some, when I talk and pray, some of them, they cry and they forgive.

JC: It's good to cry, huh?

*LEONARD: Sure. You have to let it out and forgive...the Lord, the way he done.

Aberle (1991 [1966], 156) writes that the crying of the person giving a prayer, which often causes those listening to also begin crying, is atypical for traditional Navajos: "It astonishes non-members, and often surprises novices, who consider it unmanly." My consultant *Lucy linked the consumption of Peyote with enhanced feelings of empathy, stating that when people eat Medicine, "they can feel that same feeling and this young boy, when he sang those songs, what he was feeling, I was feeling and we both cried.... [W]e made that connection." The Winnebago leader John Rave stated, "Only if you weep and repent will you be able to attain knowledge" (LaBarre 1989 [1938], 81).

Shared Suffering

Participating in Sweat Lodge rituals and Peyote Ceremonies with Native Americans led me, early in my fieldwork, to contemplate the role of ritual suffering in Native American ceremonies. This certainly reaches an extreme in the Sun Dance. LaBarre (1989 [1938], 96) writes that, among Peyotists in tribes that had the Vision Quest, "suffering is counted even a positive virtue" and that a crippled Indian at Miami told him that, to get power from Peyote, "a man must suffer to it." A Comanche informant of Simmons (quoted in LaBarre 1989 [1938], 96) evokes the flavor of this ritual suffering:

If there is suffering, this is the time. That's the reason I took a good rest: so I could stand it. Many a time I have fallen over at this time. It's getting on to what they call the dark hour, the hour of the Crucifixion. Everyone here is suffering now.

The Peyote Meeting shares with the Sweat Lodge and the Sun Dance a focus on the enactment and the strengthening through practice of the maintenance of composure in the midst of psychologically and physically challenging situations. In my interpretation of this form of spirituality, a transformation is sought at the level of the subject's basic way of experiencing. Composure becomes a ritual matter, and one can draw upon one's religion or spiritual strength in order to control oneself and endure life's hardships, just as one controlled oneself in ceremony. The transformation of suffering from a solitary thing to a shared thing is also another likely therapeutic factor, as is the concept of "stress inoculation": the idea that induction of manageable amounts of stress helps one to better cope with future stress in real-life situations (Meichenbaum 1996). In terms of my own clinical training in dialectical behavior therapy (Linehan 1993), a potential benefit would be the development of "distress tolerance" skills that enhance resilience.

One final passage from an interview with Hoskie, which took place after an especially challenging Sweat Lodge ritual, of the type that staff and clients of Hoskie's treatment facility called a "skin peeler," illustrates the ideology of ritual suffering, as well as its relation to clinical intervention and recovery:

I guess it's like in life, even in the NAC meeting they teach that. They say there's gonna be hard times in life and there's gonna be times when it's gonna be very uncomfortable. What we tend to do is stay in the comfort zone. We don't want to take a risk. We don't want to make ourselves uncomfortable. But in life sometimes you have to get out of that comfort zone to develop. We have to say to ourselves, "I'm gonna take a chance. I'm gonna experience something different and I'm gonna push myself and I'm gonna challenge myself." So what we believe in that Sweat Lodge is that we're part of all those elements that are in that ceremony. We're part of the fire, we're part of the medicine water, we're part of mother earth and the atmosphere. Those sustain us as human beings and so they're the ones that are doing the ceremony. Sometimes you have a hard time, sometimes you don't. It depends on really where you're at in your self-evaluation. The suffering part of it is that can you challenge yourself? At the same time, you've got to remember I can run out from this sweat. If I want, I can leave here, but if I do that, then I'm going to do that every time something gets difficult. In other words, it comes back to the treatment thing about do I really want to look at myself and go through all that emotional suffering, or yes I'm willing to go to any length for recovery and look at all the issues I have and suffer that pain, but still challenge myself because I know down the road it's going to help me. So that suffering part is that kind of physical suffering, but there are all other kinds of suffering: relational suffering, spiritual suffering. So that heat, it's doing the ceremony for you. It's healing you. At the same time somewhere along the way in your mind again you're gonna say, "I sat through worse than this in the Sweat Lodge. It was really hot. Now look at what's happening to me. This little thing right here and I'm getting so upset. This little thing right here I'm starting to run from it again." So that suffering part comes in with that. The suffering part says, "I'm challenging myself and I'm willing to suffer for it." (Hoskie)

Concluding Reflections on Ritual Process

This chapter has argued that the Peyote Ceremony has a ritual process that involves a dialectic between therapeutic emplotment and consciousness modification. Ritual symbolism emplots the patient in a drama of sacred reflexivity, divine communication, and transformative redemption aimed at changing the patient's personal narrative and view of his or her life. Pharmacologically, Peyote ingestion supports this process by altering attentional processes, suggestibility, and self-awareness in a way that makes the mind more malleable and open to change.

Peyotist ritual experiences are self-referential, often revealing aspects of the Peyotist's life that need to be worked on, and these experiences become important memories and guides for the individual. These experiences may or may not be in the form of visions. When there is a vision, Native American Church members emphasize the informational content or spiritual significance that is transmitted in the vision rather than its impressive visual qualities. Ritual experiences are typically interpreted as messages from the Creator or the Peyote Spirit. In addition to the spiritual dimension of these sorts of experiences, members of the Native American Church also report that rituals help them make important decisions, solve problems, set goals in such a way that they become spiritually binding commitments, and express important emotions and thoughts in the context of a shared ritual ordeal. Healing in the Native American Church also involves the mobilization of help networks and interpersonal support from the family and larger community.

The therapeutic process at the heart of the Peyote Ceremony clashes with modern Euro-American understandings of psychotherapeutic and psychopharmacological intervention. Euro-American theories of psychotherapeutic efficacy tend to be dyadic and focused on the quality of the patient/healer relationship (e.g., warmth, empathy, and genuineness) in the context of rational conversations. In contrast, therapeutic efficacy in the Native American Church seems to be built into cultural structures of meaning and practice, what I have referred to as culturally embedded therapeutic emplotment. The dynamics of the patient/healer relationship is often not as important in the Native American Church as the ritual process, unless one considers the healer to be the Creator or the Peyote Spirit. Euro-American theories of psychopharmacology derive from a materialistic agonist/antagonist paradigm, whereas Peyotist psychopharmacology can be described in terms of a semiotic/reflexive paradigm, aimed at generating rich spiritual experiences and deep transformative insights.

My understanding of the Peyote Ceremony may also clash with the ways in which some readers understand "religion" because of the way I analyze the Peyote Ceremony in terms of its therapeutic functions. Certain readers may believe that there is necessarily a contradiction between seeing Peyote as a "living presence" and understanding its therapeutic use. This sort of view has resulted in boundaries between "religious studies" writing and clinically informed medical anthropology writing focused on healing and intervention. However, I see this neat separation of spirituality and therapeutic function as itself an ethnocentrism of Western civilization, in which a particular historical division of labor has separated religion and medicine. Other societies, such as many Native American societies, have not made this separation and still view spirituality and healing as intimately linked rather than opposed domains. We should remember that the original religious practitioner in human societies (often called the "shaman") was also the original medical practitioner. In this book, I am consciously trying to bring together the perspective of ritual studies or religious studies and the perspective of a clinically informed analysis of therapeutic process.

These cultural differences in understandings of the therapeutic process, on the one hand, and the "proper" form of religious belief and practice, on the other, have resulted in the "Othering" of Native American Church members by the dominant Euro-American society and in the reduction of the complex postcolonial healing experiences described in this chapter to "harmful drug use" that can be punished in line with the War on Drugs. Such an understanding does not resonate with the ethnographic data presented here or with the lived realities of members of the Native American Church.

7

Kinship, Socialization, and Ritual in Navajo Peyotist Families

THE CLASSIC ETHNOGRAPHERS of the Native American Church, including Mooney, LaBarre, Aberle, Stewart, Opler, Slotkin, and the Spindlers, encountered a young religion that had more new converts than members from childhood. But today the Native American Church is no longer a new "cult" (a very stigmatizing term these days) but is rather a multigenerational religious and ethnomedical tradition that has developed distinctive childrearing strategies and goals for human development. Aberle could foresee this historical development, as he wrote that, because the Native American Church had been present among the Navajos long enough so that some young people were raised in the tradition from childhood, we can expect that more and more frequently, the reason for initial membership in the church will be a matter of "parental choice for children" (Aberle 1991 [1966], 187).

Socialization, parenting, childhood, and the life course represent neglected areas of the ethnographic literature on the Native American Church. This sensitive topical domain, given the communal use of the Peyote cactus, calls for a theoretical approach that is informed by a familiarity with the multiple paths of normal human development that are manifest in the world's societies, including diverse modes of socialization, family behavior, therapeutic intervention, and psychopharmacology. Contextualization of Peyotist socialization within the breadth of world cultures, many of which institutionalize the use of psychedelic plants, makes the tradition much more comprehensible. This topic area also calls for a reflexive approach that is able to question the ideological and cultural roots of conventional knowledge, including Euro-American legal, ethical, and medical knowledge. Finally, statements about human development in the Native American Church should be based on a real familiarity with it, derived from observing and getting to know actual Native American Church families in the context of long-term ethnographic fieldwork as I have done.

In this chapter, I want to draw attention to the fact that the Native American Church structures family contexts and human development beyond the ritual. I thus want to give Native American Church studies life historical and sociohistorical depth. A family/kinship perspective humanizes studies of the Native American Church while simultaneously expanding our understanding of normal human development and the range of viable family values. The relevance of a focus on socialization in the Native American Church is supported by the prevalence of parental symbolism in the Peyote Meeting and by the child–parent form of relations with Mother Peyote, Father Peyote, and the Creator in this tradition. The relevance of a focus on the life course is supported by the symbolism of the Peyote Road as the arc of one's life from birth to death. Finally, the family dimension simply stands out in my field experiences. Most salient are the loving parenting styles and approaches to communication between family members that I observed in and out of ceremonies. One Native American Church member I interviewed expressed this approach to parenting perfectly:

> Parents really love their kids and in there you see it. You hear the prayers that parents pour out—the love they have for their kids. And that's just between the creator and them and you hear it. And that's very special. And that's what I always tell people that judge our church. (*Mary)

Among the Native American Church families I got to know in my fieldwork, children were encouraged to attend Peyote Meetings and consume the sacrament when they decided they were ready. I observed several family rituals in which Peyote was consumed communally, passed from grandparent to parent to child. The culture clash with mainstream American family values is obvious. Few things push contemporary Americans into a moral fervor as much as the idea of drug use by children. For parents to lovingly give their four- or five-year-old a "powerful psychedelic drug" in any quantity is, for many Euro-Americans, incomprehensible. However, from a broad anthropological perspective, enlightened by study of the entire range of the world's cultures, this behavior is not shocking at all. Socialization in human societies often takes place in connection with communal rituals, such as initiation rituals or rites of passage (Van

Gennep 1960 [1909]). Furthermore, these rituals often utilize consciousness alteration induced by psychoactive plants or painful ritual ordeals
(Grob and Dobkin de Rios 1994; Herdt 1987). My field observations reveal
that socialization, along with healing, is a central function of the Native
American Church, and Peyote plays an integral role. Peyote Meetings are
held for children to support their schoolwork, and ingestion of the sacrament is thought to benefit children, as well as adults. I have mentioned
the Peyotist father who told me a charming story of how he gave his young
son a little Peyote, which helped him to learn to tie his shoes. Another
young man said that he began attending Native American Church meetings in a cradle board (a piece of wood to which babies are swaddled). So
Peyote is used across the life course from "cradle board to grave." What,
many will ask, can be good about this?

I will summarize my argument. From a psychopharmacological stand-
point, as I have argued previously, ingestion of Peyote alters suggestibility and openness to social messages (Sjoberg and Hollister 1965). Chief
among these messages in the context of the Native American Church
are the family values of honoring one's relatives and avoiding alcohol. In
addition, communal Peyote ingestion (and use of tobacco) provides positive role modeling of a controlled and respectful pattern of use of sacred
psychoactive substances by adults. Most importantly, perhaps, Peyote also
has the role of a guardian spirit. As I have argued, Peyote is seen not
only as a sacred medicinal herb but also as an omniscient spiritual entity.
If socialization is successful, the omnipresent gaze of the Peyote Spirit
will become a constant companion of the young Native American Church
member, preventing the child from alcohol consumption and other sins
even when the parents are absent. The Peyote Spirit is thus itself a sort of
parent, and this role further clarifies why it is called "Mother Peyote" or
"Father Peyote."

Here I will bring in the term *panoptical*, but without its negative
Foucauldian connotations. The term derives from Greek roots meaning
"all-seeing." Foucault's (1979) book *Discipline and Punish* was inspired
by Jeremy Bentham's design for the perfect prison, which he called the
Panopticon. In the Panopticon, prisoners were always visible, but they
never knew when they were being watched because the observer was
never visible. Bentham believed that the prisoner's belief that he was
always being observed was sufficient to reform his behavior. But the term
can also be applied to potentially useful aspects of religious belief, such as
guardian spirits or omniscient divinities like the Peyote Spirit.

I speak here as someone who has done clinical work on the Navajo reservation with Native American adolescents having very severe problems with alcoholism and substance abuse. I found that the usual approaches of Western clinical sciences (individual therapy sessions, psychoeducation, and Alcoholics Anonymous) were often not appealing to these young people. But most had some interest in Native American ceremonies and spirituality, and it was standard practice for me to attend a weekly Sweat Lodge ritual with my patients. Self-disclosure in this ritual context was not a personal choice but a cultural duty, and a lot of useful clinical information was made available in these sweats. Clinically relevant information deriving from these rituals was summarized in a therapy note added to the patient's chart, as will be described more in the next chapter.

I also witnessed the deep impact of Peyote Ceremonies on children, especially the rituals I attended with the Native American Church family I lived with during the summer of 1990. One family ritual stands out in my memory. It was near the end of the summer, and the children were preparing to return to their high school on the other side of the reservation. The purpose of the meeting was to help the children be receptive to the teachings in school and avoid substance abuse while they were away from home. This is a typical situation among the Navajos, and this type of Native American Church ritual is called an "Education Meeting." The ceremony was formal but marked by the weeping and fervent prayer of the Peyotist mothers for their children. This obviously had an impact on the children, who began to cry themselves. It is in these ritual contexts that relationships are forged between children and the Peyote Spirit, they make binding promises to follow the teachings of their elders and avoid alcohol and other sins, and they come to believe that the omniscient Peyote Spirit will know their actions and punish their sins. These spiritual orientations have significant potential to establish a panoptical form of control, instilling the belief that Peyote is always watching and helping children to avoid the harms caused by alcohol abuse and other risk behaviors when they are out of the sight of their parents.

The Interdisciplinary Study of Socialization and Human Development

Psychological studies of human development have been dominated by reductionist intrapsychic theories such as those of Piaget, for whom mental development was primarily an unfolding of an autonomous internal rational process. Piaget's famous lab-based studies largely overlooked the social world (Shweder 1984). Knowledge construction was prototypically characterized as self-constructed by the child in response to trial-and-error discovery of physical laws. Freudian approaches to human development also tended to be individualistic and intrapsychic in their focus on the acquisition of impulse control and in their frequent reduction of the sociocultural to the psychological. However, Freudian theories incorporated the social world to a greater extent, for example, in their understanding of the pressure of social norms and the internalization of these norms in the superego.

A much more explicitly social perspective on the psychology of human development was developed in the work of George Herbert Mead (1934) at the University of Chicago and Lev Vygotsky (1978), who worked in post-revolutionary Russia. For both Mead and Vygotsky, social experience is primary and foundational. Self arises out of observation of, and participation in, social interaction. It arises with the use of language and with the child's modeling and responding to the attitudes of other people.

Anthropological approaches to human development are the most socially encompassing in that they include not only the influence of particular social interactions but also the entire social milieu and the shared structures of meaning in which the child is "enculturated." Anthropological studies have revealed many areas of cultural divergence in approaches to socialization, family structure, family behavior, and family values. These include polygamous families (Altman and Ginat 1996); divergent sexuality and gender development (Herdt 1987); divergent child sleeping practices, including cosleeping (Shweder, Jensen, and Goldstein 1995); divergent age of weaning (Stuart-Macadam and Dettwyler 1995); divergent swaddling (such as the Navajo cradle board); greater emphasis on nonmaternal care and other differences in maternal care practices (LeVine et al. 1996); and divergent learning styles (Kommers and Venbrux 2008). Many of these areas of cultural divergence are areas of existing or potential culture clash. The anthropological approach has the potential to revolutionize our understandings of human development. However, anthropological perspectives often have their own limitations. Many influential segments of the discipline tend to banish psychological and biological realities and see everything in terms of public meanings and communication.

This chapter adopts an interdisciplinary approach to the study of socialization and human development in the Native American Church. It stresses the role of what LeVine (1982) has called "deliberate socialization" responsive to cultural values and developmental goals. It also incorporates the influence of psychology and biology in its examination of the dialectical relationship between Peyotist superego development and Peyotist psychopharmacology. Studies of socialization add an important dimension to the intrapsychic focus of developmental psychology. They also make an important contribution to anthropology in that they seek to explain how culture is acquired and transmitted and how persons are formed by society.

The Peyote Spirit as Omnipresent Socializer

As my analysis of ritual symbolism in the previous chapter demonstrates, maternal and birth-related symbols dominate the ritual, and Peyote and other divinities are approached using parental forms of address. God is often referred to as "Our Father" or even, as Aberle (1991 [1966], 153) reports, "Our Father and Our Mother," while participants describe themselves as "Your children," or "Your babies." Peyote is referred to in the same way, though the relationship with Peyote seems more proximate than the relationship with the Creator. Evidence supporting this view that Peyote is a more proximate deity than "the Creator" or "God the Father" includes the frequent identification of Peyote with Jesus (rather than "God") and the frequent characterization of Peyote's role as a "mediator" between God and the Native American Church member. One of my Peyotist consultants told me, "They say Peyote is like your brother." But it is much more typical to address this spiritual entity as "Mother Peyote" or "Father Peyote":

> This Peyote was put down with certain properties by the Holy Spirit. That's the mediator between you and the Creator. It's also got properties and a spirit of its own. And so we call it "Mother Peyote," "Father Peyote." ... We believe that we tell our problems to this Medicine here, then it's gonna help us to overcome whatever problems we're having. (Hoskie)

In my analysis of panoptical socialization in the Native American Church, Peyote is understood as a psychoculturally constituted surrogate parent who, being omniscient and omnipresent, is experienced by the child (or adult) to be monitoring his or her behaviors and thoughts. When the child is socialized into a belief in the Peyote Spirit and an understanding that a relationship with this omniscient spirit has been formed, this perceived relationship supports behavioral self-control, self-monitoring, and superego development. This may partially explain how so many members of the Native American Church are able to avoid the problems with alcohol that affect many other Native Americans: they have a relationship with the all-seeing Peyote Spirit and thus have an internalized system of panoptical control. Thus, the reason for the high rates of abstinence from alcohol in the Native American Church may not be as much in the pharmacology of Peyote as in the personal relationship between the spiritual aspect of Peyote and the Native American who ingests it, though pharmacology is instrumental in creating the ritual experiences interpreted as evidence for the presence and omniscience of the Peyote Spirit. In many cases, this relationship, whether interpreted as a relationship with Peyote or a relationship with God *through* Peyote, takes the form of a contract or pledge. Promises or pledges or setting a goal are especially associated with prayers using tobacco. As one of Aberle's (1991 [1966]) Navajo consultants stated, you are "branded by your smoke."

Peyote's gaze makes itself known through visions, voices, and other sorts of communications interpreted as warnings or revelations about the self. These experiences can influence feelings of guilt (or perhaps more properly "shame" depending on how the presence of the Peyote Spirit is understood metaphysically). One of D'Azevedo's (1985, 13) Washoe Peyotist consultants stated, "This Medicine...keeps pushing you to go the right Way." But the Peyote Spirit provides not only guilt but also the opportunity for redemption—a renewal that resolves the guilt.

Some Native American Church members emphasize the role of the Peyote Spirit as a guardian and protector, and others emphasize that Peyote can punish one for misbehavior. One wonders whether these contrasting views may derive from different parenting styles and thus be transferences onto Peyote of feelings about one's parents. Spindler and Spindler (1984) quote a Menominee Peyotist who described a vision of Peyote as a police officer with a club beating the message into him. Radin (1914) wrote of the guilty conscience that a person has if he eats Peyote and does not repent openly. Peyote use is thus implicated in superego development. The Peyote Spirit functions in ways similar to a superego or conscience. In fact, Aberle (1991 [1966], 145) describes a prayer in which a Navajo Peyotist prayed not only for a clear mind but also for "his conscience." The process of Peyotist socialization is exemplified in the following account by one of the teenage grandsons of the Road Man *Mike whose family I lived with in 1990:

> I grew up in a Native American Church family and attended since I was small. I heard that I used to go with my Dad to Peyote Meetings in a cradleboard. He would give me to the ladies that were sitting inside the tipi....At five or seven or something, that's when I started eating Peyote....I just used to take it in a holy way but I never took much. And then from fifteen on, that's when I started kind of like going crazy and I started getting into peer pressure and all, and I guess I didn't take it seriously. I stopped going to meetings with my Dad and started going to parties and all. And then my grandpa's teaching. He used to talk to us...when we were small, he used to tell us that we had a spirit. And I started going into meetings....I used to start praying. When I would go in and I would pray it seemed like I got more—kinda like—shaped up from all the substance abuse....It kinda wised me up. I started praying and I had a change like. Somehow through prayers I began to believe that. It helped me and my family. (*Adam)

As this story illustrates, some children raised in Native American Church families may go through a period of rebellion and succumbing to peer pressure to join in drinking parties. But continuing socialization efforts, as well as the church connections developed and the teachings instilled at a younger age, may bring them back into line with the church's teachings as they mature. In the previous passage, *Adam refers to "grandpa's teaching...when we were small" as the prelude to his return to the church. This is the change point in this short illness and recovery narrative. The impact of family and church teachings on children's thoughts and behavior between rituals is also apparent in the following passage: "Sometimes when I don't go to prayer meetings it's like I feel like doing something bad...but I remember what I said or what was said to me and I try to make not too many mistakes" (*Adam).

But the impact of ritual experiences and the relationship with the Peyote Spirit is also apparent:

> When I first took it, when I was like all drinking and all—I took a whole bunch of Peyote—it tripped me out that time because it showed me how bad I was doing—that's what I thought. I felt like

the ground was this high and I was this close to the fire. I felt—
like—small. But right now when I'm serious about it—right now it
knows me—it knows who I am. If I've been having hard times—I
did something bad—and I go in—when I puke it shows that I've
been bad that way. (*Adam)

My knowledge of *Adam derives from the summer I spent with his
family in 1990 and from the several visits I made on subsequent summers. I was able to observe a growing maturity and respect in his approach
to Native American Church membership. For example, when I first got to
know *Adam, he and his cousins were very much into "heavy metal" music
and wore the black shirts with angry slogans that are characteristic of this
musical genre. The boys would even wear these shirts to ceremonies. But
on one of my last visits to the family, I noticed that *Adam dressed more
conservatively, like an adult church member. I asked him about this and
he explained it this way:

We don't wear those black shirts no more. It kind of turned us
around. Like I said, it used to work on me like that....Now when
I'm in a Peyote Meeting, I get really close to the Grandpa Fire. Like
this past weekend, I went to a meeting. The fire was really huge. I
talk to the Grandpa Fire. You have to set aside your jealously, your
hatred, your bad habits....(*Adam)

Superego development as a parental goal is also suggested in the following description of a Native American Church father:

We do want to be good parents. We want to raise our kids so they
won't get into trouble. And we can protect them from everything in
the world physically. But when it comes to their own selves, it's their
choice. (*Henry)

I interpret this passage in the context of the social changes that the
Navajos have gone through. With the breakdown of many traditional
forms of social control, stronger internal forms of control were needed. For
example, with the need to fit into a new Anglo-dominated North America
and its wage economy, Native American children and parents are often
separated in new ways. Students may have to go away to school if there
are none close to home. Also, parents may be absent from the household

for work at various shifts. In this new situation, a guardian deity monitoring children's actions may be seen as a very useful cultural adaptation. And if Peyote ingestion and other ritual techniques facilitate a powerful experience of the existence of the Peyote Spirit and its omniscience, then Peyote Ceremonies are adaptive rather than regressive. Thus, similar to what LeVine (1990) wrote about parenting among the Gusii, the Native American Church provides a form of socialization that contrasts strongly with mainstream American values and assumptions but which is oriented toward the survival and continued health of children.

K'é: The Ethic of Navajo Kinship

Beyond the ritual and its visionary experiences, the Native American Church is associated with a particular sort of social and emotional milieu: one emphasizing feelings of brotherhood, sisterhood, and other valences of kinship and belonging. Among the Navajo, this sort of milieu is identified with the term *k'é*. *K'é* is a central concept of the Navajo worldview, perhaps as central as the concept of *hózhǫ́* but much less discussed in the literature (but see Witherspoon 1975, 37, 120–126, and Willging 2002). *K'é* is not easily translatable. From one perspective, it can be described as a code of behavior based on traditional kinship relations, kinship etiquette, and forms of introduction and address. It also encompasses a more general ethic or ideology that extends these sorts of kinship-based forms of relationship beyond blood relatives to include other Navajos and, especially among Peyotists, to other tribes, to people generally, and even to animals and other forms of life. Witherspoon emphasizes the ethical/ideological aspect when he writes that *k'é* means "love," "kindness," "peacefulness," and "cooperation":

> At the conclusion of any war, fighting, or confrontation, one often hears the phrase "k'e nahasdįį́" which means conditions have returned to "k'e." "Doo k'e nizin da" means he does not think according to k'e, or he is unfriendly, uncooperative, or does not think like a kinsman. (Witherspoon 1975)

K'é is used a lot in the Navajo Native American Church. Traditional forms of address and introduction not only help Navajos to establish clan identities (which clarifies appropriate etiquette, as well as who can date whom) but also are also used with nonkin to show respect, express solidarity, or establish harmonious relationships. Among the Peyotist clinicians I interviewed and worked with, *k'é* was explicitly used to establish therapeutic relationships and was itself considered a sort of intervention:

> You know, too—another Navajo way of healing is to reach out to Andrea and say Andrea, you're gonna be my daughter and making Andrea feel good that way... we accept you in this way. I think that does more than anything... relations, *k'é*, I've gained a sister, I've gained a brother... so in this way, everybody is healed. They're gonna feel good about themselves. (*Henry)

The emotional impact of invoking *k'é* through traditional forms of address using Navajo kinship terms is apparent in the following passage from *Henry:

> That's what makes us feel good. When somebody says *shiyáázh*, *shizházhí*, meaning "little one" or "my baby," oh man, you hear that from a grandmother, that's the best feeling in the world. It just gets all warm in here [gestures at his heart]. The best thing you can have in a traditional family setting is a grandma calling you that. Nowadays, what do we call our relatives or our patients? We call them *'adláaniis* right? "Drunks," right? "Get out of here! You're still drinking over here!" You get shunned away from the family 'cause you're drinking a lot. But now when they come in, maybe they might be my uncle or grandpa and we'll address them by that. And that sense of belonging will come: "Yeah, I didn't hear that in a long time. It makes me feel good." So we try to bring that sense of belonging back into that family instead of saying, "Hey pops," "Hey dude," "Hey moms," "Hey man." We start—I guess you could say conditioning—to use that *k'é* back again....

In another area of the reservation, *Mary expressed similar feelings:

> The way I see it is that people in the Church—the Native American Church—they're like your own family. Even though they're not blood family, they're still your family—they respect you in that way. And that's what I really like. And it's just done so much for my family.

Another young woman, when asked to give a definition of the Peyote Ceremony, gave the following, very family-oriented definition:

A ceremony is kind of like a gathering of relatives and friends to support someone who's having trouble with things in their life that may be confusing—maybe they're not in harmony with themselves. A ceremony brings together the family so that person can have support. People need support. I guess it's a good way to get through hard times instead of being alone. (*Florence)

The centrality of multigenerational families in the Navajo Native American Church is represented in many cultural productions. For example, the Peyote song album by Eli Secody called *The Following Generation* (on Canyon Records) includes songs titled "Families Walking in Beauty," "God Bless You My Child," and "Good Education." There are many other family-oriented Peyote song albums that could be analyzed in a similar way, for example, *My Father's Chapel* by Paul Guy, Jr. and Paul Guy, Sr. (also on Canyon Records). All of this is in agreement with Aberle's (1991 [1966]) statement that an ethic of kinship responsibility was alive and well among Peyotists.

Peyote Use in Early Childhood

Peyotism functions in all ways as a living religion: peyote christens the new-born and protects their early years, teaches the young, marries young men and women, rewards and punishes the behavior of adult years, and buries the dead—offering throughout consolation for troubles, chastening for bad deeds or thoughts, and serving as the focus for tribal and intertribal life.

—LaBarre (1989 [1938], 103)

When do children start taking Peyote? For many, the correct answer would be "just before birth." This is because pregnant women who are members of the Native American Church sometimes ingest Peyote as they prepare to deliver their child. This practice is not as threatening as it sounds in that it likely involves use of a low dose (as a sacrament) by an experienced user. However, it alarmed doctors at the local Indian Health Service hospital to such an extent that, when faced with the situation, they were known to say things like, "Oh no...we have another 'Peyote baby.'...[G]et ready for a sick baby" within earshot of the mother who was about to deliver. I interviewed a Peyotist nurse who worked at the hospital. She had overheard such incidents and was shocked and insulted. The analogy is clear: Peyote babies are assumed to be like crack babies or babies with fetal alcohol syndrome because Peyote is seen as a "drug." However, I am not aware of any data from human studies indicating that this practice endangers the mother or child in any way and have heard many stories of such births completed without problems.

In one published account, Dr. Lois Van Tol (2009), a family doctor working at a tribal clinic, describes a young Native American mother who was given Peyote tea by her grandmother shortly before giving birth. The young mother explained, "This is a very holy thing. I want to take it to help my baby be born safely. Peyote will help me have an easy labor, and it will bless my baby and help him to be strong and healthy" (Van Tol 2009, 184). This upset the doctor and other clinical staff members very much. However, aside from a temporarily elevated heart rate, there were no complications. Before consuming the Peyote tea, the mother was described as "quite uncomfortable" with her contractions, and she was calm and much less troubled by pain after having the tea. Both mother and infant were healthy after the birth, and the mother was described as loving and conscientious in bringing her baby for his check-ups. At the end of Van Tol's two years at the tribal clinic, at her going-away party, the patient's father, Tommy, thanked her:

> "I just want to thank you for taking care of my daughter when she had her baby. You helped her give birth safely. But most of all, you listened to us and you respected our ways."
>
> "What do you mean?" I protested. "I disagreed with you. I argued with you. I tried to stop you from giving peyote to Hattie!"
>
> Tommy laughed. "I didn't say you agreed with us. I said you listened to us. You respected our ways. And we will never forget that."
> (Van Tol 2009, 187)

My interviews suggest that young children of Native American Church families learn about Peyote informally, through participating in normal family activities. When young, they are often given a little piece of Peyote as a sacrament or as a home remedy. The dosage is typically so small that it causes little consciousness alteration if any. A larger dose, often in the form of tea, may be given if the illness is more serious. The following account from a middle-aged woman is somewhat typical, though the age of three or four years old is on the young side for a first use:

> I remember my aunt had Peyote buttons. I didn't really know what they were for but she would cut them and dry them out. So I saw it, and then I helped her clean it, I helped her prepare it and she would tell me to take it. . . . I remember that experience—I must have been about 3 or 4 years old. . . . When I first took the Medicine when I was real young, I remember I was sitting there—and I remember (laughing), "What's going on?" I'm sitting here thinking to myself, "What's going on with me?" . . . I felt kinda weird, things were moving around, I didn't really understand what was going on. . . . I don't know if I had visions or what—but that's the first time I ever took it. . . . I remember I kinda got physically sick, and it got to my stomach like I wanted to vomit or something—I don't know if I vomited or not. But I remember just feeling like I was dizzy or in a trance. And when I got older, I took it again—which was like in the early '70s. . . . I remembered and I would just take a little bit because I thought that it was pretty potent stuff—and it would work on me a lot. I think I was kind of scared of it—'cause I didn't like that feeling it gave me—that dizziness, so I'd just take a little bit of it. But when I got older, I found out that it was not really the Medicine, it's really me—how I affected it. And now I look at it differently. (*Beatrice)

Another woman recalls that every Sunday, while she was growing up, her father used to "make the sacrament in a certain shape and give it to us after a prayer for our well-being" (*Ruth). An account of first use during an illness, at the age of six or seven, was given by *Edgar:

> Well, my mom was a part of the NAC since she was a teenager and we were raised with it. That's how I got into it. There's different stories of how it came into our family. And how I got involved in it is when I became sick one time. That was when I was about seven or six years old. I got sick and they didn't know what was wrong. So my mom fed me a lot of Peyote—the hot tea. In the morning I got OK because a lot of it was psychological. So that was one of my first experiences with the Peyote.

The age of first use in these passages (three or four years old for *Beatrice, five to seven years old for *Adam, and six or seven years old for *Edgar) will alarm many readers. But the accounts given in the previous section were offered by two clinicians (*Beatrice and *Edgar) and a teacher (*Ruth) whom I knew for more than a year and who were fully functioning, healthy members of their community. They did not appear damaged in any way by their early Peyote use. Furthermore, no Native American Church members I interviewed reported that they were forced to take Peyote at a certain age. The consensus was that it was a choice for the child to make after observing the role of Peyote in his or her family. One Peyotist father made the following statement:

> What I say is don't force it on your kids. I don't force it on my kids. But they still gotta respect it. The way you conduct yourself, the way your parenting skills will show with your kids is "Yeah Dad, I like the way you conduct yourself and I want to participate in the ceremony." I don't force them in there, especially at a young age. (*Henry)

I asked my consultants how children are expected to behave in rituals. The typical answer was that children were welcome to attend but should be respectful and not disruptive. *Mary began attending as a little girl but often slept through the ceremony, waking up at midnight to go outside at the short midnight water ceremony. I have witnessed children asleep in meetings. Some adults felt that the religion had become more tolerant of children sleeping in the ritual and that adults were stricter when they were growing up. I also asked what children are taught about participating in the ritual. The following response from *Beatrice seems typical:

> They have kind of a little idea of being supportive...and my son, we're trying to teach him to have a certain mindset even when he goes into a Sweat Lodge—to have a mindset to help, you're sacrificing your time...so we're slowly teaching him and I think he's grasping but he's still little—he's still a lot egocentric. But my older daughters, they understand you go in there and you help people.

The Peyotist college student *Florence gave another account of what things children are taught in the Native American Church:

> There were teachings, especially going into Hoskie's meetings. His teachings. I think when I first started—maybe the first couple times

I was going in—it was a meeting with Hoskie. He kinda knows when people don't understand. And then the next morning, he just sits there and just starts talking to you, explaining things. The first few times was maybe how important the instruments are and the explanations of the songs—things that were done the night before. What also made it easier whenever I went to a meeting with him is the language barrier: maybe the patients speak fluent Navajo. And he was always sitting there, being able to translate for me and my brother—just to let us know what's going on and make us more aware of what's going on—the purpose of what's going on that night.

Another parent described the Peyote Ceremony as a context for the modeling of adult gender roles in the family. Here two ritual officiants, the Road Man and Dawn Woman (typically a married couple), are role models of harmony between the sexes and particularly between husband and wife:

That lady that brings in the water...you can't do a ceremony without a female in there. So both of them has to work together and they demonstrate that, where he does the talking and singing, where that lady does the prayers and they talk about how the water is used and she tells about the role of the mother and father, the mom and the wife, or the sister. So she talks about some traditional role. Then he talks about the male role and how they come together as a family. And that part we pray about. (*Henry)

Several Peyotists described an educational process in the Native American Church in which lessons are planted in the child's mind like seeds and only later become relevant and useful in the child's life. This is consonant with findings in the interdisciplinary study of human development that suggest that much socialization is implicit or indirect. Consider the following passage from *Mary:

A lot of teachings from the elders that are passed down, some you may have heard but you don't understand it. But later down the road, when you come across an obstacle, you're going to say, "Oh, this is what they had meant back then." So you learn from that too.

*Mary went on to give a concrete example of this process in her own life:

> When I got married and had my own son—that's when I really started to go to it. Because at the time you're a teenager you're like—"oh gosh—staying up all night, dragging all this"—and you really don't know the meaning to it until you grow up and have kids of your own—that's when you start to change your mind toward it.

In line with *Mary's comments, which hint at the support many parents receive from Native American Church membership, the following extended passage from *Beatrice illustrates that Peyote visions can energize the process of parenting and allay the parent's anxieties about the process:

> One [ceremony] I can particularly remember is my son. I think it was last year. I was really happy when I was pregnant. And when he was born, I got kind of ambivalent because sometimes I had lots of questions. What do I need to do with him and how should I raise him? And the last time we had a meeting, it was for a patient of Hoskie's. I was at that point where my daughter was into drugs and I didn't know what to do to help her. It was a really stressful time. I started thinking about my son—how can we help him to understand so, hopefully, he doesn't grow up to be like all these kids that wind up here: the anger problems, identity problems. And we tried to put him on the path... "Son, I want you to be a leader." That's how I talked to him. I'd tell him, "One of these days you're gonna be a leader of your people." We did that for him. But it comes to the point where he's getting older and older. He starts to learn to think. He gets reactive at times, started to act out. I really struggled with that and didn't know what to do. And I turned to the meeting. And I had an experience that was like a revelation to me. [Her voice becomes hushed:] There's an angel that appeared right in the middle of the tipi. And she said, "This is your son" and she gave him to me. It was so beautiful [she begins to weep]. And from there I got this really peaceful feeling that this is right. He was going to take on a purpose. We could be serious about training him. He was going to become a good leader for his people, a good person. From there on, we started trying to teach him about his background, what

happened in the past, have him understand what leaders were like, started having him to Sweat Lodges to be strong, learn to discipline himself. Ever since then he has started to participate more actively in NAC meetings and Sweat Lodges. So that was a big change in my life for me.

Ritual Education in the Native American Church

Traditional societies typically alter the psychobiological state to enhance attention, feelings of significance, and suggestibility (Bourguignon 1973; Grob and Dobkin de Rios 1994). This is frequently done in the context of healing or socialization efforts. For example, the Chumash Indians of California administered *Datura meteloides* (jimson weed) to adolescents at their rite of passage into adulthood. Another *Datura* species (*Datura fatuosa*) is used in the girl's initiation ritual among the Shangana-Tsonga of Mozambique. The Sambia of New Guinea, studied by Herdt (1987), and many other societies use painful or exhausting ordeals to alter the psychobiological state. This induction of an altered state of consciousness is usually followed by the revelation of important teachings, secrets, and warnings.

The Native American Church follows this cross-cultural pattern of psychobiologically assisted intergenerational education or socialization. During the ritual, prayers are often spoken that are primarily aimed at influencing young people, especially concerning their behavior and well-being. Most prominent are the moral lectures given in the morning, immediately after the all-night ritual. The Comanche chief and early Native American Church missionary Quanah Parker is reported to have lectured young people in the morning after Peyote Meetings. Sometimes stories or jokes are told that have a moral message. In one of the few descriptions of Peyotist socialization in the literature, LaBarre writes,

Old men often lecture younger members on behavior at this time, "preaching" directly to a relative, and more indirectly to others. When he has finished another old man may exhort: "You must do as that old man has said. He's had experience. What he's telling you is good." ... Polonian obviousness is usually the note in these harangues (sit up straight and keep awake in meetings, wear clean clothes and bathe before coming, wear a blanket, keep your mind on good things in the ceremony, don't look around the tipi, don't drink whiskey, don't lie to your wife or show off, but pray for your wife and children, respect old people, humble yourself, go home again if you come to a crowded meeting)— but occasionally specific admonitions are made. (LaBarre 1989 [1938], 52)

Why are psychobiologically assisted forms of education prevalent in world cultures? They generally reflect a cultural need to enhance the delivery of certain messages, such as messages intended to aid the survival of individuals, to facilitate transition of an individual between social roles, or to preserve social harmony. Central concerns of Native American Church socialization are that children do not consume alcohol or other illicit substances, are kind and respectful to others, and take care of their families. All of these concerns relate to social harmony, and the first relates to personal survival. Modification of psychobiology before the presentation of educational messages is likely done for many reasons. We need look no further than the use of Ritalin in mainstream American culture to find evidence that drugs are used to focus attention to facilitate education. In addition to focusing or "grabbing" the attention of young people, certain modified states of consciousness, such as those induced with psychedelics, are associated with increased states of suggestibility (Sjoberg and Hollister 1965). From this perspective, post-consciousness modification teachings are like hypnotic suggestions. Still another mechanism by which modified psychobiological states facilitate education or socialization is their ability to stimulate highly personal religious experiences that nevertheless reflect cultural values.

Visions and other forms of religious experience are believed to have educational value in the Native American Church. They make a unique impact on church members, given their mystical interpretation as lessons (recall *Ruth's comparison of visions with "Aesop's fables" in the previous chapter). Peyotists typically characterize Peyote as a teacher or as a conduit for God's teachings. When I asked members about the Native American Church, I would often be told that to learn anything about the tradition, one has to ingest the sacrament and learn directly from Peyote. One of Aberle's (1991 [1966], 388) Peyotist consultants stated, "Through the Native American Church we don't say to live this way, do this, know this, we let the medicine do it." This statement supports my argument about panoptical socialization, superego development, and internal forms of social control. Another of Aberle's consultants described the teachings of Peyote as follows:

> [M]y mind said, "You've got to think straight and smooth if you really want to believe the medicine and God; you've got to be clean." And the chief peyote started to talk to me: "Put away the bad things." It told me what I did. I didn't know what to say. (Peyotist interviewed in Aberle 1991 [1966], 159)

The Native American Church and Formal Education

The previous sections of this chapter have described some of the supportive roles that ceremonial Peyote use plays in parenting and early childhood socialization. This supportive role also extends throughout the school years. There is, in fact, a special type of Peyote Ceremony among the Navajos called an Education Meeting, called specifically to support the education of students. I collected several accounts of these meetings, as well as attending one. According to *Ruth,

> All along, when I was in school my dad used to have all these prayer services for me so that I could get an education. And I just went along with it because I didn't really understand. . . . [Now] I feel strongly that it did help me because every year in August or September we'd have an education meeting—even when I was in grade school and high school. And we just went along with it. Our priority was to get an education. And so when I was in college my freshman year, I guess like everybody else we didn't know what independence was. We experienced all that and I partied my first semester and got bad grades. But toward the end of my first semester, I began my second semester, and I thought about the prayer services that were being done for me. And so I decided to turn my life around because of that strong bond with my parents.
>
> JC: So you were able to remember back to those meetings?
>
> *Ruth: Yes. Those ideals and morals that they taught us. You could hear all the words of wisdom that the elders spoke about. And I really didn't understand at the time but it came through.

A Peyotist student living away from the reservation to attend college described the impact of ceremonies as follows:

> I was away for four years of high school and then went directly to college. And I just basically went away. And distance has made it hard to be able to participate as much as I wanted to. But whenever I did go in, it was like a cleansing time for me because I've been away for too long. And it was a time for me to be able to regather my thoughts. Get my mind in focus again. Like starting all over—a clean slate—because I just feel so rejuvenated. I think what it has done for me every time, my belief in the religion itself is so strong because I have experienced how it feels being away from home and going back and going into a meeting. It just makes me feel like I wasn't that far. I wasn't as far as I thought I was from home. It kind of brings me back. (*Florence)

I interviewed this student's mother and she stated proudly that whenever her daughter runs into difficulty, she goes back to the Native American Church: "She goes back to the Medicine, she goes back to tobacco. It seems like that's her strength." Several other consultants mentioned that Peyote had helped them throughout their school years.

Adult Development in the Native American Church

In adulthood, Peyote guides Native American Church members in the areas of higher education, career development, marriage, giving birth, parenthood, health maintenance, sobriety, major life transitions, and religious salvation or redemption. This is true of both later converts and those raised in the religion. According to one young man who converted to the Native American Church in early adulthood,

> I wasn't there to see, hallucinate, or to see visions like people sometimes that go there. I wasn't looking for that. I was looking for something to mature in my sobriety. I was looking for that spirituality part. I was looking for that strength, the values and how I could become a better person. Just like guidelines in the Bible. (*Henry)

As with child development, adult participants learn from each other, as well as from Peyote. They benefit from the supportive environment and expressions of kinship. Between healing experiences and experiences of mystical communication or insight, there is a gradual accumulation of wisdom from the words and experiences of others:

> I was taught a little about it—not really in detail, just little things would come in each church service. So I learned a little about it. But then I learned a lot while I was going along from other people—their experiences and their teachings—because everybody has teachings to give each other. And they respect you and they treat you like their own child. So that's the good thing about it. (*Mary)

This woman went on to describe how the church helped her establish a functional marriage, a career, and a home:

> I had always prayed for a person to marry that was a certain way: that believed in my religion, that respected me as a woman, that was very understanding and worked for us and provided for us. And that's the person I married—everything I wanted was what I have now. And my job I got through my prayers, my home, everything I have now is through my Church. (*Mary)

According to another female member, her participation taught her to see that there are many challenges in life but that Peyote would help her through them:

> I always think back to the Medicine. When I fall down, I make a mistake, I think back to the Medicine and think, "OK. What are you trying to teach me today?" or "Why did you put this in front of me?" (*Gladys)

*Gladys went on to describe her daughter and her daughter's boyfriend, who she said comes from "a very good NAC family," and how both families support them as a young couple. Here it is obvious that older adults mentor young adults in the Native American Church:

> The way I feel about NAC and the way the guy's parents feel about NAC, we give them the guidance and tell them that you know where your answers are. You know the teachings, you know the values that you need to make the moves that you want to make in

life. I've come to realize my goal in life is to reach out to the next generation. At least it won't be so dysfunctional, they won't have to go through so much hardship. Life will be a lot easier for them as far as knowing that there is a higher power out there that's there watching over them.... [W]hat I'm beginning to see now is that my nieces and nephews are reaching out—asking Auntie can you help me with this problem? It seems like they're more than willing to listen, more than willing to learn. It seems like that's where my future is heading as far as the purpose of my life. (*Gladys)

By the end, this passage hints at the role of elder, which is a much venerated role among the Navajos.

Peyotist Attitudes toward Death and the Afterlife

Both traditionalist Navajos and members of the Native American Church seem to greatly value a life lived well and ending in old age. However, the ways in which Navajo members of the Native American Church talk about death and relate to the dead contrast with the pattern of traditional Navajo culture. Traditional Navajo burial practices involve rapid disposal of the body with a minimum of ceremony and efforts to avoid contact with the chʼįįdii, a spiritual component of the dead person (often translated with the word "ghost") believed to cause illness or misfortune. If a person died at home, the house was abandoned or destroyed (Levy 1978). In contrast, Navajo Peyotists I interviewed mentioned seeing visions of the spirits of the departed in ceremony that were not disturbing to them. Many participants encounter their own death in ritual experiences, such as Hoskie's discussed in the previous chapter, and death has a role in the symbolism of the Peyote Ceremony. A different relationship with death is also expressed in Peyotist burial practices, in which the body may even be buried close to the house. Aberle (1991 [1966], 217) wrote that, while this practice was a matter of concern for traditionalist Navajos, it was a matter of pride for members of the Native American Church.

Understandings concerning an afterlife varied among the Native American Church members I knew. Hoskie told me that he still had not found an answer to the question of an afterlife. However, a discussion with *Adam revealed an interesting teaching:

My Dad...used to tell me...and like—my grandpa. When we go inside the Peyote Meeting, we like have a half moon like this and...they have the fire here.... Here would be the altar...and here would be the fire...and the wood like this. And where the fire is at, they say that there's another moon on that side...[a]nd another fire. That makes a whole full moon like this. This is reality [the visible moon altar] and this is the spiritual [a mirror image of the altar,' completing a circle]...that makes a full moon. And this side is the people that have gone beyond...like, passed on.... [I]t shows you there's like a freeway...running with the moon too, clock-wise....There's this one [he sketches a semicircle in the air]...but there's this one that's just like this [he completes the circle]. This one has a whole bunch of lanes...and this one is like real hard....They say we don't know how long we're going to live here on earth— Mother Earth...but life don't end—it continues for us. After we leave, our body goes to the ground but our spirit goes up.

*Adam's discussion of the mirror crescent moons was a revelation to me as a student of Peyotist iconography. It revealed the presence of the sacred circle symbol of Native Americans discussed by Geertz (1973, 128) as "a natural form with a moral import." It also suggested the existence of conceptions of the afterlife and/or reincarnation for certain Native American Church members.

Appreciating a Unique Form of Family Life and Human Development

This chapter has examined the Native American Church from the perspectives of socialization and human development in the context of Peyotist families. The Native American Church has become a multigenerational tradition and has developed unique approaches to socialization and the life course. We now have multigenerational Peyotist families and we can study how the religion is acquired by children and adults, what the salient family values and parental goals are, and the role of ritual experiences in Peyotist childhood and development. A human development perspective enlightens the literature on the Native American Church and such ethnographic research broadens our understanding of socialization and human development across cultures.

In procedures of socialization, some societies resemble modern Euro-American society in that they rely heavily on verbal education. Other societies, however, rely on ritual-based forms of socialization, often including altered psychobiological states. This chapter has outlined several distinctive approaches characteristic of Navajo Peyotist socialization. Among the Navajo Native American Church families I have studied, ritual Peyote use is a cherished family value. Children are typically encouraged to participate in family rituals at whatever age they become interested in doing so. They are not forced, however, and only a small dose of Peyote is typically used initially. Many Navajos raised in Peyotist families had their first taste of Peyote when they were as young as five or even three years old. Peyote use pervades family life and development. There is thus a "moral model" of drug use operating in the Native American Church that contrasts strongly with the moral model of the dominant Euro-American culture but that, nevertheless, results in well-adjusted and productive adults.

In the Native American Church, socialization and education are psychobiologically assisted and supported by ritual. This approach allows society to focus the attention of children on important messages. In addition, use of Peyote likely alters suggestibility and often stimulates visions and other numinous religious experiences. These experiences tend to be culturally structured and congruent with Peyotist values. The Native American Church also supports students in formal education through Education Meetings.

As with the Gusii studied by LeVine and colleagues (1996), Native American Church socialization has a safety/survival focus. If socialization is successful in installing the gaze of the omniscient Peyote Spirit in the consciousness of the child, this spiritual guardian will help the child avoid the risks associated with alcoholism, drug abuse, driving while intoxicated, and other risky behaviors. In addition, through participating in the Native American Church, children are frequently exposed to role modeling by adults of controlled, prosocial use of substances within a sacred context. They learn to relate to psychoactive plants as beings that are to be respected and not misused. The Native American Church continues to provide guidance through the school years and into adulthood, supporting stable careers, marriages, parenting, elderhood, and a relationship with death.

8

Postcolonial Hybridity
and Ritual Bureaucracy
in New Mexico

PARTICIPANT OBSERVATION IN A NAVAJO
PEYOTIST HEALER'S CLINICAL PROGRAM

AS PART OF my ethnographic research among the Navajos, in addition to more traditional field activities of interviewing and participating
in community life and community rituals, I spent a full year providing
clinical services at a treatment program for Native American adolescents
with severe substance abuse and mental health problems. I will refer to
the facility at which I worked using the pseudonym "Navajo Adolescent
Treatment Center." This federally funded treatment facility was run by a
Peyotist healer and a clinical psychologist and administered by the Navajo
tribe. At the time I worked there, the facility was accredited by the Joint
Commission on Accreditation of Healthcare Organizations (JCAHO) to
treat substance abuse and associated mental disorders.

This position allowed me to do participant observation from a vantage point similar to that of Alfred Smith, the Peyotist substance abuse
counselor whose termination triggered the *Smith* case.[1] It also allowed
me to work alongside Native American clinicians and to observe how
the Peyote Ceremony is used in federally funded clinical settings as an
intervention recognized and coded by the US Indian Health Service.
As mentioned earlier, Kunitz and Levy (1994, 202) documented the
Indian Health Service's recognition of the Peyote Ceremony in the list
of "client service codes" used for reporting provision of services to the
Indian Health Service (which enables reimbursement). The entry for
Native American Church treatment specifies "Participation in Native
American Church Ceremonies...conducted primarily for the purpose

of treating persons with alcohol and drug problems" as a reimbursable category of treatment.

As the code description suggests, not only is the Peyote Ceremony of the Native American Church recognized and accepted as a treatment for alcohol and drug problems by the US government's Indian Health Service, but also it has been bureaucratized and subjected to quality control (perhaps the most convincing proof of its acceptance by the US health care system). The code specified that the Road Man conducting the ceremony be "recommended by a local NAC chapter." Thus, there is a method of clinical privileging at this level. The CEO of the Navajo clinical program at which I worked (Hoskie, whom I have previously mentioned) explained the clinical privileging process for practitioners of ceremonial treatment at his facility as follows:

> We wanted to make sure those who did it [ritual treatment] knew how to do it within a treatment concept. Remember what we were talking about earlier, about the blaming [a reference to witchcraft accusations]—that sometimes you get somebody who helps the client to do more blaming rather than self-responsibility? That can happen in NAC. That can happen in sweats. If we have somebody who is a Sweat Lodge leader who is still using alcohol or drugs and they might be running Sweat Lodges, they could unravel everything....If somebody is going to provide a ceremony, they need to know what they're doing. We go through a clinical privileging process. Dave and I and Mark are the only ones authorized to run sweats—because we've proven it through documentation that we've been given the authority to do that. Now, you have others that may be knowledgeable about that but if they don't have the clinical privileging to do it, they don't do it. If somebody decides that they want to get their fan out, and their whistle, and their cedar and do a ceremony for a client, then if they don't have the clinical privilege they're in violation of the therapeutic process....That's just like if you don't have the training and background to do families [family therapy], then you don't do families.

The previous chapters have described the traditional contexts of the Native American Church in Native American families, communities, and religious life. However, as the Native American Church has become established as a religious tradition in the United States, it has moved into new contexts as well. My work adds another dimension to studies of the Native American Church by documenting the clinical use of the Native American Church in treatment programs serving Native American communities. This chapter will focus on describing the Navajo treatment facility at which I worked. It is thus a clinical ethnography within a clinical ethnography.

Working at Hoskie's Clinical Program

The Navajo Adolescent Treatment Center was a twenty-four-bed, sixty-day residential treatment program for Native American youths, male and female, between the ages of twelve and nineteen years old. It opened in 1989. Patients were referred from courts, schools, social services, and families, with some self-referrals as well. The patients came not only from the Navajo Nation but also from many other Native American tribes both near and far. This program provided substance abuse treatment and education; individual, group, and family counseling and psychotherapy; assessment and evaluation; and aftercare/recovery planning.

The Navajo Adolescent Treatment Center incorporated modern clinical, traditional tribal, contemporary intertribal, Christian, Native American Church, and other traditions of intervention (e.g., Alcoholics Anonymous) into an approach that was responsive to the unique backgrounds and individual needs of particular clients. There were five Medicine People on staff, representing the perspectives of traditional Navajo religion, the Native American Church, Lakota-influenced intertribal spirituality, and the Sun Dance. Traditions incorporated into treatment at the center included the Sweat Lodge, talking circles, traditional storytelling, powwow drumming and singing, tipi building, and Christian teachings. With the proper parental permissions, clients were also taken off-grounds to attend traditional Navajo healing ceremonies, Christian church meetings, or Peyote Ceremonies. The program's brochure describes their combination of traditional cultural and standard clinical approaches as follows:

> In addition to the traditional western therapeutic approach, services rendered include the integration of Native American cultural activities to meet relevant cultural needs of the target population being served. These cultural activities promote enhancement of self-identity as a Native American, and also promote knowledge of basic cultural values for establishing self harmony.

The emphasis seemed to be on using what works in particular tribal traditions while avoiding what seems to cause problems. For example, treatment tended to reinforce self-reliance and questioning of one's own actions rather than blaming others. It thus de-emphasized certain traditional reactions to illness that involve witchcraft accusations. Kluckhohn's (1944) functionalist analysis notwithstanding, I would argue that witchcraft is an aspect of traditional cultures that is often very dysfunctional in its results. Hoskie described the importance of culturally relevant treatment with Navajo clients as follows:

> The Navajo Nation at that time didn't have its own rehab program. The states were providing services to the Navajo. Then they said, hey we have a unique population here. The Navajo Nation said we want to form our own rehab program. And based on that we went on to develop a culture-relevant program...which includes our own people to provide the service because a lot of Navajo won't talk to a non-Navajo about their ceremonial needs. And it came back to that spiritual thing. Like when I went through the whole rehab process due to my vision loss, I had an Anglo counselor and there's no way I would talk to him about my usage of Native American Church and the use of Peyote because he would say, "What? You're taking drugs? No wonder you can't see!" All this kind of stuff, so....Now, if he knew that, maybe he would have been able to support me a little bit more. So yes I can talk to him but he's not giving me culture-relevant services.

The clinician working among the Navajos should be aware of several aspects of the local culture that can affect the therapeutic relationship. An interesting list of these aspects was put together by the Navajo Area Indian Health Service (2003). I will mention a few of the most relevant. Direct eye contact is typically avoided in Navajo culture. Thus, a lack of eye contact should not be misinterpreted as disinterest or inattention. Handshakes involve a touching of the hands rather than a firm gripping. Many Navajos still point directionally with their lips (which can surprise the uninformed) and do not point with their fingers. A Navajo may arrive for health care with their skin blackened with charcoal, which indicates that they have recently had a traditional ceremony performed for them. In addition, many Navajos believe that "stating something may happen in the future (potential complications including death for example) will cause the event to occur" (Navajo Area Indian Health Service 2003).

The Navajo concept of well-being is a spiritually based concept in which physical, psychological, and social health depend upon spiritual harmony or balance. This holistic view of health, which does not separate the mental from the physical in the same way as modern medicine, is typical of many nonindustrial cultures. Spiritual harmony is called *hózhǫ́* in the Navajo language and the concept occupies a central position in Navajo religious beliefs (Kluckhohn 1949). If this harmony is upset, the spirit is put into a vulnerable state. This spiritual imbalance may result in health problems as Hoskie indicated: "Your mind gets tired, your spirit gets tired. When your mind gets tired and your spirit gets tired it affects your body." When the spirit is strengthened, or the spiritual problem is remedied, physical problems may be alleviated. Navajos classify illness by its supernatural cause rather than by its symptoms (Levy, Neutra, and Parker 1987, 3). Harmony may be upset by violation of a taboo, such as coming into contact with the location of a lightning strike or a death. Navajos refer to this class of things as *báhádzid*, "dangerous to do."

Harmony may also be upset by the power of evil thoughts, as studies of Navajo witchcraft concepts and mythology demonstrate. In a legend described by Gladys Reichard (1950), the mythological character First Woman threatens, "When I think, something bad will happen. People will become ill. Coyote will know [and presumably carry out] all my thoughts." In Reichard's opinion, the main cause of illness for Navajos is not the presence of germs but the absence of a positive psychological state: "Fear, the primary cause of illness, is established, confidence undermined. Fear may be combated by a power who will stand up to it, refuse to abandon courage. By turning inward, using one's own powers, one may find the strength to overcome evil" (1950, 106). Therefore, when we are dealing with traditional Navajo theories of healing, we must be aware that what is really being treated is the spiritual or psychological imbalance.

The Navajo Adolescent Treatment Center was mostly federally funded (via the Indian Health Service) but also received some Medicaid support. Given the program's use of evidence-based treatment approaches, such as a level system, coping skills training, and relapse prevention, as well as the fact that research studies support the efficacy of bicultural competence approaches (LaFromboise and Rowe 1983), gaining access to Medicaid and Medicare funding became a goal. One way Hoskie's program pursued this goal was through the implementation of a user-friendly computer-based clinical information management system created by the company Accurate Assessments. This system tracked clinicians' billable hours for Medicaid and Medicare services, tracked clients' response to treatment and the need for additional services, and supported reporting requirements and outcome-based treatment. I found this system to be more sophisticated than the systems at my other training sites, including the University of Chicago Hospitals. As Hoskie stated in an interview for the American Indian newspaper *Indian Country Today*, "We're going to help Indian tribes access Medicare dollars that they didn't know they could get because they didn't have an evidence-based treatment model" (Ross 2003).

According to Hoskie, Navajos were sometimes able to take time off work for ceremonies, and sometimes these rituals were covered by insurance. This reveals the local acceptance of traditional forms of intervention and the growing recognition of the importance of culturally relevant treatment more generally. At his previous place of employment, Hoskie said that they allowed illness time off for ceremonies. However, he said, "It had to be: how's your illness impacting your ability to do your job. It can't be just a blessing ceremony." Hoskie also reported that at his brother's place of employment, "they do insurance coverage on ceremonies. Matter of fact, I helped them put that together, I served on the panel.... People do it within their own arena of operation."

Hoskie and his clinical director reported that, prior to the implementation of their bicultural approach incorporating Native American traditions, just 54 percent of the adolescent clients completed the two-month program. However, following the introduction of the bicultural approach, the graduation rate was consistently 80 percent or above. In addition, prior to the bicultural program, only one-third of the parents of these adolescents supported their children by visiting the facility. After the bicultural approach was implemented, this number doubled and, by 2001, had reached 92 percent (Ross 2003).

A typical weekly schedule at the time I was at this facility is summarized as follows. Clients woke up early for a morning run or exercise, followed by a shower and breakfast. Clinical staff met for a staffing meeting at 8 AM. There was an all-community group on Mondays from 9:30 to 11 AM. Then there were psychoeducational groups on topics such as substance abuse, child abuse, or domestic violence. There were also hours devoted to the Education Lab, my psychotherapy group, Adventure-Based Counseling,

AA meetings, individual counseling, or various therapeutic assignments. I also met weekly with the clinical director, a licensed clinical psychologist, for individual supervision. On weekends, clients could go to church, other rituals, or other approved activities.

At the treatment center, what I would describe as a loving and supportive spiritual milieu was created through a focus on shared therapeutic goals, kinship-related terms of address, and other practices that reduced the separation between staff and clients, in line with psychiatric rehabilitation and psychosocial clubhouse perspectives, as well as the Navajo kinship ideology of *k'é*. Reflecting *k'é*, I heard staff at the center address even the housekeeper as *shimá* ("my mother"). I often had the thought that many janitorial workers at Euro-American hospitals would love to be treated with as much kindness. Rituals were used to maintain or reestablish harmony in both clients and staff. For example, a smoking ceremony (involving ritual use of tobacco) for staff was called when the Anglo nurse at the facility was thrown off her horse and injured.

There was a level system, which is a typical behavior modification technique in Euro-American clinical approaches. Clients were encouraged to progress up the level system by exhibiting appropriate behavior and engaging in treatment. Clients could advance through bear, buffalo, and eagle levels. These levels were associated with increasing privileges. An honoring ceremony was held for clients advancing to the next level, which was positive reinforcement for the advancing clients and a motivation builder for the other clients. If clients became violent, they were isolated in a room called the "Seventh Direction Room" until they were stabilized to the point that they were able to return to the group. To explain the concept of "Seventh Direction," which refers to self-reflection or introspection, the first six directions are north, south, east, west, up, and down. The Seventh Direction is "inward."

Cases at this facility tended to be very severe. There were cases of severe alcohol addiction, high-risk abuse of inhalants and crystal methamphetamine, histories of physical and sexual abuse, and violent acting out. Approximately 80 percent of the clients had an identifiable mental health disorder in addition to a substance abuse problem. I encountered adolescents with self-cutting behaviors characteristic of borderline personality disorder and suicide attempts. In many of the clinical cases I worked with, the substance abuse behaviors were so severe and rational discussion of costs and benefits so ineffective that it was no stretch of the imagination to think that an impressive ritual intervention might be the only kind of thing that would have any impact. This clinical work revealed the usefulness of native methods in this context and sometimes revealed the irrelevance of many Euro-American approaches that were said to be "empirically validated" (e.g., the traditional one-to-one therapy hour, rational discussion and cost/benefit analysis, expectations of self-disclosure to a professional stranger, etc.).

Parents specified which forms of spiritual intervention their child could attend on an intake document called the Consent Form for Spiritual Participation. During the first week of my clinical work at the treatment center, I was reviewing the intake evaluation forms and found this form. It asked the parent to identify which spiritual options their child could be exposed to from the following list: NAC, Traditional Navajo Practices/ Ceremonies, Sweat Lodge, or "Christian Domination, please specify." I realized immediately what a beautiful Freudian slip I had encountered: instead of "Christian Denomination," it said "Christian Domination!" I brought this to the attention of the clinical director, who had the form revised immediately.

I asked one of the clinical staff if there had been any objections to the use of spirituality in treatment. He said not to the general philosophy. But there were sometimes disagreements on the specific implementation of the general philosophy, given the particular beliefs of the members of the governing body or staff. Some examples of reactions he gave are as follows: "Well, but I'm born again I don't believe in that stuff" or "Well I'm from the Mohawk tribe and we don't do that stuff in the east." Hoskie pointed out that people who had problems with the treatment center's use of spirituality simply did not know the mainstream approaches of the addiction field (e.g., Alcoholics Anonymous) in which a relationship with a higher power is considered essential. In addition, the use of rituals like the Sweat Lodge or Native American Church Meeting in treatment was responsive to the cultural needs that many clients already had:

> We have some on the board of directors [who ask], "So where does this Sweat Lodge have a place in recovery and rehabilitation?" They can't put it together. Then we have those that say, "Well, we're supposed to be certain Navajos and we're not supposed to do intertribal sweats." Then we have those that are Christian that are saying, "How come we're letting kids go to NAC? You guys aren't pushing Christianity enough." Really that's not what we're trying to do. We're again going back to the needs of the client. If the client grew

up in NAC and wants to return back that way, that's a need that's being fulfilled (rather than us saying to them NAC's not good for you or Christianity not good for you). And people have a problem with that, because again of their particular biases rather than coming to understand the needs of the client. (Hoskie)

The Sweat Lodge

One ritual that was attended by most clients regardless of their particular tribal or religious background was the Sweat Lodge. As a counselor, I was expected to attend a weekly Sweat Lodge with my clients. These shared ordeals were effective in building a sense of community. They were definitely very effective in helping the adolescent clients to express their emotions and discuss their problems, which they usually would not do in individual therapy sessions. The material that was brought up in the Sweat Lodge and the client's level of participation was then documented in the client's chart and could be discussed later in individual sessions. Ritual leaders might also discuss what the client expressed and how he or she participated in the ritual during treatment team meetings or family meetings. Sometimes very important information was gained in a sweat or other ritual; for example, one girl reported that she had been sexually abused. Hoskie described voluntary participation in the Sweat Lodge as follows:

> All of those were signed up for sweats by their parents. The choice is theirs. They can either go into sweat or they can stay on and work on some treatment assignments. So the ones that weren't in there were working on treatment assignments and the ones that were in there, they chose to be in there. Nobody is forced. So every time we have sweats, we take a count of how many want to have sweats and if there's enough saying, "yeah, we want a sweat" then we'll do it. (Hoskie)

The weekly Sweat Lodge usually took place each Thursday at around noon, though sometimes it was held early in the morning. It lasted four or five hours. First a fire was burned to heat the "stone people" (as the large volcanic rocks used in the Sweat Lodge are called). Clients typically participated with staff in this activity, which was considered an honor, as well as a therapeutic activity. A sample progress note for this activity is given here:

Client participated in preparing the Inipi for the early morning sweat ceremony. Client prepared the eight main logs that run from east to west, and logs from south to north. Client then took the stones and placed them on the logs beginning from the east, south, west, north and the center. The remaining stones were placed counter clock-wise beginning from the east. A prayer was offered and smudging of sage took place as the client was in a state of positive thinking while preparing the Inipi.

Participants would assemble in swimsuits with towels and stand around the fire for a while. Then all would enter the lodge and the heated stones would be brought in (by the person tending the fire) and placed in the central pit with a pitchfork. This was an intertribal lodge, about eight to ten feet across. There were separate lodges, on opposite sides of the facility's grounds, for the male and female clients. The most common Sweat Lodge leaders were Hoskie, who typically sang Peyote songs, and Dave, a Lakota Medicine Man and Sun Dancer, who often sang Sun Dance songs. When I came to the sweat and I saw Hoskie with his eagle wing fan, I would know that it would be a very hot ceremony. Hoskie would use the eagle wing to fan the stones, causing waves of searing heat (but never more than we could take). I was a regular attendee at these sweats and sometimes wrote the progress notes. Here is a general progress note on a Sweat Lodge ritual written by Dave:

> Clients attended Sunrise Inipi ceremony that was very emotional for all that attended. Clients prayed throughout all four doors, with the first door having them develop a relationship with a personal Higher Power the everywhere spirit, then onto the next door for 7th Direction work. In the third door Grief was explored and much healing took place with all clients shedding tears and sharing the losses that made them want to numb out with chemicals and now by sharing these same losses they want healing and recovery. Fourth door was looking back at life and assessing all that we can be thankful for and develop self love and identity. Etchetu Welo Mitakuye Oyasin.

Notes specifically describing a particular client's behaviors in the ritual were also entered into charts. A few sample descriptions from charting on Sweat Lodge participation are included here to give a flavor of the sorts of things evaluated: "Did well. Struggled yet was able to stay"; "Especially emotional during the third round, focused on grief and healing through acceptance"; "Client verbalized how in the past he exhibited poor attitude but now knows he can't change the past, but just to accept it and move on for a positive future"; "Some acting out but was confronted by staff. Gave support and appeared reverent"; "Client shared he had not respected his peers the way he should. He made amends and shared that he wanted to change."

I often think of the Sweat Lodge, and, to some extent, the Peyote Ceremony, in terms of shared suffering, as well as emotional expression. Suffering together in ritual is not only a particular shared experience but also can function as a potent metaphor of our sharing of life's suffering more generally. It would seem that, when suffering ceases to be individual for the clients and becomes something that can be shared, then they will be more likely to reach out to others for support and to be supportive themselves.

Modeling of Respectful Use of Psychoactive Substances

Sweat Lodge rituals and certain other rituals were also clinically useful in that they modeled proper use of psychoactive substances. The traditional smoking of tobacco or Navajo herbal "mountain smoke" in a pipe was used in the Sweat Lodge and in smoking ceremonies, which were done in-house (at the treatment center). Traditional respectful use of Peyote could be experienced in off-grounds rituals to which clients could be taken.

A particularly revealing example of this modeling of the proper use of psychoactive substances occurred after a male resident was caught smoking a cigarette. He had gotten the cigarette from a friend on the outside who handed it to him over the fence. Two others saw him but failed to report the incident. The clinical director decided to use peers to get the troublesome individuals in line. At the community group (9:30 AM), the boys were "hot seated" in the center of the room and were made to answer for their crimes. The other residents, when asked to express their feelings about the incident, mostly registered disappointment that they had let the community down. It is true that these are ritually expected responses, but they rang true because the other residents knew the contraband might cause community-wide repercussions. The issue was also discussed in a subsequent Sweat Lodge ritual in which tobacco was smoked in the proper Indian way (in a pipe and with prayers).

This example of a culturally disvalued use of tobacco being treated by participation in a traditional ritual involving culturally valued use of tobacco (in a pipe rather than a cigarette) demonstrates that substance use is culturally mediated in divergent ways. This example also contrasts with standard Euro-American ideology, which tends to demonize the substance or the user rather than the *manner* in which the substance is used. Euro-American treatment approaches would almost never involve modeling of controlled and respectful use of a psychoactive substance. But this modeling, which would occur in many traditional contexts, is permitted in the context of a culturally relevant treatment philosophy.

Though use of certain traditional psychoactive substances was allowed, it had to be within the proper respectful frame of mind. A respectful ritual context in which the substance was treated as a being was acceptable. An unreflective, habitual use of the substance was not acceptable. For this reason, staff had to evaluate the purposes for which a client might ask for a ritual involving tobacco or mountain smoke. Hoskie described the following incident:

> One time I had a situation where three or four of the boys said we're really stressed out and we want to know if you can go into the Sweat Lodge with us and have some mountain smoke [a traditional Navajo herbal smoking mixture]. Right away I knew what they were up to. I knew they just wanted to go over there and smoke—just the addiction to cigarettes. And I said OK let's go do it then. But when I got out there, I said no—all we're going to use is sweet grass [a traditional incense]. Then their enthusiasm was lost. So you have to been kind of mature about it, insightful about it. It should complement it [treatment], move them towards their treatment plan, objective, goals.... [T]hat's what we try to tell the governing board here. It's all treatment. And some of them can't understand it. It's hard for them to understand it.

In addition to my provision of clinical services at the Navajo Adolescent Treatment Center, I was also involved in training staff at the facility and presenting training sessions to Indian Health Service staff and staff of the Navajo Nation Department of Behavioral Health. Many of the sessions for Indian Health Service staff focused on educating health care workers about the Native American Church and were done in collaboration with Hoskie, who covered the traditional spiritual perspective while I covered the anthropological perspective and research literature. For example, we presented training sessions on traditional Navajo medical and spiritual practices to the obstetrics unit at the local Indian Health Service Medical Center. There had been particular conflicts with obstetrics staff who did not know how to interpret the desire of Native American Church mothers to take Peyote before giving birth (see the discussion of this topic in the previous chapter). I also helped present case-management training sessions to the Navajo Nation Department of Behavioral Health in Tuba City, Arizona.

Many of the staff members at the treatment center were Native American Church members, but others were not. Peyote songs were sung during Sweat Lodge rituals conducted by Hoskie. There were no Peyote Ceremonies done in-house on the grounds of the facility. But off-grounds Peyote Ceremonies could be attended by clients during their treatment if the parents had checked "Native American Church" on the Consent Form for Spiritual Participation. Peyote Ceremonies could be written into treatment plans and also into aftercare plans reviewed at the patient's discharge meeting. I remember a particular discharge meeting in which a female client wept and told her mother that she had planned a Native American Church meeting as part of her aftercare and that it would really make her happy if her mother would come in (the mother had previously preferred not to participate in meetings, though she did serve food for the participants). This case illustrates one way in which a family Peyote Ceremony could provide the context for a family reconciliation that supports recovery for the adolescent client.

Reflections on Local Clinical Practice

This chapter has described my yearlong clinical placement working at a treatment facility run by a Navajo Peyotist Road Man, done as an aspect of my dialectically structured clinical ethnographic fieldwork. The relativistic understanding of the Native American use of Peyote that I developed in my first two ethnographic publications (Calabrese 1994, 1997) was further tested through my immersion in a program that exposed me to the range of drug problems experienced by Native American adolescents. During this immersion, I observed no cases of Peyote abuse among the adolescents I treated (based on their clinical histories and self-reports). Instead, this immersion revealed the clinical uses of the Peyote Ceremony and its important role in treatment programs serving Native American communities.

Integrative medicine, as exemplified in this treatment center, is often criticized within medical disciplines because the "empirically validated" medical approaches are assumed to be effective in all cases and the alternative or traditional approaches with which they are combined are assumed to be unsupported, inferior, and potentially damaging. However, at this Navajo clinical facility, given the cultural differences in models of illness and treatment and the often conflicting cultural ideologies embedded in modern psychotherapeutic approaches, the traditional ritual methods were the ones that actually appeared to be the most relevant and effective. In this situation, the undermining of traditional healing networks and a flourishing indigenous revitalization movement in favor of modern clinical techniques that have little local cultural relevance is a very real risk to indigenous mental health and community stability.

When I began working at the Navajo clinical program, I was amazed not only by the fact that rituals like the Peyote Ceremony were incorporated into federally funded and accredited health care but also by the bureaucratization of ritual healing that occurred in this process. Max Weber famously argued that the bureaucracy is a distinctive organizational structure that has become dominant in the modern world. Rather than relying on the authority of a charismatic leader, bureaucracies are rule governed and characterized by a "legal-rational" form of authority. This sort of institutional structure tends to be impersonal, predictable, standardized, and routinized. An "official" (or "bureaucrat") needs a particular form of credential, a particular sort of professional training, a particular jurisdiction, and a particular place in a chain of command. The person dealing with the bureaucrat is often said to be treated as a number rather than an individual. A beneficial aspect of this form of control is that it may result in "the leveling of social and economic differences" as everyone is supposed to be treated equally. However, as Weber (1946) warned, when fully established, bureaucracy and bureaucratic structures are among the hardest of all social structures to destroy and they may result in an "Iron Cage" of bureaucratic rationality.

This chapter demonstrates that even ritual interventions such as the Peyote Ceremony or the Sweat Lodge, which are radically different from standard Euro-American treatment modalities, can be incorporated into existing health care bureaucracies if those involved pay attention to certain issues. This situation creates a fascinating instance of postcolonial hybridity in the medical sphere in which healing rituals are coded as interventions and practitioners are credentialed to provide ritual treatments. Hoskie's clinical program skillfully dealt with religious and tribal diversity (as well as the cultural differences with mainstream Euro-American society) by using clinical paperwork such as the Consent Form for Spiritual Participation. The program conducted and documented rituals like the Sweat Lodge in such a way that they were reimbursable as group therapy. And Hoskie worked toward gaining access to Medicaid and Medicare funding through meeting accreditation requirements and implementing a sophisticated computer system that could track billable hours and produce quantitative data on clients' responses to treatment. It is certainly an interesting multicultural world when clinical progress notes done on an ancient healing ritual are being fed into a state-of-the-art computer-based clinical information management system!

However, remembering Max Weber's warnings about the Iron Cage, there is a potential danger that the incorporation of rituals into a Euro-American health care bureaucracy will alter the rituals in unexpected ways. One question is this: if sacred healing rituals like the Peyote Ceremony are bureaucratized, offered at clinical facilities that the White Man built and funds, and administered with the White Man's approval, how effective can they be as part of an indigenous effort at self-healing and the postcolonial identity formation that is often at its heart? This tension is not easy to resolve, especially given that the Supreme Court has abandoned religious freedom for minority religious traditions. It may be that more toleration will be offered for the Peyote Ceremony as a culturally appropriate treatment modality than as a sacred ritual. As such, it is possible that the movement of the Peyote Ceremony into modern clinical contexts, demonstrating its relevance within health care bureaucracies, is a necessary adaptation to a changing United States.

9

Decolonizing Our Understandings of the Normal and the Therapeutic

Although it is medicinal, yet in its use there are many superstitions, which the Holy Tribunal of the Inquisition had at times punished.

—FATHER ANDRES PEREZ DE RIBAS (1645)

THE PRIMARY INTENT of this book has been to present a case that challenges the reader's notions about the use of psychoactive plants, religious traditions, childrearing, and health practices. This book has described the Peyote Ceremony as it is used in Native American family contexts and in federally funded clinical programs for Native American patients. It has immersed the reader in descriptions of the lives of members of the Native American Church in a way that allows their unique voices to be heard and that, hopefully, facilitates empathic understanding and an opening of minds even given the centuries-old clash of cultural paradigms.

For many, hearing Native American voices can be difficult. When we allow ourselves to listen to Native Americans, and especially if we are willing to immerse ourselves in issues of Native American mental health, we often find very painful experiences. Like the children of Jewish Holocaust survivors, contemporary Native Americans have "a pervasive sense of pain from what happened to their ancestors and incomplete mourning of those losses" (Brave Heart and DeBruyn 1998, 68). However, listening to each other can be a healing process and, in addition to learning about the pain, we can learn much about the resilience of indigenous peoples, the resilience of the human spirit, practices of meaning and self-reflection, the multiplicity of the normal, and the many paths toward healing.

In the aftermath of conquest, attempted genocide, and forced acculturation, Native Americans today face health problems and social disorganization that are, compared to many other groups within the United States, uniquely severe. "Postcolonial disorders" (M-J. Good et al. 2008) has been employed as a useful term for drawing attention to the links between the sociopolitical and the personal in such contexts. This book builds on the postcolonial disorders perspective, developing a focus on postcolonial *healing* to gain a more complete and nuanced view of the postcolonial situation and the resilience of indigenous populations. This book has presented an immersive study of the practices and personal experiences of postcolonial healing in the Native American Church, which occur simultaneously at the levels of society (cultural revitalization and social reorganization) and experiences of the person (socially produced and culturally structured healing experiences). It also provides a critique of the neocolonialist view that interprets the Native American Church as a social pathology and as a mandate for intrusive intervention. In this case, ethnocentric intervention actually disrupts a hard-won mental health equilibrium for thousands of Native American people who have adjusted in their own way to the postcolonial situation.

Assessing the Clash of Cultural Paradigms

The case of the ritual use of the Peyote cactus takes us into an area of cultural conflict that has endured for centuries in North America and that stirs very strong and often diametrically opposed emotions and moral interpretations. For many Euro-Americans, thinking on this issue begins and ends when they note that their government has found Peyote to be an illegal drug. They know what thoughts and assumptions the category of "illegal drug" stirs up in their minds: criminals, often from a minority ethnic group, injecting heroin in an alley, who are not contributing to society and who may rob you for their next fix. Many will not be able to get past these ethnocentric stereotypes to see another way of life, and, given the homogenizing effect of the Euro-American concept of "drug," many will not even be able to appreciate that Peyote is a very different substance than heroin (e.g., it does not cause addiction and is not associated with criminal behavior or deaths from overdose). However, others who are more open-minded and thoughtful may find this case helpful in allowing them to interrogate their own cultural assumptions, come to terms with difficult aspects of American history, and come to understand a different society's perspective on the use of a culturally different medicine.

During my two years among the Navajos, I lived with Navajo families, attended healing ceremonies, and, as an aspect of my clinical ethnographic fieldwork, completed a year of clinical practice as a volunteer at a Navajo-run treatment program for Native American adolescents that made use of the Peyote Ceremony and other ritual modalities. The clinical component of my fieldwork revealed a fascinating instance of postcolonial hybridity in the medical sphere. It also revealed a surprising irony: the fact that the Peyote cactus (a Schedule I substance, defined by the United States as a dangerous drug without therapeutic uses) has another coding that renders the first coding meaningless. The US Indian Health Service codes the Peyote Ceremony as a valid and reimbursable therapeutic intervention for substance abuse (Kunitz and Levy 1994, 202). It is thus obvious that the Peyote Ceremony has a therapeutic use and is intimately connected with health care and recovery for thousands of people within the United States. In fact, it was standard practice at the Navajo clinical program at which I worked to write Peyote Ceremonies into treatment and aftercare plans for clients with Native American Church backgrounds and other Native Americans who were open to this form of intervention.

Given the research findings, we can see how the current Euro-American majority opinion is as two-faced as it was during the Inquisition (as exemplified in the Inquisitor quotation that opens this chapter): an acknowledgment of Peyote's therapeutic potential, now supported by an array of scientific evidence (e.g., Halpern et al. 2005; Dorrance, Janiger, and Tepliz 1975; Bergman 1971), is met with a continuing ethnocentric desire to punish its users. This pattern of policy makers being shown the truth by the careful research completed by scientists but choosing to ignore these findings in favor of their own ethnocentric pseudo-certainties is a mainstay of the War on Drugs. It is also found in President Nixon's immediate rejection of the report of the National Commission on Marihuana and Drug Abuse—a report that he himself ordered (National Commission on Marihuana and Drug Abuse 1972). This commission, which was chaired by Republican Governor Raymond Shafer and which carefully and honestly evaluated a diverse range of research findings, concluded that the potential harm of marijuana use was not great enough to justify intrusion of criminal law into the private behavior of the citizens of the United States. The commission recommended the decriminalization of marijuana. Nixon's response was to simply assume that he knew better than the experts he had commissioned to inform him. He instead called for an all-out war on marijuana users. A similar situation took place in 2009 in the United Kingdom, when British psychiatrist David Nutt, currently the Edmund J. Safra Professor of Neuropsychopharmacology and director of the Neuropsychopharmacology Unit in the Division of Brain Sciences at Imperial College London, was fired from his position as chairman of the Advisory Council on Misuse of Drugs by the home secretary Alan Johnson because Nutt maintained that illicit drugs should be classified according to the actual evidence of the harm they cause, which would rank alcohol and tobacco as much more harmful than cannabis or many psychedelics (Travis 2009).

It is the position of this book that such ethnocentric and uninformed dismissal of expert findings is no longer tolerable in a multicultural democracy and especially not in a country that refers to itself as the "Land of the Free" or in any country that claims to base its policies on rationality or science. Beyond this position, I have argued that a special ethical issue is raised by traditional indigenous forms of therapeutic intervention that can be shown to support the health and social harmony of indigenous communities and do no demonstrable harm. When faced with this situation of multiculturalism, the ethically defensible choice is not to advocate clinical imperialism and imprisonment of those who disagree. Instead, we should strive to understand the broad differences in cultural paradigms related to psychological functioning and healing. Many studies of therapeutic process across societies search for "common factors" in psychotherapeutic intervention (e.g., Frank and Frank 1993), possibly following the assumption of the psychic unity doctrine that we are all basically the same (Stocking 1982, 115–123). My analysis suggests that healing traditions may approach intervention using structurally dissimilar and philosophically opposed rather than common factors. We need to study "uncommon factors" in therapeutic intervention, including those that are unique to particular cultural traditions or groups of traditions.

The existence of these "uncommon" paths to healing, combined with the ethnocentric certainty of members of the dominant culture that their own approach is the right one universally, helps explain the cultural paradigm clash that is the focus of this book. The paradigm clash between Euro-American and Native American Peyotist traditions of psychotherapeutic intervention is profound and multifaceted. The generative sources of these contradictions are differences in very basic cultural orientations to epistemology, the person in social context, the role of spirituality in healing, and the separation or integration of mind and body. Euro-American psychotherapy derives from a cultural orientation that can be described anthropologically as individualist, positivist, rationalist, secular, and mind/body dualist. It typically emphasizes the dyadic (one-to-one) healer/patient relationship within a positivist approach that emphasizes the single patient as a source of data to be collected in isolation from the patient's social contexts, sequestered within a private office and within the standard one-hour time slot (or a fraction of this for the psychiatrist). Therapeutic change is typically characterized as a rational decision arrived at through cost/benefit analysis or weighing of evidence. There is an expectation of calm self-disclosure and rational discussion of one's deepest emotions to a professional stranger in hour-long therapy sessions in which an individualized health-facilitating narrative is collaboratively constructed by therapist and patient. In the area of psychopharmacology, a form of mind/body dualism is revealed. Euro-American society has divided into separate clinical disciplines the psychopharmacological approaches to mental health intervention (in the discipline of psychiatry) and the semiotic and behavioral approaches (in the discipline of clinical psychology). Psychiatry and psychology have become increasingly polarized and autonomous, resulting in a situation in which psychiatric medicines are administered in an extremely technical manner with little or no effort devoted to emplotting their use in a meaningful way (Calabrese 2008).

In contrast, Native American traditions of intervention, and especially the practices of Navajo members of the Native American Church, tend to be communal, focused on experiences rather than reasoning and conversation, and embedded in a system of spiritual understandings and practices. Healing may involve ecstatic experiences or hypnotic suggestions forged in a symbolically structured ritual context that may extend for many hours or days, unlike the rather limited psychotherapeutic office hour. This process involves an integrated understanding of mind and body and a more meaningfully integrated approach to psychopharmacology. Although Euro-American psychopharmacological intervention has followed a very materialist agonist/antagonist paradigm, paying the bulk of its attention to effects at the molecular level, psychopharmacological intervention in Native American rituals like the Peyote Meeting tends to follow what I have called a semiotic/reflexive paradigm. This approach emphasizes the ability of certain psychoactive plants, working in close coordination with structures of meaning and ritual behavior, to facilitate therapeutic emplotment, meaningful emotional experiences, and insight. Rather than being institutionally separated, psychopharmacology and meaning are aspects of the same intervention, and the use of psychoactive medicines is aimed at higher-order mental processes and transformative experiences rather than micromanagement of a person's mood state and level of arousal at the molecular level.

The last two paragraphs describe two very different approaches to psychiatric intervention, each making sense in its own context, given its close fit with basic cultural orientations, but making less sense when transplanted to the other context. The differences derive from particular social histories and adaptations over time to unique local contexts. The analysis presented here illustrates the complex relationship of clinical understanding and cultural ideology and contributes to critiques of biomedical hegemony and the view that the cultural other holds culturally determined and often erroneous "beliefs," whereas Euro-American clinical sciences provide "straightforward, objective depictions of the natural order" (B. Good 1994, 22).

Coming to Recognize Uncommon Paths to Healing

This book has argued that an adequate understanding of the Native American Church should simultaneously focus on interpretive processes and on embodied experiential states (as well as their interrelationships). My analysis of the Peyote Ceremony reveals a process of pharmacologically supported therapeutic emplotment permeated with metaphors of healing, rebirth, and the dawning of a new day. These symbols of spiritual transformation provide models "of and for" (Geertz 1973, 93) what Wallace (1966) called a "religious identity renewal" that support ritual healing. Another class of symbols aids the ritual process by providing a depiction of the human life span. These "self symbols" support reflexivity: the distinctive human ability to take an objective look at one's own life and at human life in the abstract. Peyote plays a crucial role in this form of intervention, operating pharmacologically to enhance suggestibility and openness to therapeutic messages and serving as a guardian spirit and pathway to divinely-inspired understanding.

The orientation to human development, kinship, and family life adopted in this book also adds an important dimension to studies of the Native American Church. Such an approach humanizes a very exoticized and stigmatized tradition and extends our understanding of the postcolonial healing effort beyond the ritual event. I found that the socialization of children in the Native American Church has a safety/survival focus aimed at avoidance of alcohol and other significant risks. If socialization is successful, the child will learn that the Peyote Spirit knows his or her activities even in the absence of parents. The Peyote Spirit will itself become a sort of omnipresent surrogate parent for the child, and this process has implications for superego development in the Native American Church. Powerful ritual experiences help instill these beliefs. Participation in the Native American Church also exposes children to public role modeling by adults of controlled, prosocial use of psychoactive substances within a sacred context. They learn to relate to psychoactive plants as beings that are to be respected and not misused. By comparison, the typical pattern of mainstream Euro-American society is complete abstinence with no training and little rational discussion, but much unsupervised experimentation, until the child is twenty-one years old, at which time the child is largely on his or her own as far as learning about proper (or improper) use of socially tolerated psychoactive substances within a completely hedonistic and secular paradigm. The substance abuse problems of the mainstream American society, especially compared to the lack of such problems in the Native American Church's ritual pattern of Peyote use, suggest that the modern approach is the irrational, primitive approach and that the fault resides not in the substances themselves but in the manner in which they are used.

The data indicate healthy outcomes of membership in the Native American Church. In his quantitative analysis, Aberle (1991 [1966], 273) found that Peyotists and non-Peyotists were indistinguishable in random samples with respect to education, employment history, education of children, plans for the education of children, or possession of material objects such as radios or cars. The psychometric study by Halpern and his colleagues at McLean Hospital/Harvard Medical School (Halpern et al. 2005) indicates that Navajos who use Peyote regularly showed no significant differences from Navajos who use no psychoactive substances on most scales and scored significantly better on two scales of the Rand Mental Health Inventory (RMHI). In fact, greater lifetime Peyote use was associated with significantly better RMHI scores on five of the nine scales including the composite Mental Health Index. So we are obviously dealing with an area of life in which difference does not imply deficiency. As for my own study, the years that I have spent studying the Native American Church have demonstrated that this tradition, rather than being detrimental to health, creativity, productivity, or a harmonious family life, in fact supports these things. I have seen many examples of functional Peyotist lives and no examples of dysfunction that I could relate to involvement with the Native American Church. Most of the Native American Church members I have come to know lead controlled, productive lives and maintain leadership roles in their communities. These have included the CEO of a federally funded and accredited treatment center, a medically trained pharmacologist, a district prosecutor, many clinicians working for the Indian Health Service or the Navajo Nation, and many well-adjusted, active elderly people (many still active at herding sheep and cattle) who have used Peyote regularly for forty or more years.

Implications

The findings of this book call into question the standard psychopharmacological understandings of the dominant Euro-American culture and expose the ideological bias and, in some cases, the cultural and political domination of the clinical sciences. Consciousness alteration is a ubiquitous human activity across cultural space and historic time, and it often plays a central role in traditions of therapeutic and educational intervention. We must learn to distinguish normal, though culturally divergent, *use* from damaging abuse. It is no longer acceptable in a democracy representing a multicultural population to simply distinguish culturally familiar Euro-American substances from substances of cultural Others and assume that the Euro-American substances are rational to use and the Other's are irrational and criminal. This is one of the last bastions of unreflective ethnocentrism in dominant clinical and social policy structures: tobacco and alcohol together kill over half a million each year (Mokdad et al. 2004), but the United States allows their mass production and mass marketing while it pursues a life-destroying zero-tolerance policy toward those who use culturally unfamiliar substances that are demonstrably harmless. The costs to society of failing to understand cultural diversity in the area of psychoactive substance use include the unjust imprisonment of over one million nonviolent Americans (Justice Policy Institute 1999), the widespread erosion of respect for laws and government due to the ethnocentrism and irrationalism of social policies, and the unnecessary destruction of often beneficial cultural traditions. To grow beyond our destructive ethnocentrism, we must adopt an anthropological viewpoint in acknowledging those substances that have the potential for safe and controlled use and that, when used properly, may actually provide mental and physical health benefits for certain groups of people.

From the anthropological perspective adopted in this book, Native American Peyote use is an example of a tradition of controlled, prosocial use of a psychoactive substance that predates Euro-American psychopharmacology, the social movements of the 1960s, and the modern drug problem by millennia but which is still, incorrectly, viewed through the lenses of these phenomena by Euro-Americans. This tradition has been subject to attacks and attempts at control by Euro-Americans since the Spanish conquest of the Aztecs (Leonard 1942) and has been at the center of contemporary politics as a result of the Supreme Court's intervention in the case of *Employment Division of Oregon v. Smith,* 494 U.S. 872 (1990). The case of the Native American Church has many significant implications for the larger context of the War on Drugs. Under the Spanish Inquisitors, traditions of Peyote use were punished because they were seen as a barrier to Christian domination of the very souls of indigenous Americans. Today, in the United States, there are many groups of people who, like the members of the Native American Church, regularly use psychoactive plants that the dominant culture criminalizes and who cause no harm to anyone yet face the cruel imprisonment at rates and durations that make a mockery of the United States' pretensions to the title "Land of the Free." Hundreds of thousands (and millions internationally) suffer the loss of their freedom and their lives due to an unscientific and ethnocentric opinion of a cultural ruling class. Why should we continue to allow this?

The findings call for a more advanced understanding of mental health and healing practices in diverse contexts, with an accompanying reflexive awareness of the cultural and ideological biases of our own clinical sciences, social sciences, and governments. The data reviewed demonstrate that systems of diagnosis and therapy, especially in the domain of mental health, often reflect the particular sensibilities and moral assumptions of their cultures of origin. In addition, unique cultural systems of normality give culturally diverse clients unique profiles of responsiveness to clinical interventions. The role of clinicians or government agencies working with such cultural differences is not to eliminate culturally different systems of psychiatric functioning and replace them with those of the dominant society. The ethical approach in multicultural democracies is to understand existing cultural differences, take them into account when providing treatment, and, whenever appropriate, support social groups in their own efforts at self-healing. Such an approach can only improve our clinical disciplines, the ethical integrity of our governments, and our anthropological understanding of the diverse forms of the normal and the therapeutic.

Notes

1. The "prairie dog" is not actually a dog. It is a burrowing rodent similar to a squirrel.
2. Byron Good (1994, 55) describes semantic networks as networks of associative meanings that link illness perceptions to fundamental cultural values and that color the interpretation of newly encountered health phenomena.
3. The word *Peyote* is capitalized in this book because, as is discussed in chapter V, Native Americans refer to it both as a medicine and as a spiritual entity. *Peyotist* is also capitalized, as is *Medicine* when it refers specifically to Peyote.
4. Therapeutic emplotment will be more completely introduced in the second chapter. As defined in this study, the term refers to interpretive activity or the application of a preformed cultural narrative that *places events into a plot structure or story* that is therapeutic, either in that it supports expectations of a positive outcome, makes illness or treatment comprehensible, discourages unhealthy behaviors, or otherwise supports health.
5. I have introduced the word *(post)colonial* and have apparently spelled it wrong, so I should describe how I am using this word. In the case of Native North Americans and many other peoples, it is clear that colonialism has not ended. So I will use the word *postcolonial* to describe the world in the aftermath of the onset of colonialism. I am not referring to "the world after the end of colonialism" because there has been no ending of colonialism in the particular context that I describe. However, I feel that it is necessary (for the purposes of the dialectical balancing of worldviews) to emphasize that, even though neither North America nor the world in general is free of colonialism, there have been advances in the areas of international human rights and indigenous self-determination that create a contrast with the age of intense colonization, genocide, and slavery. So I will use *colonialism* to refer to this latter stage and *postcolonial* to refer to the era of

more subtle domination after "high colonialism," which was characterized by the use of absolute power to enslave or destroy target populations. Sometimes I will spell the word as *(post)colonialism* as a reminder that colonialism has not ended.

6. Ritualized consciousness alteration practices are viewed by many, even by many contemporary anthropologists, as too exotic to be taken seriously. However, in view of the War on Drugs and the massive increase in imprisonment associated with it, consciousness alteration is actually one of the most focal and divisive issues of the modern world. Much contemporary anthropology tries to distance itself from the discipline's association with the study of "exotic" rituals and other "exotic" practices through an attention to "real-world problems and issues." But what if the practices that anthropologists or others find "exotic" are, for the people involved, "real-world problems and issues"? Then, through scholarly avoidance, the practices have been not only exoticized but also marginalized.

1 INTRODUCTION

1. Though many Americans would think that the Thirteenth Amendment of the US Constitution abolished slavery, the Thirteenth Amendment actually states, "Neither slavery nor involuntary servitude, except as a punishment for crime whereof the party shall have been duly convicted, shall exist within the United States" (Marion 2009, 214). This created a loophole that has allowed the forced labor of predominantly ethnic minority prisoners to contribute to the corporate profits of the expanding for-profit prison industry. Contrary to popular opinion, slavery is not dead in the United States.

2. In fact, drug policy is so dominated by ideology that use of the word *rational* in this context most often signals a critique of current policy or advocacy of a heretical intervention strategy such as the strategy of harm reduction (Zimring and Hawkins 1992; Marlatt 1998).

3. The psychologist of intelligence Robert Sternberg (2004, 325), citing Michael Cole and colleagues, opened his American Psychological Association presidential address with a similar statement on the importance of cultural context: "Behavior that in one cultural context is smart may be, in another cultural context, stupid.... Stating one's political views honestly and openly, for example, may win one the top political job, such as the presidency, in one culture and the gallows in another."

CHAPTER 4 THE UNFOLDING CULTURAL PARADIGM CLASH

1. In a similar study of the use of another psychedelic plant, Bloom and colleagues (1970) went to the Yanomamo Indians of Venezuela and found no difference in chromosomal damage between males and females despite the fact that only males participated in ceremonial use of the plant.

2. The connections between anti-drug campaigns and the corporate profit motives of alcohol, tobacco, and pharmaceutical industries were revealed in an article by Cynthia Cotts (1992) in *The Nation*. The 1991 tax returns of the Partnership for a Drug-Free America, a specialist in anti-drug advertising, list donations of $150,000 each from cigarette manufacturers RJR Reynolds and Philip Morris and beer manufacturer Anheuser-Busch, to name a few. Cotts reported that pharmaceutical companies and their beneficiaries donated at least 54 percent of the $5.8 million the Partnership took from its top twenty-five contributors from 1988 to 1991. This suggests the possibility that anti-drug campaigns are motivated, to some extent, by the desire to eliminate competition for the sellers of profitable legal drugs. The Partnership no longer accepts alcohol and tobacco money but they continue their relationship with the pharmaceutical industry.

5 MEDICINE AND SPIRIT

1. As will be described later in the book, *k'e* can be described as the Navajo kinship ethic and the concept suggests peace, kindness, and cooperation.

8 POSTCOLONIAL HYBRIDITY AND RITUAL BUREAUCRACY IN NEW MEXICO

1. Of course, the differences included the fact that I was Euro-American rather than Native American and, unlike Alfred Smith's treatment center, the Navajo Adolescent Treatment Center considered the Peyote Ceremony an important treatment option.

References

Aberle, David F. 1991 [1966]. *The Peyote Religion among the Navaho*. Chicago: University of Chicago Press.

Adams, David Wallace. 1995. *Education for Extinction: American Indians and the Boarding School Experience 1875–1928*. Lawrence: University Press of Kansas.

Adovasio, J. M., and G. F. Fry. 1976. "Prehistoric Psychotropic Drug Use in Northeastern Mexico and Trans-Pecos Texas." *Economic Botany* 30(1):94–96.

Agar, Michael H. 1977. "Drug Use and Abuse: Some Culture-Crossing Questions." *Journal of Psychedelic Drugs* 9(1):69–73.

Albaugh, Bernard J., and Philip O. Anderson. 1974. "Peyote in the Treatment of Alcoholism among American Indians." *American Journal of Psychiatry* 131:1247–1250.

Allen, Catherine J. 1988. *The Hold Life Has: Coca and Cultural Identity in an Andean Community*. Washington, DC: Smithsonian.

Altman, Irwin, and Joseph Ginat. 1996. *Polygamous Families in Contemporary Society*. New York: Cambridge University Press.

American Anthropological Association. 1993. "Notes from Washington." *Anthropology Newsletter* 34(6):47.

American Psychiatric Association (APA). 1980. *Diagnostic and Statistical Manual of Mental Disorders*, 3rd ed. Washington, DC: American Psychiatric Association.

Aronilth, Wilson Jr. 1981. "Dine's Peyote Story" (a one-page document on Aronilth and Ashley 1981). Taos, NM: Indian House Records.

Aronilth, Wilson Jr., and Hanson Ashley. 1981. *Navajo Peyote Ceremonial Songs— Volume 1* (phonograph record). Taos, NM: Indian House Records.

Averill, James. 1990. "Emotions in Relation to Systems of Behavior." In *Psychological and Biological Approaches to Emotion*, edited by Nancy L. Stein, Bennett Leventhal, and Thomas R. Trabasso, 385–404. Hillsdale, NJ: Lawrence Erlbaum.

Babcock, Barbara. 1980. "Reflexivity: Definitions and Discriminations." *Semiotica* 30(1–2):1–14.

Barkun, Michael. 1974. *Disaster and the Millennium*. New Haven: Yale University Press.

Barrett, Leonard E. 1997. *The Rastafarians*. Boston: Beacon Press.

Basseches, Michael. 1984. *Dialectical Thinking and Adult Development*. Norwood, NJ: Ablex.

Bean, Lowell, and Sylvia Vane. 1978. "Shamanism: An Introduction." In *Art of the Huichol Indians*, edited by Kathleen Berrin, 117–128. New York: Abrams.

Becker, Ernest. 1973. *The Denial of Death*. New York: Free Press.

Bedi, Gillinder, David Hyman, and Harriet de Wit. 2010. "Is Ecstasy an 'Empathogen'? Effects of +/-3,4-Methylenedioxymethamphetamine on Prosocial Feelings and Identification of Emotional States in Others." *Biological Psychiatry* 68:1134–1140.

Bell, Catherine. 2009. *Ritual: Perspectives and Dimensions*. New York: Oxford University Press.

Benedict, Ruth. 1934. "Anthropology and the Abnormal." *Journal of General Psychology* 10:59–80.

Bergman, Robert L. 1971. "Navajo Peyote Use: Its Apparent Safety." *American Journal of Psychiatry* 128:695–699.

Bloch, Maurice. 1974. "Symbols, Song, Dance, and Features of Articulation." *European Journal of Sociology* 15:55–81.

Bloom, A. D., J. V. Neel, K. W. Choi, S. Iida, and N. Chagnon. 1970. "Chromosome Aberrations among the Yanomamma Indians." *Proceedings of the National Academy of Science* 66(3):920–927.

Botsford, James, and Walter B. Echo-Hawk. 1996. "The Legal Tango: The Native American Church v. the United States of America." In *One Nation Under God: The Triumph of the Native American Church*, edited by Huston Smith and Reuben Snake, 125–142. Santa Fe, NM: Clear Light Publishers.

Bourguignon, Erika. 1973. "Introduction: A Framework for the Comparative Study of Altered States of Consciousness: An Assessment of Some Comparisons and Implications." In *Religion, Altered States of Consciousness and Social Change*, edited by Erika Bourguignon, 3–35. Columbus: Ohio State University Press.

Brave Heart, Maria Yellow Horse. 1995. *The return to the Sacred Path: Healing from Historical Trauma and Historical Unresolved Grief among the Lakotas*. Unpublished Doctoral Dissertation, Smith College: Northampton, MA.

Brave Heart, Maria Yellow Horse, and Lemyra M. DeBruyn. 1998. "The American Indian Holocaust: Healing Historical Unresolved Grief." *American Indian and Alaska Native Mental Health Research* 8(2):60–82.

Bravo, Gary, and Charles S. Grob. 1989. "Shamans, Sacraments and Psychiatrists." *Journal of Psychoactive Drugs* 21:123–128.

Breggin, Peter R. 1991. *Toxic Psychiatry*. New York: St. Martin's Press.

Briggs, Jean. 1970. *Never in Anger: Portrait of an Eskimo Family*. Cambridge, MA: Harvard University Press.

Bromberg, Walter, and Charles L. Tranter. 1943. "Peyote Intoxication: Some Psychological Aspects of the Peyote Rite." *Journal of Nervous and Mental Disease* 97(5):518–527.

Brown, Daniel P., and Erika Fromm. 1987. *Hypnosis and Behavioral Medicine.* Hillsdale, NJ: Erlbaum.

Brown, Dee. 1970. *Bury My Heart at Wounded Knee.* New York: Hold, Rinehart, and Winston.

Bruhn, Jan G., Peter A. G. M. De Smet, Hesham R. El-Seedi, and Olof Beck. 2002. "Mescaline Use for 5700 Years." *The Lancet 359*:1866.

Bruhn, Jan G., J. E. Lindgren, and Bo Holmstedt. 1978. "Peyote Alkaloids: Identification in a Prehistoric Specimen of Lophophora from Coahuila, Mexico." *Science 199*:1437–1438.

Bruner, Edward M. 1986. "Ethnography as Narrative." In *The Anthropology of Experience,* edited by Victor W. Turner and Edward M. Bruner, 139–155. Urbana: University of Illinois Press.

Bruner, Jerome. 2008. "Culture and Mind: Their Fruitful Incommensurability." *Ethos 36*(1):29–45.

Calabrese, Joseph D. 1994. "Reflexivity and Transformation Symbolism in the Navajo Peyote Meeting." *Ethos 22*(4):494–527.

———. 1997. "Spiritual Healing and Human Development in the Native American Church: Toward a Cultural Psychiatry of Peyote." *Psychoanalytic Review* 84(2):271–289.

———. 2001. "The Supreme Court versus Peyote: Consciousness Alteration, Cultural Psychiatry and the Dilemma of Contemporary Subcultures." *The Anthropology of Consciousness 12*(2):4–19.

———. 2003. "Reality and Representation in the Cultural Psychology of Childcare: Incorporating a Critical Perspective" [invited commentary]. *Culture and Psychology* 9(4):499–506.

———. 2008. "Clinical Paradigm Clashes: Ethnocentric and Political Barriers to Native American Efforts at Self-Healing." *Ethos 36*(3):334–353.

———. 2011. "'The Culture of Medicine' as Revealed in Patients' Perspectives on their Psychiatric Treatment." In *Shattering Culture: American Medicine Responds to Cultural Diversity,* edited by Mary-Jo DelVecchio Good, Ken Vickery, and Larry Park, 184–199. New York: Russell Sage Foundation.

Calabrese, Joseph D., and Patrick W. Corrigan. 2005. "Beyond Dementia Praecox: Findings from Long-Term Follow-up Studies of Schizophrenia." In *Recovery in Mental Illness: Broadening Our Understanding of Wellness,* edited by Ruth O. Ralph and Patrick W. Corrigan, 63–84. Washington, DC: American Psychological Association.

Cappendijk, Susanne L. T., and Michailo R. Dzoljic. 1993. "Inhibitory Effects of Ibogaine on Cocaine Self-Administration in Rats." *European Journal of Pharmacology 241*:261–265.

Carrasco, David. 1988. "The Hermeneutics of Conquest." *History of Religions* 28(2):151–160.

Caudill, William. 1961. "Some Problems of Transnational Communication: Japan-U.S." *Application of Psychiatric Insight to Cross-Cultural Communication* 7:409–421.

Chuchiak, John F. 2012. *The Inquisition in New Spain, 1536–1820: A Documentary History.* Baltimore: Johns Hopkins University Press.

Clifford, James. 1986. "Introduction: Partial Truths." In *Writing Culture: The Poetics and Politics of Ethnography,* edited by James Clifford and George E. Marcus, 1–26. Berkeley: University of California Press.

Cohen, Peter. 2003. "The Drug Prohibition Church and the Adventure of Reformation." *International Journal of Drug Policy* 14:213–215.

Cohler, Bertram J. 1992. "Intent and Meaning in Psychoanalysis and Cultural Study." In *New Directions in Psychological Anthropology,* edited by Theodore Schwartz, Geoffrey M. White, and Catherine A. Lutz, 269–293. Cambridge: Cambridge University Press.

———. 1999. "Sexual Orientation and Psychoanalytic Study and Intervention among Lesbians and Gay Men." *Journal of Gay and Lesbian Psychotherapy* 3(2):35–60.

Cohler, Bertram J., and Joseph D. Calabrese. 1996. "Clinical Psychoanalysis and Ethnography," unpublished manuscript, Microsoft Word file.

Colby, Benjamin. 1991. "The Japanese Tea Ceremony: Coherence Theory and Metaphor in Social Adaptation." In *Beyond Metaphor: The Theory of Tropes in Anthropology,* edited by James W. Fernandez, 244–260. Stanford: Stanford University Press.

Colby, Benjamin N., James W. Fernandez, and David B. Kronenfeld. 1981. "Toward a Convergence of Cognitive and Symbolic Anthropology." *American Ethnologist* 8(3):422–450.

Cole, Michael. 1990. "Cultural Psychology: A Once and Future Discipline?" In *Cross-Cultural Perspectives. Nebraska Symposium on Motivation, 1989,* edited by J. J. Berman, 279–335. Lincoln: University of Nebraska Press.

———. 1996. *Cultural Psychology: A Once and Future Discipline.* Cambridge, MA: Belknap.

Cook, Noble David. 1998. *Born to Die: Disease and New World Conquest, 1492–1650 (New Approaches to the Americas).* Cambridge: Cambridge University Press.

Corrigan, Patrick W., and Joseph D. Calabrese. 2001. "Practical Considerations for Cognitive Rehabilitation of People with Psychiatric Disabilities." *Rehabilitation Education* 15(2):143–153.

———. 2003. "Cognitive Therapy and Schizophrenia." In *Cognitive Therapy across the Lifespan: Evidence and Practice,* edited by Mark A. Reinecke and David A. Clark, 315–332. Cambridge: Cambridge University Press.

———. 2004. "Strategies for Assessing and Diminishing Self-Stigma." In *On the Stigma of Mental Illness: Practical Strategies for Research and Social Change,* edited by Patrick W. Corrigan, 239–256. Washington, DC: American Psychological Association.

Corrigan, Patrick W., Joseph D. Calabrese, Sarah E. Diwan, Cornelius B. Keogh, Lorraine Keck, and Carol Mussey. 2002. "Some Recovery Processes in Mutual-Help Groups for Persons with Mental Illness I: Qualitative Analysis of Program Materials and Testimonies." *Community Mental Health Journal* 38(4):287–301.

Cotts, Cynthia. 1992. " Hard Sell in the Drug War. " *The Nation* March 9.

Crapanzano, Vincent. 1986. "Hermes' Dilemma: The Masking of Subversion in Ethnographic Description." In *Writing Culture: The Poetics and Politics of Ethnography*, edited by James Clifford and George E. Marcus, 51–76. Berkeley: University of California Press.

Csordas, Thomas J. 1990. "Embodiment as a Paradigm for Anthropology." *Ethos* 18:5–47.

———. 1995. *Embodiment and Experience: The Existential Ground of Culture and Self.* Cambridge: Cambridge University Press.

———. 2002. *Body/Meaning/Healing*. New York: Palgrave Macmillan.

D'Andrade, Roy. 1995. *The Development of Cognitive Anthropology*. Cambridge: Cambridge University Press.

d'Azevedo, Warren L. 1985. *Straight with the Medicine: Narratives of Washoe Followers of the Tipi Way*. Berkeley: Heyday Books.

Deacon, Terrence W. 1997. *The Symbolic Species: The Co-Evolution of Language and the Brain*. New York: Norton.

Deren, Maya. 1970. *Divine Horsemen: The Voodoo Gods of Haiti*. New York: Delta.

Desjarlais, Robert R. 1992. "Imaginary Gardens with Real Toads." In *Body and Emotion: The Aesthetics of Illness and Healing in the Nepal Himalayas*, 3–35. Philadelphia: University of Pennsylvania Press.

Devereux, George. 1967. *From Anxiety to Method in the Behavioral Sciences*. The Hague: Mouton.

Dewey, John. 1916. *Human Nature and Experience*. New York: Holt.

Dillehay, Tom D. 1989. *Monte Verde, A Late Pleistocene Settlement in Chile, Vol. 1, Palaeoenvironment and Site Context*. Washington, DC: Smithsonian Institution Press.

Dobkin de Rios, Marlene. 1972. *Visionary Vine: Hallucinogenic Healing in the Peruvian Amazon*. Prospect Heights, IL: Waveland Press.

———. 1977. "Drug Use and Abuse in Cross Cultural Perspective." *Human Organization* 36:14–21.

Dorrance, David L., Oscar Janiger, and Raymond L. Tepliz. 1975. "Effects of Peyote on Human Chromosomes." *Journal of the American Medical Association* 234:299–302.

Dow, James. 1986. "Universal Aspects of Symbolic Healing: A Theoretical Synthesis." *American Anthropologist* 88:56–69.

Duran, Eduardo, and Bonnie Duran. 1995. *Native American Postcolonial Psychology.* Albany: State University of New York Press.

Durkheim, Emil. 1965 [1912]. *Elementary Forms of the Religious Life.* New York: Free Press.

Ewing, Katherine P. 1987. "Clinical Psychoanalysis as an Ethnographic Tool." *Ethos* 15(1):16–39.

———. 1992. "Is Psychoanalysis Relevant for Anthropology?" In *New Directions in Psychological Anthropology,* edited by Theodore Schwartz, Geoffrey M. White, and Catherine A. Lutz, 251–268. Cambridge: Cambridge University Press.

Farella, John R. 1984. *The Main Stalk: A Synthesis of Navajo Philosophy.* Tucson: University of Arizona Press.

Fernandez, James W. 1972. "Tabernanthe Iboga: Narcotic Ecstasis and the Work of the Ancestors." In *Flesh of the Gods: The Ritual Use of Hallucinogens,* edited by Peter T. Furst, 237–260. New York: Praeger.

———. 1973. "Analysis of Ritual: Metaphoric Correspondences as the Elementary Forms." *Science* 182:1366–1367.

———. 1982. *Bwiti: An Ethnography of the Religious Imagination in Africa.* Princeton: Princeton University Press.

Fogelson, Raymond D. 1965. "Psychological Theories of Windigo 'Psychosis' and a Preliminary Application of a Models Approach." In *Context and Meaning in Cultural Anthropology,* edited by Melford E. Spiro, 74–97. New York: Free Press.

———. 1979. "Person, Self, and Identity: Some Anthropological Retrospects, Circumspects, and Prospects." In *Psychosocial Theories of the Self,* edited by B. Lee, 67–109. New York: Plenum Press.

———. 1980. "Windigo Goes South: Stoneclad among the Cherokees." In *Manlike Monsters on Trial: Early Records and Modern Evidence,* edited by Marjorie M. Halpin and Michael M. Ames, 132–151. Vancouver: University of British Columbia Press.

———. 1985. "Interpretations of the American Indian Psyche: Some Historical Notes." In *The Social Contexts of American Ethnology, 1840–1984,* edited by June Helm, 4–27. Washington, DC: American Anthropological Association.

Fortes, Meyer. 1973. "On the Concept of the Person among the Tallensi." In *La Notion de Personne en Afrique Noire,* edited by G. Dieterlen, 283–319. Paris: Editions du CNRS.

Foucault, Michel. 1979. *Discipline and Punish.* New York: Vintage Books.

Frank, Jerome D., and Julia B. Frank. 1993. *Persuasion and Healing: A Comparative Study of Psychotherapy.* Baltimore: Johns Hopkins University Press.

Frohnmayer, D. 1989. *Oral Arguments in Employment Division, Oregon Department of Human Resources v. Smith, 494 U.S. 872. Audio Recording, The Oyez Project.* Evanston, IL: Northwestern University.

Gaines, Atwood D. 1982. "Cultural Definitions, Behavior and the Person in American Psychiatry." In *Cultural Conceptions of Mental Health and Therapy,* edited by Anthony J. Marsella and Geoffrey M. White, 167–192. Dordrecht: D. Reidel.

———. 1992. "Ethnopsychiatry: The Cultural Construction of Psychiatries." In *Ethnopsychiatry: The Cultural Construction of Professional and Folk Psychiatries,* edited by Atwood D. Gaines, 3–50. Albany: State University of New York Press.

Geertz, Clifford. 1973. *The Interpretation of Cultures.* New York: Basic Books.

Gellner, David. 1994. "Review of Robert Desjarlais Body and Emotion: The Aesthetics of Illness and Healing in the Nepal Himalayas (Univ. of Pennsylvania Press, 1992)." *Man (N.S.)* 29:509–510.

Gill, Merton M. 1994. *Psychoanalysis in Transition: A Personal View.* Hillsdale, NJ: Analytic Press.

Gilmore, Kim. 2000. "Slavery and Prison—Understanding the Connections." *Social Justice* 27:195–205.

Gluckman, Max. 1954. *Rituals of Rebellion in South-East Africa.* Manchester: Manchester University Press.

Gone, Joseph P. 2008. "Introduction: Mental Health Discourse as Western Cultural Proselytization." *Ethos* 36(3):310–315.

Good, Byron J. 1977. "The Heart of What's the Matter: The Semantics of Illness in Iran." *Culture, Medicine and Psychiatry* 1:25–58.

———.1992."Culture and Psychopathology: Directions for Psychiatric Anthropology." In *New Directions in Psychological Anthropology,* edited by Theodore Schwartz, Geoffrey M. White, and Catherine A. Lutz, 181–205. Cambridge: Cambridge University Press.

———. 1994. *Medicine, Rationality and Experience: An Anthropological Perspective.* Cambridge: Cambridge University Press.

Good, Byron J., Henry Herrera, Mary-Jo DelVecchio Good, and James Cooper. 1982. "Reflexivity and Countertransference in a Psychiatric Cultural Consultation Clinic." *Culture, Medicine and Psychiatry* 6:281–303.

———. 1985. "Reflexivity, Countertransference and Clinical Ethnography: A Case from a Psychiatric Cultural Consultation Clinic." In *Physicians of Western Medicine: Anthropological Approaches to Theory and Practice,* edited by Robert A. Hahn and Atwood D. Gaines, 193–221. Dordrecht: D. Reidel.

Good, Mary-Jo DelVecchio, Sandra Teresa Hyde, Sarah Pinto, and Byron J. Good, eds. 2008. *Postcolonial Disorders.* Berkeley: University of California Press.

Good, Mary-Jo Del Vecchio, Tseunetsugu Munakata, Yasuki Kobayashi, Cheryl Mattingly, and Byron J. Good. 1994. "Oncology and Narrative Time." *Social Science and Medicine* 38:855–862.

Gray, James. 2001. *Why Our Drug Laws Have Failed: A Judicial Indictment of War on Drugs.* Philadelphia: Temple University Press.

Green, Melanie C., and Timothy C. Brock. 2000. "The Role of Transportation in Persuasiveness of Public Narratives." *Journal of Personality and Social Psychology* 79(5):701–721.

———. 2002. "In the Mind's Eye: Transportation-Imagery Model of Narrative Persuasion." In *Narrative Impact: Social and Cognitive Foundations,* edited by

Melanie C. Green, Jeffrey J. Strange, and Timothy C. Brock, 315–342. Mahwah, NJ: Erlbaum.

Grinspoon, Lester, and James Bakalar. 1986. "Can Drugs Be Used to Enhance the Psychotherapeutic Process?" *American Journal of Psychotherapy* 40:393–404.

Grob, Charles S., Alicia L. Danforth, Gurpreet S. Chopra, Marycie Hagerty, Charles R. McKay, Adam L. Halberstadt, and George R. Greer. 2011. "Pilot Study of Psilocybin Treatment for Anxiety in Patients with Advanced-Stage Cancer." *Archives of General Psychiatry* 68(1):71–78.

Grob, Charles S., and Marlene Dobkin de Rios. 1994. "Hallucinogens, Managed States of Consciousness, and Adolescents: Cross-Cultural Perspectives." In *Psychological Anthropology*, edited by Philip K. Bock, 315–329. Westport, CT: Praeger.

Grof, Stanislav. 1976. *Realms of the Human Unconscious: Observations from LSD Research*. New York: E. P. Dutton.

Hall, J. L. 1886. Report of the Kiowa, Comanche, and Wichita Agency. *U.S. Bureau of Indian Affairs, Annual Report* 1886:127–132.

Hallowell, A. Irving. 1955. "The Self and Its Behavioral Environment." In *Culture and Experience*, 75–110. Philadelphia: University of Pennsylvania Press.

Halpern, John H. 1996. "The Use of Hallucinogens in the Treatment of Addiction." *Addiction Research* 4(2):177–189.

Halpern, John H., Andrea R. Sherwood, James I. Hudson, Deborah Yurgelun-Todd, and Harrison G. Pope Jr. 2005. "Psychological and Cognitive Effects of Long-Term Peyote Use among Native Americans." *Biological Psychiatry* 58:624–631.

Harner, Michael. 1980. *The Way of the Shaman*. San Francisco: Harper and Row.

Herdt, Gilbert. 1987. *The Sambia: Ritual and Gender in New Guinea*. New York: Holt, Rinehart and Winston.

———. 1990. "Sambia Nosebleeding Rites and Male Proximity to Women." In *Cultural Psychology: Essays in Comparative Human Development*, edited by James W. Stigler, Richard A. Shweder, and Gilbert Herdt, 366–400. Cambridge: Cambridge University Press.

Herdt, Gilbert, and Robert Stoller. 1990. *Intimate Communications: Erotics and the Study of Culture*. New York: Columbia University Press.

Hollan, Douglas. 1988. "Staying 'Cool' in Toraja: Informal Strategies for the Management of Anger and Hostility in a Nonviolent Society." *Ethos* 16:52–71.

———. 1992. "Cross-Cultural Differences in the Self." *Journal of Anthropological Research* 48(4):283–300.

Human Rights Watch. 2003. "Incarcerated America." http://www.hrw.org/legacy/backgrounder/usa/incarceration/.

Indian Health Service. 2004. "Trends in Indian Health." http://www.ihs.gov/NonMedicalPrograms/IHS_stats/files/Trends_02–03_Entire%20Book%20(508).pdf.

International Centre for Prison Studies. 2012. "World Prison Brief." http://www.prisonstudies.org.

Iser, Wolfgang. 1978. *The Act of Reading. A Theory of Aesthetic Response*. Baltimore: Johns Hopkins University Press.

Jahoda, Gustav. 1993. *Crossroads between Culture and Mind*. Cambridge, MA: Harvard University Press.

James, William. 1958 [1902]. *The Varieties of Religious Experience*. New York: New American Library.

Justice Policy Institute. 1999. "America's One Million Nonviolent Prisoners." Washington, DC: Justice Policy Institute. http://www.justicepolicy.org/research/2070.

Kirmayer, Laurence J. 1989. "Cultural Variations in the Response to Psychiatric Disorders and Emotional Distress." *Social Science and Medicine* 29(3):327–339.

———. 1994. "Is the Concept of Mental Disorder Culturally Relative?" In *Controversial Issues in Mental Health*, edited by S. A. Kirk and S. Einbinder, 1–20. Boston: Allyn and Bacon.

Kleinman, Arthur M. 1974. "Medicine's Symbolic Reality: On a Central Problem in the Philosophy of Medicine." *Inquiry* 16:206–213.

———. 1977. "Depression, Somatization, and the 'New Transcultural Psychiatry'." *Social Science and Medicine* 11:3–9.

Kleinman, Arthur. 1981. "Culture, Health Care Systems, and Clinical Reality." In *Patients and Healers in the Context of Culture*, 24–70. Berkeley: University of California Press.

———. 1988. *Rethinking Psychiatry: From Cultural Category to Personal Experience*. New York: Free Press.

Kleinman, Arthur, Veena Das, and Margaret Lock, eds. 1997. *Social Suffering*. Berkeley: University of California Press.

Kleinman, Arthur, and Lilias H. Sung. 1979. "Why Do Indigenous Practitioners Successfully Heal?" *Social Science and Medicine* 13B:7–26.

Kluckhohn, Clyde. 1944. "Navaho Witchcraft." *Papers of the Peabody Museum of American Archaeology and Ethnology, Harvard University* 22(2).

———. 1949. "The Philosophy of the Navajo Indians." In *Ideological Differences and World Order*, edited by F. S. C. Northrop, 356–384. New Haven: Yale University Press.

———. 1956. "Toward a Comparison of Value-Emphases in Different Cultures." In *The State of the Social Sciences*, edited by Leonard D. White, 116–132. Chicago: University of Chicago Press.

Kohut, Heinz. 1959. "Introspection, Empathy, and Psychoanalysis: An Examination between Mode of Observation and Theory." In *The Search for the Self: Selected Writings of Heinz Kohut, 1950–1978*, edited by P. Ornstein, 205–232. Madison, CT: International Universities Press.

———. 1971. *The Analysis of the Self*. New York: International Universities Press.

———. 1982. "Introspection, Empathy, and the Semi-Circle of Mental Health." *International Journal of Psychoanalysis* 63:395–407.

————. 1985. *Self Psychology and the Humanities: Reflections of a New Psychoanalytic Approach*. New York: Norton.

Kommers, Jean, and Eric Venbrux. 2008. *Cultural Styles of Knowledge Transmission: Essays in Honour of Ad Borsboom*. Amsterdam: Amsterdam University Press.

Kracke, Waud. 1979. "Dreaming in Kagwahiv: Dream Beliefs and Their Psychic Uses in an Amazonian Indian Culture." *The Psychoanalytic Study of Society* 8:119–171.

————. 1987. "Encounter with Other Cultures: Psychological and Epistemological Aspects." *Ethos* 15(1):58–81.

————. 1991. "The Self and Kagwahiv Dream Beliefs." *The Psychoanalytic Study of Society* 16:43–54.

————. 1994. "Reflections on the Savage Self: Introspection, Empathy, and Anthropology." In *The Making of Psychological Anthropology II*, edited by Marcelo Suarez-Orozco, George Spindler, and Louise Spindler, 195–222. Fort Worth: Harcourt Brace.

Kuhn, Thomas. 1970. *The Structure of Scientific Revolutions*. Chicago: University of Chicago Press.

Kunitz, Stephen J., and Jerrold E. Levy. 1994. *Drinking Careers: A Twenty-Five Year Study of Three Navajo Populations*. New Haven: Yale University Press.

LaBarre, Weston. 1939. "Note on Richard Schultes' 'The Appeal of Peyote'." *American Anthropologist* 41:340–342.

————. 1972a. "Hallucinogens and the Shamanic Origins of Religion." In *Flesh of the Gods: The Ritual Use of Hallucinogens*, edited by Peter T. Furst, 261–278. New York: Praeger.

————. 1972b. *The Ghost Dance: Origins of Religion*. New York: Dell Publishing Company.

————. 1989 [1938]. *The Peyote Cult*. Norman: University of Oklahoma Press.

LaBarre, Weston, David P. McAllester, J. S. Slotkin, Omer C. Stewart, and Sol Tax. 1951. "Statement on Peyote." *Science* 114:582–583.

LaFromboise, T. D., and W. Rowe. 1983. "Skills Training for Bicultural Competence: Rationale and Application." *Journal of Counseling Psychology* 30:589–595.

Lakoff, George, and Mark Johnson. 1980. *Metaphors We Live By*. Chicago: University of Chicago Press.

Lamphere, Louise. 1969. "Symbolic Elements of Navajo Ritual." *Southwestern Journal of Anthropology* 25:279–305.

Las Casas, Bartolomé de. 1971. *History of the Indies*, translated and edited by Andree Collard. New York: Harper and Row.

Leder, Drew. 2004. "Imprisoned Bodies: The Life-World of the Incarcerated." *Social Justice* 31:51–66.

Leonard, Irving A. 1942. "Decree Against Peyote, Mexican Inquisition, 1620." *American Anthropologist* 44:324–336.

Lévi-Strauss, Claude. 1963. "The Effectiveness of Symbols." In *Structural Anthropology*. New York: Basic Books.

LeVine, Robert A. 1982. *Culture, Behavior, and Personality*. New York: Aldine.

———. 1990. "Infant Environments in Psychoanalysis: A Cross-Cultural View." In *Cultural Psychology: Essays in Comparative Human Development*, edited by James W. Stigler, Richard A. Shweder, and Gilbert Herdt, 454–474. Cambridge: Cambridge University Press.

LeVine, Robert A., Suzanne Dixon, Sarah LeVine, Amy Richman, P. Herbert Leiderman, Constance H. Keefer, and T. Berry Brazelton. 1996. *Child Care and Culture: Lessons from Africa*. Cambridge: Cambridge University Press.

Levy, Jerrold E. 1978. "Changing Burial Practices of the Western Navajo: A Consideration of the Relationship between Attitudes and Behavior." *American Indian Quarterly* 4(4):397–405.

Levy, Jerrold E., Raymond Neutra, and Dennis Parker. 1987. *Hand Trembling, Frenzy Witchcraft, and Moth Madness: A Study of Navajo Seizure Disorders*. Tucson: University of Arizona Press.

Lewton, Elizabeth L., and Victoria Bydone. 2000. "Identity and Healing in Three Navajo Religious Traditions: Sa'ah Naagháí Bik'eh Hózho." *Medical Anthropology Quarterly* 14(4):476–497.

Lin, Keh-Ming, Michael W. Smith, and Viviana Ortiz. 2001. "Culture and Psychopharmacology." *Psychiatric Clinics of North America* 24(3):523–538.

Linehan, Marsha M. 1993. *Cognitive-Behavioral Treatment of Borderline Personality Disorder*. New York: Guilford Press.

Littlewood, Roland. 1996. "Psychiatry's Culture." *The International Journal of Social Psychiatry* 42:245–268.

———. 2001. "Psychotherapy in Cultural Contexts." *Psychiatric Clinics of North America* 24(3):507–522.

Lucy, John. 1992. *Language Diversity and Thought: A Reformulation of the Linguistic Relativity Hypothesis*. Cambridge: Cambridge University Press.

Luhrmann, Tanya M. 2000. *Of Two Minds: The Growing Disorder in American Psychiatry*. New York: Alfred A. Knopf.

MacLean, Katherine A., Matthew W Johnson, and Roland R Griffiths. 2011. "Mystical Experiences Occasioned by the Hallucinogen Psilocybin Lead to Increases in the Personality Domain of Openness." *Journal of Psychopharmacology* 25(11): 1453–1461.

Marion, Ryan S. 2009. "Prisoners for Sale: Making the Thirteenth Amendment Case against State Private Prison Contracts." *William & Mary Bill of Rights Journal* 18(1):213–247.

Marlatt, G. Alan, ed. 1998. *Harm Reduction: Pragmatic Strategies for Managing High Risk Behaviors*. New York: Guilford Press.

Mash, Deborah C., Craig A. Kovera, John Pablo, Rachel F. Tyndale, Frank D. Ervin, Izben C. Williams, Edward G. Singleton, and Manny Mayor. 2000. "Ibogaine: Complex Pharmacokinetics, Concerns for Safety, and Preliminary Efficacy Measures." *Neurobiological Mechanisms of Drugs of Abuse, Annals of the New York Academy of Sciences* 914:394–401.

Matchett, N. F. 1972. "Repeated Hallucinatory Experience as Part of the Mourning Process among Hopi Indian Women." *Psychiatry* 35:185–194.

Mattes, Merrill J. 1960. "The Enigma of Wounded Knee." *Plains Anthropologist* 5(9):1–11.

Mattingly, Cheryl. 1994. "The Concept of Therapeutic Emplotment." *Social Science and Medicine* 38(6):811–822.

McAllester, David. 1949. *Peyote Music.* New York: Viking.

McDermott, John D. 1990. "Wounded Knee: Centennial voices." *South Dakota History* 20(4):245–298.

McGinnis, J. Michael, and William H. Foege. 1993. "Actual Causes of Death in the United States." *Journal of the American Medical Association* 270:2207–2212.

Mead, George Herbert. 1934. *Mind, Self, and Society.* Chicago: University of Chicago Press.

Meichenbaum, Donald. 1996. "Stress Inoculation Training for Coping with Stressors." *The Clinical Psychologist* 49:4–7.

Menninger, Karl. 1971. "Comment." *American Journal of Psychiatry* 128(6):699.

Moerman, Daniel. 1979. "Anthropology of Symbolic Healing." *Current Anthropology* 20(1):59–80.

Mokdad, Ali H., James S. Marks, Donna F. Stroup, and Julie L. Gerberding. 2004. "Actual Causes of Death in the United States, 2000." *Journal of the American Medical Association* 291:1238–1245.

Myerhoff, Barbara G. 1976. *Peyote Hunt: The Sacred Journey of the Huichol Indians.* Ithaca, NY: Cornell University Press.

Nadelmann, Ethan A. 1988. "U.S. Drug Policy: A Bad Export." *Foreign Policy* 70:83–108.

National Commission on Marihuana and Drug Abuse. 1972. *Marihuana: A Signal of Misunderstanding.* Washington, DC: U.S. Government Printing Office.

Navajo Area Indian Health Service (NAIHS). 2003. "Cross Culture Medicine." http://www.ihs.gov/facilitiesservices/areaoffices/navajo/naihs-cross-culture-medicine.asp

Nisbett, Richard E., Kaiping Peng, Incheol Choi, and Ara Norenzayan. 2001. "Culture and Systems of Thought: Holistic vs. Analytic Cognition." *Psychological Review* 108:291–310.

Obeyesekere, Gananath. 1981. *Medusa's Hair: An Essay on Personal Symbols and Religious Experience.* Chicago: University of Chicago Press.

———. 1990. *The Work of Culture: Symbolic Transformation in Psychoanalysis and Anthropology.* Chicago: University of Chicago Press.

Opler, Morris. 1939. "A Description of a Tonkawa Peyote Meeting Held in 1902." *American Anthropologist* 41:433–439.

Ornstein, Robert, and David Sobel. 1999. *The Healing Brain.* Cambridge, MA: Malor Books.

Palgi, Phyllis, and Henry Abramovitch. 1984. "Death: A Cross-Cultural Perspective." *Annual Review of Anthropology* 13:385–417.

Perez de Ribas, Andres. 1645. *Historia de los Triumphos de Nuestra Santa Fe en los Missiones de la Provincia de Nueva Espana*. Madrid (passage cited and translated in Stewart 1987).

Perry, Mary Elizabeth, and Anne J. Cruz. 1991. *Cultural Encounters: The Impact of the Inquisition in Spain and the New World*. Berkeley: University of California Press.

Prucha, Francis Paul. 1984. *The Great Father: The United States Government and the American Indians*. Lincoln: University of Nebraska Press.

Quinn, Naomi. 1991. "The Cultural Basis of Metaphor." In *Beyond Metaphor: The Theory of Tropes in Anthropology*, edited by James W. Fernandez, 56–93. Stanford: Stanford University Press.

Radcliffe-Brown, Alfred R. 1945. "Religion and Society." *Journal of the Royal Anthropological Institute of Great Britain and Ireland* 75:33–43.

Radin, Paul. 1914. "A Sketch of the Peyote Cult of the Winnebago: A Study in Borrowing." *Journal of Religious Psychology* 7(1):1–22.

Reichard, Gladys. 1950. *Navajo Religion: A Study of Symbolism*. Princeton: Princeton University Press.

Ricoeur, Paul. 1973. "The Model of the Text: Meaningful Action Considerations as a Text." *New Literary History* 5(1):91–117.

———. 1984. *Time and Narrative*. Chicago: University of Chicago Press.

Rogers, Carl. 1957. "The Necessary and Sufficient Conditions of Therapeutic Personality Change." *Journal of Consulting Psychology* 21:95–103.

Ross, Matt. 2003. "Expertise Offered on Alcohol and Drug Treatment." Indian Country Today. http://indiancountrytodaymedianetwork.com/ictarchives/2003/12/19/expertise-offered-on-alcohol-and-drug-treatment-89726.

Sahagun, Bernardino de. 1969 [c. 1570]. *Historia General de las Cosas de Nueva Espana*. Mexico: Editorial Porrua.

Sapir, Edward. 1932. "Cultural Anthropology and Psychiatry." *Journal of Abnormal and Social Psychology* 27:229–242.

Schaefer, Stacey B., and Peter T. Furst, eds. 1997. *People of the Peyote: Huichol Indian History, Religion, and Survival*. Albuquerque: University of New Mexico Press.

Schafer, Roy. 1959. "Generative Empathy in the Treatment Situation." *Psychoanalytic Quarterly* 28(3):342–373.

Schieffelin, Edward L. 1985. "Performance and the Cultural Construction of Reality." *American Ethnologist* 12:707–724.

Schlosser, Eric. 1998. "The Prison-Industrial Complex." *The Atlantic Monthly*. http://www.theatlantic.com/magazine/archive/1998/12/the-prison-industrial-complex/4669/.

Schultes, Richard Evans. 1938. "The Appeal of Peyote as a Medicine." *American Anthropologist* 40:698–715.

———. 1972. "An Overview of Hallucinogens in the Western Hemisphere." In *Flesh of the Gods: The Ritual Use of Hallucinogens*, edited by Peter T. Furst, 3–54. New York: Praeger.

————. 1998. "Antiquity of the Use of New World Hallucinogens." *The Heffter Review of Psychedelic Research* 1:1–7.

Schultes, Richard Evans, and Albert Hofmann. 1992. *Plants of the Gods.* Rochester, VT: Healing Arts Press.

Schurr Theodore G., and Stephen T. Sherry. 2004. "Mitochondrial DNA and Y Chromosome Diversity and the Peopling of the Americas: Evolutionary and Demographic Evidence." *American Journal of Human Biology* 16:420–439.

Shore, Bradd. 1996. *Culture in Mind: Cognition, Culture, and the Problem of Meaning.* New York: Oxford University Press.

Shweder, Richard A. 1984. "Anthropology's Romantic Rebellion against the Enlightenment, or There's More to Thinking than Reason and Evidence." In *Culture Theory: Essays on Mind, Self, and Emotion,* edited by Richard A. Shweder and Robert A. LeVine, 27–66. New York: Cambridge University Press.

Shweder, Richard A., and Edmund Bourne. 1984. "Does the Concept of the Person Vary Cross-Culturally?" In *Culture Theory: Essays on Mind, Self, and Emotion,* edited by Richard A. Shweder and Robert A. LeVine, 158–199. New York: Cambridge University Press.

Shweder, Richard A., Lene Jensen, and William A. Goldstein. 1995. "Who Sleeps by Whom Revisited: A Method for Extracting the Moral Goods Implicit in Practice." *Cultural Practices as Contexts for Development* 67:21–39.

Shweder, Richard, Manamohan Mahapatra, and Joan G. Miller. 1990. "Culture and Moral Development." In *Cultural Psychology: Essays in Comparative Human Development,* edited by James W. Stigler, Richard A. Shweder, and Gilbert Herdt, 130–204. Cambridge: Cambridge University Press.

Sisko, Bob. 1994. "Remarks to the 56th Meeting of the National Institute of Health's National Advisory Council on Drug Abuse, January 26th, 1994." *MAPS* 4(4):12–14.

Sjoberg, B. M., and L. E. Hollister. 1965. "The Effects of Psychotomimetic Drugs on Primary Suggestibility." *Psychopharmacologia* 8:251–262.

Slotkin, James Sydney. 1975 [1956]. *The Peyote Religion.* New York: Octagon.

Smith, Alfred. 1996. "Response to the Supreme Court's Outlawing of Peyote." In *One Nation under God: The Triumph of the Native American Church,* edited by Huston Smith and Reuben Snake, 68. Santa Fe, NM: Clear Light Publishers.

Smith, Huston, and Reuben Snake, eds. 1996. *One Nation under God: The Triumph of the Native American Church.* Santa Fe, NM: Clear Light Publishers.

Spindler, George D., and Louise S. Spindler. 1984. *Dreamers with Power: The Menominee.* Prospect Heights, IL: Waveland Press.

Spiro, Melford E. 1965. "Religious Systems as Culturally Constituted Defense Mechanisms." In *Context and Meaning in Cultural Anthropology,* edited by Melford E. Spiro, 100–113. Glencoe, IL: Free Press.

————. 1982. "Collective Representations and Mental Representations in Religious Symbol Systems." In *On Symbols in Anthropology,* edited by J. Maquet, 45–72. Malibu, CA: Undena Publications.

Spitzer, Manfred, Markus Thimm, Leo Hermle, Petra Holzmann, Karl-Artur Kovar, Hans Heimann, Euphrosyne Gouzoulis-Mayfrank, Udo Kischka, and Frank Schneider. 1996. "Increased Activation of Indirect Semantic Associations under Psilocybin." *Biological Psychiatry* 39:1055–1057.

Stannard, David E. 1992. *American Holocaust: Columbus and the Conquest of the New World.* New York: Oxford University Press.

Sternberg, Robert J. 2004. "Culture and Intelligence." *American Psychologist* 59(5):325–338.

Stewart, Omer C. 1987. *Peyote Religion: A History.* Norman: University of Oklahoma Press.

Stigler, James W., Richard A. Shweder, and Gilbert Herdt, eds. 1990. *Cultural Psychology: Essays on Comparative Human Development.* Cambridge: Cambridge University Press.

Stocking, George W. Jr. 1982. *Race, Culture, and Evolution: Essays in the History of Anthropology.* Chicago: University of Chicago Press.

Straub, Patrick. 2009. *It Happened in South Dakota: Remarkable Events That Shaped History.* Guilford, CT: Globe Pequot Press.

Straus, Anne. 1977. "Northern Cheyenne Ethnopsychology." *Ethos* 5:326–357.

Stuart-Macadam, Patricia, and Katherine A. Dettwyler, eds. 1995. *Breastfeeding: Biocultural Perspectives.* Hawthorne, NY: Aldine de Gruyter.

Surgeon General of the U.S. Public Health Service. 2005. "Statement on Suicide Prevention among Native American Youth before the Indian Affairs Committee, U.S. Senate." http://www.hhs.gov/asl/testify/t050615.html.

Tamm, Erika, Toomas Kivisild, Maere Reidla, Mait Metspalu, David Glenn Smith, Connie J. Mulligan, Claudio M. Bravi, Olga Rickards, Cristina Martinez-Labarga, Elsa K. Khusnutdinova, Sardana A. Fedorova, Maria V. Golubenko, Vadim A. Stepanov, Marina A. Gubina, Sergey I. Zhadanov, Ludmila P. Ossipova, Larisa Damba, Mikhail I. Voevoda, Jose E. Dipierri, Richard Villems, Ripan S. Malhi, and Dee Carter. 2007. "Beringian Standstill and Spread of Native American Founders." *PLoS ONE,* 2(9): e829. doi:10.1371/journal.pone.0000829

Tanner, H. 1982. "A History of All the Dealings of the United States Government with the Sioux." Unpublished manuscript. Prepared for the Black Hills Land Claim by order of the United States Supreme Court. On file at the D'Arcy McNickle Center for the History of the American Indian, Newberry Library, Chicago.

The Lakota Times. 1990. "Wounded Knee Remembered." The Lakota Times (December, Special Edition).

Thornton, Russell. 1987. *American Indian Holocaust and Survival: A Population History since 1492.* Norman: University of Oklahoma Press.

Todorov, Tzvetan. 1984. *The Conquest of America: The Question of the Other.* New York: Harper and Row.

Travis, Alan. 2009. "Chief Drug Adviser David Nutt Sacked over Cannabis Stance." *The Guardian*. October 30, 2009. http://www.guardian.co.uk/politics/2009/oct/30/david-nutt-drugs-adviser-sacked.

Trigger, Bruce. 1991. "Early Native North American Responses to European Contact: Romantic versus Rationalistic Interpretations." *The Journal of American History* 77(4):1195–1215.

Turner, Victor W. 1967. *The Forest of Symbols: Aspects of Ndembu Ritual*. Ithaca, NY: Cornell University Press.

———. 1969. *The Ritual Process: Structure and Anti-Structure*. New York: Aldine.

———. 1985. *Dramas, Fields and Metaphors: Symbolic Action in Human Society*. Ithaca, NY: Cornell University Press.

Van Gennep, Arnold. 1960 [1909]. *The Rites of Passage*. Chicago: University of Chicago Press.

Van Tol, Lois. 2009. "I Promise I Won't." *Families, Systems, and Health* 27(2):183–187.

Voget, Fred W. 1968. "Review of the Peyote Religion among the Navaho." *American Anthropologist* 70:118–119.

Vygotsky, Lev S. 1978. *Mind in Society: The Development of Higher Psychological Processes*, edited by Michael Cole, Vera John-Steiner, Sylvia Scribner, and Ellen Souberman. Cambridge, MA: Harvard University Press.

Wacquant, Loïc. 2001. "Deadly Symbiosis: When Ghetto and Prison Meet and Mesh." *Punishment and Society* 3(1):95–134.

———. 2004. *Body and Soul: Notebooks of an Apprentice Boxer*. New York: Oxford University Press.

Wagner, Roland. 1975. "Some Pragmatic Aspects of Navajo Peyotism." *Plains Anthropologist* 20(69):197–206.

Wallace, Anthony F. C. 1956. "Revitalization Movements." *American Anthropologist* 58:264–281.

———. 1966. *Religion: An Anthropological View*. New York: Random House.

Walsh, Roger. 1990. *The Spirit of Shamanism*. Los Angeles: Jeremy Tarcher.

Weber, Max. 1946. "Bureauacracy." In *From Max Weber*, edited by Hans Gerth and C. Wright Mills, 196–244. New York: Oxford University Press.

White, Hayden. 1981. "The Value of Narrativity in the Representation of Reality." In *On Narrative*, edited by William John Thomas Mitchell, 1–24. Chicago: University of Chicago Press.

Whorf, Benjamin Lee. 1941. "The Relation of Habitual Thought and Behavior to Language." In *Language, Culture and Personality, Essays in Memory of Edward Sapir*, edited by Leslie Spier, 75–93. Menasha: Sapir Memorial Publication Fund.

Wikan, Unni. 1990. "Hidden Hearts and Bright Faces." In *Managing Turbulent Hearts: A Balinese Formula for Living*, 41–62. Chicago and London: University of Chicago Press.

Willging, Catherine E. 2002. "Clanship and K'é: The Relatedness of Clinicians and Patients in a Navajo Counseling Center." *Transcultural Psychiatry* 39(1):5–32.

Winkelman, Michael, and Thomas B. Roberts, eds. 2007. *Psychedelic Medicine: New Evidence for Hallucinogenic Substances as Treatments.* Westport, CT: Praeger.

Witherspoon, Gary. 1974. "The Central Concepts of the Navajo World View (I)." *Linguistics* 119:41–59.

———. 1975. *Navajo Kinship and Marriage.* Chicago: University of Chicago Press.

Young, Allan. 1982. "The Anthropology of Illness and Sickness." *Annual Review of Anthropology* 11:257–285.

———. 1995. *The Harmony of Illusions: Inventing Post-Traumatic Stress Disorder.* Princeton: Princeton University Press.

Zimring, Franklin E., and Gordon Hawkins. 1992. *The Search for Rational Drug Control.* Cambridge: Cambridge University Press.

Zinberg, Norman. 1984. *Drug, Set, and Setting.* New Haven: Yale University Press.

Name Index

Aberle, David F., 19, 67, 83–85, 87–88,
    92, 94, 99, 103–107, 112, 116,
    124–127, 129, 135–136, 139–140,
    143–145, 150, 155–156, 161, 168–169,
    172, 196
Adams, David Wallace, 7, 80, 90
Adovasio, J. M., 78
Agar, Michael H., 27
Albaugh, Bernard J., 20, 92, 97, 116
Anderson, Philip O., 20, 92, 97, 116
Aronilth, Wilson Jr., 104, 111,
    128–129, 136
Averill, James, 37

Babcock, Barbara, 58–59
Barkun, Michael, 83, 85
Bean, Lowell, 130
Becker, Ernest, 25
Bedi, Gillinder, 96, 138
Bell, Catherine, 121
Benedict, Ruth, 3, 15, 17
Bergman, Robert L., 19, 92–94, 192
Black Dog, 130–131
Blackmun, Justice Harry, 92
Bloch, Maurice, 35
Boas, Franz, 19
Botsford, James, 90
Bourguignon, Erika, 13, 25, 167
Brave Heart, Maria Yellow Horse,
    4, 7–9, 190
Bravo, Gary, 137

Briggs, Jean, 21
Brown, Daniel P., 118
Bruhn, Jan G., 10, 45, 78
Bruner, Edward M., 81
Bruner, Jerome, 4

Cappendijk, Susanne L. T., 95, 137
Carrasco, David, 5
Caudill, William, 71
Christ, Jesus, 4–5, 31, 98–99, 104, 114,
    136, 142–143
Clifford, James, 60
Cohen, Peter, 27, 40
Cohler, Bertram J., 18, 40, 52, 63, 65
Colby, Benjamin N., 65, 133
Cole, Michael, 4, 16, 37, 43
Collier, John, 88
Cook, Noble David, 4
Corrigan, Patrick W., 17, 34, 65, 66,
    112, 122
Crapanzano, Vincent, 54
Crashing Thunder, 109, 139
Creator, the, 14, 33, 38, 87, 102–105, 107,
    110, 130–131, 141–142, 144, 147–148,
    151, 155–156, 168–169
Csordas, Thomas J., 43, 54

D'Andrade, Roy, 38
d'Azevedo, Warren L., 105, 156
Deacon, Terrence W., 37
Deren, Maya, 55

Desjarlais, Robert R., 35, 54–57
Devereux, George, 18, 59, 61, 62
Devil, the, 6, 79, 114, 116
Dewey, John, 37, 43
De Wit, Harriet, 96, 138
Dobkin de Rios, Marlene, 13, 27, 43, 98,
   137, 152, 167
Dorrance, David L., 93, 192
Dow, James, 25, 33, 117, 121, 126
Duran, Eduardo and Bonnie, 49, 110
Durkheim, Émil, 41, 120

Echo-Hawk, Walter B., 90
Ewing, Katherine P., 52–54, 58, 63

Farella, John R., 119
Fernandez, James W., 13, 54, 56–57, 95,
   133, 137
Fogelson, Raymond D., 16, 21, 39, 43,
   101
Fortes, Meyer, 102
Foucault, Michel, 47, 69, 152
Frank, Jerome D. and Julia B., 193
Freud, Sigmund, 31, 47, 64, 122, 154
Frohmayer, David, 92
Fromm, Erika, 118
Furst, Peter T., 10

Gaines, Atwood D., 22, 24, 47
Geertz, Clifford, 29, 35–38, 53–54, 64,
   134, 173, 195
Gellner, David, 56
Gill, Merton M., 64
Gilmore, Kim, 11–12, 99
Gluckman, Max, 120
God (*see* Creator)
Gone, Joseph P., 49
Good, Byron J., 14, 16, 21, 24, 25, 29,
   40, 42, 43, 47, 52, 70, 117, 119, 195,
   199n2
Good, Mary-Jo DelVecchio, 4, 7, 29,
   30, 191
Green, Melanie C., 30
Grinspoon, Lester, 27

Grob, Charles S., 96, 98, 137–138,
   152, 167
Grof, Stanislav, 130, 137

Hall, J. Lee, 86
Hallowell, A. Irving, 114, 125
Halpern, John H., 20, 95, 137, 192, 196
Harner, Michael, 55
Herdt, Gilbert, 4, 16, 18, 21, 43, 52–54,
   58, 111, 117, 119, 152, 154, 167
Hofmann, Albert, 45, 99
Hollan, Douglas, 21, 32
Hollister, L. E., 118, 152, 168

Iser, Wolfgang, 29

Jahoda, Gustav, 38–39, 111
James, William, 44
Janiger, Oscar, 93, 192

Kirmayer, Laurence J., 43
Kleinman, Arthur M., 4, 21, 24, 25, 43,
   47, 119,
Kluckhohn, Clyde, 22, 81–82, 178–179
Kohut, Heinz, 28, 63
Kracke, Waud, 18, 21, 43, 52, 59,
   63–65, 71
Kroeber, Alfred, 19
Kuhn, Thomas, 14
Kunitz, Stephen J., 19, 97, 116, 175, 192

LaBarre, Weston, 19, 45, 78, 84–85, 94,
   99, 104–109, 124, 128, 132, 135–137,
   139, 142–145, 150, 161, 167–168
LaFromboise, T. D., 179
Lakoff, George, 133
Lamphere, Louise, 127
Las Casas, Bartolomé de, 4–5
Leach, Edmund, 127
Leary, Timothy, 46
Leder, Drew, 11
Leonard , Irving A., 6, 79, 198
LeVine, Robert A., 4, 21, 43, 52, 154, 155,
   159, 174

Lévi-Strauss, Claude, 25, 35, 58, 113, 117, 121
Levy, Jerrold E., 19, 97, 116, 172, 175, 179, 192
Lewton, Elizabeth, 119
Linehan, Marsha M., 15, 65, 146
Littlewood, Roland, 43
Lucy, John, 37
Luhrmann, Tanya M., 120

MacLean, Katherine A., 96, 138
Malinowski, Bronislaw, 41
Marion, Ryan S., 12, 99
Mash, Deborah C., 96, 138
Matchett, N. F., 28
Mattingly, Cheryl, 25, 29–31, 33–35
McAllester, David P., 94, 132
McGillycuddy, Valentine, 8–9
Mead, George Herbert, 154
Mead, Margaret, 58–59
Meichenbaum, Donald, 146
Menninger, Karl, 19, 94, 116
Moerman, Daniel, 25, 121
Mokdad, Ali H., 12, 197
Mooney, James, 86, 150
Myerhoff, Barbara G., 10

Nadelmann, Ethan A., 11
Nisbett, Richard E., 15, 21
Nutt, David, 193

Obeyesekere, Gananath, 4, 41, 111, 117, 119, 122, 139
Opler, Morris, 133, 150
Ornstein, Robert, 42

Palgi, Phyllis, 130
Parker, Quanah, 98, 167
Peyote Spirit, 33, 95, 98, 101–102, 104–115, 135, 152–159
Piaget, Jean, 153–154
Pratt, Richard, 79

Quinn, Naomi, 133, 135

Radcliffe-Brown, Alfred, 41
Radin, Paul, 107, 156
Reichard, Gladys, 179
Ricoeur, Paul, 42, 64, 117
Roberts, Thomas B., 118, 138
Rogers, Carl, 32

Sahagun, Bernardino de, 78
Sapir, Edward, 3, 17, 23
Satan (*see* Devil)
Scalia, Antonin, 92, 97–98
Schaefer, Stacey B., 10
Schieffelin, Edward L., 35–36
Schlosser, Eric, 11
Schultes, Richard Evans, 10, 13, 45, 78, 79, 85, 86, 99, 103, 116
Shafer, Roy, 63
Shell, Charles E., 87
Shore, Bradd, 28, 36, 43
Shweder, Richard A., 4, 22, 43, 111, 119, 154
Sisko, Bob, 95
Sjoberg, B. M., 118, 152, 168
Slotkin, James Sydney, 19, 80, 83, 86, 94, 103–104, 129, 131, 150
Smith, Alfred, 68, 90–92, 97, 100, 175
Spindler, George D. and Louise S., 109, 114, 150, 156
Spiro, Melford E., 24, 41
Spitzer, Manfred, 137
Stannard, David E., 4, 6–7
Stewart, Omer C., 6, 19, 78, 79, 86, 87, 89, 94, 116, 150
Stocking, George W. Jr., 38, 193
Straus, Anne, 102
Surgeon General of the U.S. Public Health Service, 7, 80

Tax, Sol, 19, 94
Thornton, Russell, 4
Todorov, Tzvetan, 4
Trigger, Bruce, 5
Turner, Victor W., 32, 35, 101, 117, 120–121, 125–126, 128, 135

Van Gennep, Arnold, 117, 120–121, 125, 152
Van Tol, Lois, 162
Voget, Fred W., 84, 86
Vygotsky, Lev S., 43, 154

Wacquant, Loïc, 12, 17, 99
Wagner, Roland, 81–82, 84, 86
Wallace, Anthony F. C., 8, 120, 121, 195
Walsh, Roger, 130
Weber, Max, 188–189
White, Hayden, 29

Whorf, Benjamin Lee, 37
Wikan, Unni, 21
Willging, Catherine E., 159
Wilson, John, 132, 136
Winkelman, Michael, 118, 138
Witherspoon, Gary, 119, 159
Wovoka, 8

Young, Allan, 43

Zinberg, Norman, 44, 56

Subject Index

Addiction, 9, 22, 82–83, 95–96, 100,
   110, 120, 122, 137, 181–182, 186, 191
Peyote use misunderstood as, 82–83,
   100, 110, 191
psychedelics as credible treatment
   for, 95–96, 120, 137
role of spirituality in treatment
   of, 182
to alcohol, 9, 22, 181
to cigarettes, 186
twelve-step programs for, 122
Alcohol, 12, 99, 106, 110, 129, 153, 168,
   193, 197
as a sin in the Native American
   Church, 106, 129, 153, 168
as more harmful than cannabis or
   many psychedelics, 193
death rates associated with use of,
   12, 197
industry, 99
the spirit of, 110
Alcoholics Anonymous, 90, 177
as not appealing to some Native
   Americans, 153
personal narratives in, 34, 44, 122
Alcoholism, 7, 51, 68, 80, 82–83, 90,
   103, 114, 116, 143, 153, 174, 176, 181
among Native Americans, 82,
   90, 153

as an aspect of Native American
   health disparities, 7, 51, 80
as an explicit focus of the Native
   American Church, 80, 195
biological explanations of, 80
co-occurring with depression, 68
Native American Church as effective
   treatment for, 94, 97–99, 103, 114,
   116, 156, 174, 176
American Anthropological Association,
   statement in support of the NAC, 94
Archaeological evidence, 10, 45, 77–78
Assimilation, 79, 81
Aztecs, 9–10, 78, 103, 198

Bible (Christian), 48, 104, 125, 170
knowledge of Bible as a psychological
   measure of "intelligence," 48
Black Dog (early Peyotist), 130–131
Blackmun, Justice Harry (Associate
   Justice of the Supreme Court), 92
Boarding schools, 7, 79–80, 89–90
Brain, human, 36–37, 42, 45–47, 114,
   142–143, 193
Bwiti, 56–57, 95, 137

Capitalism, 11, 28, 45, 71, 99, 102
Childhood (see Native American
   Church, childhood in)

Christ, Jesus, 4–5, 31, 98–99, 104, 114,
    136, 142–143
  death and resurrection story as
    therapeutic emplotment, 31
  Peyote identified with, 99, 104, 114
  Quanah Parker's claim that Peyotists
    have a more direct relationship
    with, 98
  representations in Peyotist ritual
    symbolism, 136, 142–143
  torturing of Native Americans to
    death to honor, 4–5
Christianity, 5–6, 15, 31, 34, 55, 68, 77,
    86–87, 98, 100, 104, 114, 122, 125,
    130, 144–145, 177, 182–183
  death/rebirth symbolism as central
    to, 34, 130, 136
  forced conversion to, 5–6, 79–80,
    86–87, 198
  Peyote use seen as a threat to, 86–87,
    100, 198
  ritual use of alcohol in, 13
Clinical ethnography, 17–18, 39,
    51–74, 177
  clinical practice as a field technique
    in, 20–21, 67, 175–189
Clinical training of the ethnographer,
    16–17, 51–52, 58, 60, 62,
    64–66, 146
Collier, John (head of the Bureau of
    Indian Affairs), 88
Colonialism, 4, 6–8, 10–11, 22, 48, 80,
    83, 85–86, 191, 199n5
Communication
  from/with the Divine, 14, 33, 102, 104,
    106, 111–113, 140–142, 147, 156, 171
  human symbolic, 37
  in Peyotist families, 151
  in religious enculturation, 97
  in ritual, 33, 144–145, 151
  therapeutic, 20, 33, 97, 120, 144–145, 151
  to self, 46
Confession, 79, 144–145

Consciousness
  as culturally mediated, 37, 41, 44, 64
  decentering of normal consciousness
    in anthropology and
    psychoanalysis, 64
  diversity of states of, 44, 62, 71, 73
  self-, 59–60 (*see also* reflexivity)
Consciousness modification, 13, 17–18,
    25–28, 33, 40, 43–45, 49, 90,
    98–99, 117–118, 135–142, 167
  as a domain of conflict, 90
  as central to many ritual-based
    interventions, 13, 25, 27, 98–99,
    117–118, 152, 167, 197
  near-universality of, 13, 45, 197
  paired with emplotment in ritual, 49,
    117, 167
  Peyotist technology of, 136–139
  reasons for, 27, 98
  to facilitate enculturation and
    education, 98, 117, 167
  to facilitate therapeutic
    emplotment, 117
Consent Form for Spiritual
    Participation, 21, 68, 182, 187, 189
Countertransference, 64
Crashing Thunder (Winnebago
    Peyotist), 109, 139
Creator, the, 14, 33, 38, 87, 102–105, 107,
    110, 130–131, 141–142, 144, 147–148,
    155–156, 168–169
  as healer, 148
  child-parent form of relationship
    with, 151, 155
  ritual experiences as messages
    from, 147
  Peyote as allowing communication
    with, 102, 104, 110, 141
  Peyote as given songs by, 105
  Peyote as placed on earth by, 14,
    103–104
Cultural destruction, policy of, 4, 22,
    79–80, 90

Cultural diversity, 22, 28, 40, 48–49,
52, 74, 77–78, 102, 197
depathologizing, 48, 190–198
ethical imperative to understand, 22,
52, 197
scientific understanding of, 74
Cultural paradigm clash, 3–5, 10–15, 23,
28, 42, 69–70, 86, 100, 114, 137,
148, 151, 154, 190–195
defined, 14
dialectical study of, 14–15
psychopharmacological, 137
related to understandings of
therapeutic process, 148, 193–198
surrounding divergent forms of
family behavior and approaches to
socialization, 151, 154
surrounding Peyote and the Native
American Church, 10, 69–70,
77–100, 151, 191
surrounding psychoactive plant
medicines, 11, 192–193
Cultural psychiatries, 16–17, 21,
23–50, 110–111, 116–117, 119–120,
122, 136
conflicts between, 23, 28, 193–195
diversity of, 49, 120, 122
See also dialectic of culture and
mental health

Death, 7, 12, 31, 80, 121, 127–128, 134–136,
151, 172–173, 179
awareness of, 25, 130–131
Peyotist attitudes toward,
172–173, 179
Death/rebirth symbolism, 34–35, 71–73,
95, 112, 122, 129–136
Decision making (in ritual), 142–143
Depathologization, 46, 48
Deviance, 39
Devil, the, 6, 79, 114, 116
Diagnosis
anthropological study of, 47–48, 53

as a culturally situated process, 28,
47–48, 198
as a tool of cultural imperialism,
48–49
ethnocentric, 48
Navajo traditional, 68
Navajo Peyotist, 124
Diagnostic and Statistical Manual of
Mental Disorders, 40
Dialectic (as a particular relationship
of interacting/interrelated
phenomena)
of biological, psychological and
social systems in human evolution,
37, 39
of clinical and ethnographic
understanding (clinical
ethnography), 17–18, 51, 58–61, 68,
187
of collective and personal, 3–4, 31,
110–113, 119
of cultural diversity and general
humanity, 39
of culture and mental health (cultural
psychiatry), 16, 24–25, 41, 110–111
of culture and mind, 36–39, 42–44,
111–113
of emplotment and consciousness
modification, 26, 117, 136, 147
of local medical knowledge
and systems of ideological/
metaphysical assumption, 40, 195
of meaning and embodied practice/
experience, 35–36, 57, 195
of Peyotist superego development and
Peyotist psychopharmacology, 155
of psychotherapeutic orientations, 65
of public and private, 53
of relativism and universalism, 15, 17,
39, 60 (*See also* meta-relativism)
of symbolic analysis and embodied
experience in ethnographic study,
54–57

Dialectical approach, 3–4, 14–18, 24–25, 39, 60–61, 65, 68, 85, 129
 to cultural paradigm clashes, 14–15
 to interdisciplinary theory, 24–25
 to methodology, 17, 39
Dialectical balancing, 17, 60–61, 199n5
Dialectical behaviour therapy, 65, 146
Dichotomization, 15, 38
 of mind and body (*see* dualism)
 of religious experience and
   therapeutic efficacy, 85, 148
 of society and nature, 127
 of symbolic analysis and study of
   embodied experience, 35, 56–57
 of the public and private, 53
 of the social and personal, 41,
   53, 121
 traditions based on, 15
Disease, 4, 6, 22, 79
Disparities, health, 7, 80
Dreams, 21, 42, 59, 66–67, 69–73, 79,
   106, 110, 111–112, 131, 135
 and reflexivity in ethnographic
   research, 59, 66–67, 69–73
 as self-emplotment, 42
 culturally diverse understandings
   of, 21
 in the Peyotist Origin Myth, 111–112
 Peyotist, 106, 131
Drugs. *See* substances, psychoactive
Dualism, Cartesian, 15, 26

Education, 19, 21, 92, 97–98, 106, 135,
   161, 169–170, 173, 174, 177, 180,
   196–197
 psychobiologically assisted,
   167–169, 174
 through Peyote, 106, 165, 168
Embodiment, 44, 54–57, 69
Empathic understanding, 15, 17–18,
   33, 51, 59, 62–66, 71–74, 96, 145,
   148, 190

 as goal of the book, 15, 17–18, 69,
   73–74, 190
 in ethnographic research, 51, 59, 62,
   66, 69, 71, 73
 in psychotherapy and psychoanalysis,
   33, 51, 62–63, 148
 reported as enhanced by
   consumption of Peyote, 145
Empathy-facilitating texts, 18, 62, 66,
   73–74
Emplotment, 29, 33–35
 self-emplotment, 31, 42, 73
Emplotment, therapeutic, 25–27, 29–31,
   33–35, 42, 117–139
 clashes between diverse forms of, 42
 culturally embedded, 31, 33–34, 39,
   42, 120, 148
 definition of, 31–32
 in occupational therapy, 30
 in the Peyote Ceremony, 117–139
 in the Peyote origin myth, 113
 psychobiologically assisted, 49,
   117–118, 195
Enculturation, 33, 37, 117, 150–174
 in the Native American Church,
   97–99, 106, 135, 152–170, 195–196
Entheogen, 46 (*see also* psychedelic
   plants)
Ethics, 22, 193
Ethnocentrism, 5–6, 12–13, 15, 19–23,
   28, 37, 39, 44–45, 47–48, 64, 82,
   87–90, 97–100, 114, 148, 191–3, 197
 anthropological understanding as a
   struggle to free our minds from,
   23, 64, 197
 as disrupting Native American efforts
   at postcolonial healing, 191
 as embedded in terminology, 46
 as resulting in violations of human
   rights, 198
 European, 5–6
 in diagnosis, 48

in dismissal of expert findings, 193
in systems of health care, 47
in understandings of psychoactive
  substances, 12–13, 19, 21, 45–46, 82,
  87, 90, 100, 114, 191, 197
of the US Supreme Court, 97–98
tendencies toward dichotomization/
  polarization as, 15
Ethnography, 38, 81
as a holistic, world open research
  method, 62
clinical utility of, 52
critiques of, 57–58
person-centered, 62
reflexivity in, 57–60, 70–73
See also clinical ethnography
Experiences, sacred, 33, 45–46, 68, 73,
  83–85, 87, 95–96, 106, 108, 112–113,
  130–134, 138–142, 147–149, 156–159,
  166–168, 172–174, 191, 194–196
and therapeutic efficacy of the Peyote
  Ceremony, 95–96
approaches to study of, 46, 54–57, 73
as a goal of the semiotic/reflexive
  paradigm of psychopharmacology,
  194–195
as divine communications, 147
as providing knowledge, 106, 141, 168
as revealing Peyote's ongoing and
  omniscient gaze, 156
as self-referential, 147
as shaped by cultural norms and
  ritual behaviors, 138–139
as shaped by how the person
  approaches the experience, 141
as supporting parenting, 166–167
emotional impact of, 142
empathic understanding of, 73
Hoskie's, 68
in experimental subjects, 96
in the form of a death and rebirth,
  130–133
involving an encounter with
  death, 172
modeled in the Peyote Origin Myth,
  112–113
of Charles E. Shell, 87
of singing voices, 108
role of in the spread of the Native
  American Church, 85
therapeutic processes in, 33
triggered by psychedelic plants,
  45–46, 68, 83
variety of in the Native American
  Church, 139–142
See also transformation, personal

Families (see kinship, enculturation)
Felony, 92
Fieldwork, 67–71 (see also clinical
  ethnography)
emotions and dreams during, 69–73
Navajo consultants, 67–69
models of ethnographer's experience
  during, 71
relationships in, 53–54, 62–67, 74
Freudian slip, 182
Frohmayer, David (attorney general of
  Oregon), 92
Functionalism, 120

Genocide, 4–9, 79
Ghost Dance, 8–10, 83
Goal-setting (in ritual), 143–144, 147
God (see Creator)

Hall, J. Lee (Indian agent), 86
Hallucination, 46, 83 (see also visions,
  experiences)
Hallucinogen, 46 (see also psychedelic
  plants)
Healer
  role of, 32–33, 120, 121, 148, 194
  See also psychotherapist

Healing
 anthropological understandings of, 33
 experiences of, 68, 84 (*see also*
  experiences, sacred)
 postcolonial, 16, 23, 149, 191, 195
 See also psychotherapeutic
  intervention
Healing rituals, 18, 20, 22, 25, 31–34, 45,
  49, 117–118, 189
 bureaucratization of, 188–189
Health care system
 as an instrument of social control, 47
Hózhǫ́ 119, 126, 159, 179
Human development
 diversity of normal, 150–151, 154,
  173–174
 theories of, 153–155
Human Rights Watch, 11, 12, 45

Ideologies
 collectivist, 32
 individualist, 15, 24, 32, 34, 40, 79,
  119, 154, 194
Illness, 29, 32–33, 50, 52, 58, 162–163,
  172, 178–180
 as a focus of emplotment, 33, 113, 117,
  122, 157
 as culturally expressed and
  interpreted, 14, 16, 21, 24–25, 28,
  52, 55, 85, 179, 188
 See also mental illness
Immersion (in fieldwork), 17–18, 38, 51,
  54, 59, 61–62, 66–67, 69, 74, 187
Imperialism, cultural, 22, 86
Indian Health Service, 19–20, 97, 175,
  192
Individualism, 15, 24, 32, 34, 40, 79, 119,
  154, 194
Inquisition, Spanish, 5–6, 11, 77, 79, 86,
  190, 192
Intelligence tests, 48
Interdisciplinarity, 16–18, 60, 116–117

Justice Policy Institute, 11, 45, 197

K'é, 108, 159–161, 181
Kinship, 107, 150–174, 181, 195

Lakota, 8–9, 68, 140, 177, 184
Law, antidrug, 6
Life course, 73, 95, 119, 123, 126, 134,
  150–174
Liminality, 27, 120–121, 125–126, 128

Manifest Destiny doctrine, 6
Maya, 45
McGillycuddy, Valentine, 8–9
Meaning therapy, 42–43
Medical knowledge, 14, 16, 23, 47, 52
Mental health, 16–18, 20, 40–41, 122,
  188, 190–191, 198
 as a creative emplotment rather than
  a biological given, 39, 42, 122
 local understandings of, 24, 40–41,
  198
 of Native American Church
  members, 20, 196
Mental illness, 44, 65, 93–94, 181
Metaphors, 55–56, 129, 133–135, 185, 195
Meta-relativism, 16, 18, 60–61
Mooney, James (early ethnographer of the
  Native American Church), 86, 150
Movement, revitalization, 3, 8–10, 16, 41,
  80, 86, 90, 100, 188
Multiplicity of the normal. *See* Normal,
  multiplicity of

Narratives, 34–35, 39, 42, 80–81, 112, 144
  (*see also* emplotment)
 personal, 34, 66, 122, 144, 147
National Commission on Marihuana
  and Drug Abuse, 192
Native American Church, 79–80, 100
 adult development in, 170–172
 and formal education, 169–170

attitudes toward death and afterlife, 172–173
childhood in, 150–153, 155–159, 161–170
conflicts with Navajo tribal government and traditional Navajo religion, 69, 87–88
enculturation and socialization as a focus in, 152, 195–196
jailing of members by the Navajo Tribal Council, 87–88
mental health of members of, 20
multigenerational families in, 20, 107, 150–174
opposition to, 86–100, 192
spread of, 9–10, 80–86
Native Americans, 77, 80
conquest of, 111
Navajo Adolescent Treatment Center, 68, 175–189
clinical privileging process for ceremonial treatment at, 176–177
modeling of respectful use of psychoactive substances at, 185–187
Ndembu (African tribe), 32
Neurotransmitters, 45
Normal, multiplicity of, 15, 17, 21, 24, 39–41, 47, 52, 150–151, 190, 198

Ontogeny, human, 36
Oregon v. Smith case, 68–69, 90–100, 175, 198

Panoptical control/gaze, 69, 152–153, 155–156, 169, 174
Parker, Quanah (Comanche Peyotist), 98, 167
Personhood, 39–40, 64, 101–102, 104–115
Persuasion, narrative, 30
Peyote, 101–115
and mental health, 20

as a sacred herbal medicine, 102–104
as a serotonergic substance, 45
as placed on earth by the Creator, 103–104
as sacrament, 114
bitter taste of, 104
European understandings of, 6, 19, 23, 77, 79, 82–83, 86–100, 192
experimental studies of, 20, 196
Native American understanding and use of, 9–10, 78, 83–85, 101–115
origin myth, 105, 110–113
prehistoric use of, 10, 45, 78
preparation of, 103–104
safety of use by Native Americans, 92–94
sold as a medicine by Euro-American pharmaceutical companies, 87
taken before giving birth, 161–162
therapeutic reputation of, 84, 94–97, 103, 116, 192
therapeutic use of, 19–20, 84
Peyote Ceremony, 57, 68, 80, 116–149
as a context for modeling of adult gender roles, 165
as a context for modeling proper use of psychoactive plants, 174
clinical ethnographic study of, 57
education meetings, 123–124, 152–153, 169
expressive/communicative aspects of, 144–145
Indian Health Service coding as a treatment modality, 19–20, 116, 175–176, 192
reflexivity in, 118
ritual process of, 49, 116–149
role in bureaucratized health care, 68
self-control developed in, 146–147
shared suffering in, 145–147
symbolism in, 124–136 (*see also* symbolism)

Peyote Road, 123, 127–129, 134, 151
Peyote Spirit, 33, 95, 98, 101–102,
    104–115, 135, 152–159
    as omniscient, 106–107, 152–159
    as parental, 107–109, 152, 155–159
    gender of, 107–109
    metaphorical understandings of,
        109–110
    relationship with, 153, 156–159
    role in parenting/socialization,
        152–159
Pharmaceuticals industry, 87, 90, 99
Plot structures, 34–35 (*see also*
    emplotment)
Postcolonial healing, 16, 23, 149, 191, 195
Pratt, Richard (director, Carlisle Indian
    School), 79
Prison industrial complex, 11–12,
    99–100
Prisoners, United States 11–12, 99–100,
    197
Psychedelic plants, 45–46, 78, 133–134,
    192–193 (*see also* Peyote, plants)
    and neurotransmitters, 45
    as explaining the development of
        religious beliefs in humans, 45
    eboka, 56, 95
    experimental studies, 95–96, 137
    Mescal bean, 78
    Morning Glory, 78
    mushrooms, 45, 78
    therapeutic potential of, 137–138
Psychiatry, Euro-American, 120
    biologically reductionist position of,
        47
    use of psychoactive substances in, 49
Psychic unity, doctrine of, 28, 38–39
Psychoactive plants, 6, 11
    European punishment of, 6, 13,
        18–19, 22, 77, 79
    European understandings of, 11–14,
        18–19, 22, 82–83, 191–192

human use of, 13–14
Native American understandings of,
    11, 14
therapeutic use of, 46
See also psychedelic plants
Psychoanalysis, 58, 62–64
Psychopharmacology
    clashes between different cultural
        systems of, 44–45, 137, 148
    paradigms of, 25–26, 44
    semiotic/reflexive paradigm of,
        25–26, 96, 137, 148, 194
    See also substances, psychoactive
Psychotherapeutic intervention
    dyadic conversation-based approach
        to, 32, 119
    Euro-American approaches to,
        26–27, 32–33
    pluralism versus standardization
        debate in Euro-American, 49
    ritual-based approaches to, 32–33,
        119–120
    role of communication in, 33
Psychotherapist
    as ideally nondirective, 34
    importance of the personal properties
        of, 32

Racism, 12, 38, 48, 59
Realism, naive, 37–38, 48
Reductionism, biological, 60
Reflexivity, 17–18, 29, 42, 52, 70–74, 95,
    118–119, 125, 138–139, 150, 181, 195
    clinically naive, 58
    in ethnographic fieldwork, 57–60,
        66, 69–74, 150
    traditions of (psychological,
        sociocultural, and disciplinary),
        59–60
    See also ethnography
Relationships
    fieldwork, 53–54, 62–67, 74

Relative deprivation, 83
Relativism, 15–16, 18, 38, 60–61, 68, 187
  challenging through field
    experiences, 61, 68, 187
  See also meta-relativism
Religious freedom, 90–100
Revitalization, cultural, 8, 80–81, 90
Rites of passage, 120–121, 125–126
Ritual symbols. *See* symbolism, ritual
Rituals
  anthropological theories of, 120–122
  education in, 98, 106 (*see also*
    enculturation)
  healing, 20, 34–35
Road Man, 18–20, 33, 67–69, 88, 98,
    103, 109, 112, 123–124, 128, 132, 134,
    138, 145, 165, 176, 187
  Aronilth, Wilson, 104, 111, 128–129, 136
  as guide to the NAC member, 128
  as modeling male gender role in
    ritual, 165
  behavior during rituals, 33, 123
  Hoskie, 68
  *Leonard, 69, 88, 109, 112–113, 132,
    138, 145
  *Mike, 88, 98, 103
  Parker, Quanah, 98
  term related to ritual symbolism, 134

Sacrament, 33, 45, 69, 90–92, 98–99,
    110, 114, 122, 151–152, 161–163, 168
Scalia, Antonin (Associate Justice of the
    Supreme Court), 92, 97–98
Self-communication, 46, 73
Self-understanding, 46
Shamanism, 55, 130, 148
Shell, Charles E. (Indian agent), 87
Shumla Cave, 78
Slavery, 5, 7, 12, 99–100
Smith, Alfred (Klamath Peyotist),
    68, 90–92, 97, 100, 175 (*see also*
    Oregon versus Smith)

Sobriety, 23, 144, 170
Social control, 47
Stigma, 44
Stories. *See* emplotment
Subjectivity, 47, 54, 58–59, 62
Substances, psychoactive
  abuse of, 14, 18, 153
  anxieties related to, 69–70
  deaths due to, 12, 197
  role modeling of appropriate
    use, 152
  Schedule I, 19, 93–94, 192
  therapeutic use of, 46
  See also psychoactive plants
Suggestibility, 95, 117–118, 152,
    168, 195
Suicide, 80
Superego, 69, 154–156, 158, 169, 196
Supreme Court, US, 68–69, 90–100
Surgeon General of the U.S. Public
    Health Service, 7, 80
Sweat lodge, 20, 68, 153, 182–185
Symbolism, 124–136, 195
  analysis of, 55–56, 124–136
  generativity of, 135–136
  in dreams, 70–73
  multivocality of, 126
  of death and rebirth, 34–35, 71–73,
    129–133
  of the dawn, 132–133
  of the half moon, 126–131
  of the Peyote origin myth, 111–113
  ritual, 33–35, 73, 95, 101, 109, 119,
    124–136, 147
  self symbolism, 112, 119, 125, 127–136,
    195
  transformation symbolism, 121–122,
    125–136, 195
Tobacco, 14, 78, 144, 181, 185–186, 197
  death rates associated with use of,
    12, 197
  industry, 99

Transformation, personal, 9, 26, 119–121, 129–133, 148, 195 (*see also* experiences, sacred)

Trauma, 7, 9, 16, 80, 85, 112, 190–191

Twelve-step groups, 34

Visions, 8, 33, 57, 68, 73, 84, 106, 124, 139–141, 147, 156, 166–168, 172

Vodou (Haitian), 55

War on Drugs, 10–11, 21–23, 45–46, 59, 79, 89–90, 99–100, 149, 192, 198

Wilson, John (Peyotist), 132, 136

Witchcraft, 178

Wounded Knee, 9

Wovoka, 8